T0246054

THE OTHER
SIGNIFICANT
OTHERS

THE OTHER
SIGNIFICANT
OTHERS

Reimagining Life with
Friendship at the Center

Rhaina Cohen

ST. MARTIN'S PRESS
NEW YORK

First published in the United States by St. Martin's Press, an imprint of
St. Martin's Publishing Group

THE OTHER SIGNIFICANT OTHERS. Copyright © 2024 by Rhaina Cohen.
All rights reserved. Printed in the United States of America. For informa-
tion, address St. Martin's Publishing Group, 120 Broadway, New York,
NY 10271.

www.stmartins.com

Designed by Jen Edwards

Library of Congress Cataloging-in-Publication Data available upon
request.

ISBN 978-1-250-28091-6 (hardcover)
ISBN 978-1-250-28092-3 (ebook)

Our books may be purchased in bulk for promotional, educational, or
business use. Please contact your local bookseller or the Macmillan Cor-
porate and Premium Sales Department at 1-800-221-7945, extension
5442, or by email at MacmillanSpecialMarkets@macmillan.com.

First Edition: 2024

10 9 8 7 6 5 4 3

For M and Coco

The richest relationships are often those that don't fit neatly into the preconceived slots we have made for the archetypes we imagine would populate our lives—the friend, the lover, the parent, the sibling, the mentor, the muse . . . We then must either stretch ourselves to create new slots shaped after these singular relationships, enduring the growing pains of self-expansion, or petrify.

—MARIA POPOVA

Why do we choose what we choose?
What would we choose if we had a real choice?

—ELLEN WILLIS

CONTENTS

AUTHOR'S NOTE

This book goes into the depths of people's personal lives to illuminate a type of relationship that's been hidden in plain sight. The people featured in this book, who represent a fraction of the approximately seventy people I interviewed, decided to share so much about themselves because they hoped they could make friendships like theirs visible. I use their real names. In a few cases, I use only their first names or an initial.

I also write about myself, and, at times, it was relevant to refer to people in my personal life. Whereas the people I interviewed actively chose to participate in this book, my loved ones merely opted to be my friend or partner. Some of these people asked for pseudonyms, which I use to preserve their privacy.

INTRODUCTION

The second half of 2022 was my Wedding Tour of America. Friends who had delayed their weddings because of the COVID pandemic were like shoppers lined up outside Target on Black Friday, ready to seize the earliest days for safe celebration as soon as the doors opened. Over six months, I attended six weddings and missed two others because of travel conflicts. Each wedding featured personalized touches. There was the groom who formed a one-night-only band with his friends, euphoric and sweating through his gilded traditional Pakistani suit with each strike of his drumsticks. A bride who's a poet commanded the attention of hundreds of guests as she shared the poem she'd written for the occasion. Holding a microphone in one hand, the printed-out poem in the other, and her veil a waterfall tracing the back of her dark hair, she read aloud, "We do not belong to ourselves alone."

I silently chided myself for not having worn waterproof mascara that day.

As distinct as these weddings were, a commonality surfaced: again and again, brides and grooms referred to their spouse-to-be as their "best friend." One officiant began the vows section of the ceremony by instructing the bride and groom to "hold the hand of your best friend." I looked at the best man, who was just as lean and towering in his three-piece suit as he'd been the day that he and the groom became college roommates—a moment that predated the bride and groom's romantic relationship by more than a year. When the officiant asked the bride and groom to promise, as part of their lifelong vows, to be the other's best friend, I wondered what the best man was thinking. His title had been swiped.

For the last stop on my wedding tour, I officiated the ceremony between two friends who, in my mind, have the consummate romantic partnership. I prepared by reading speeches from people in my social circles who had officiated weddings. I was struck by a few lines in a speech from a woman who introduced herself as the best friend of the bride (her title was, so far, uncontested). After welcoming the guests, she announced, "The most important moment in life is when you meet the person with whom you want to spend the rest of your life. The person who makes you see the world as a beautiful and magical place, who validates your every breath. For [the bride], that happened twenty-three years ago when she met me."

Cue laughter.

The officiant continued, "But eight years ago, she met [the groom]."

I thought it was a brilliant joke. But then, journalist killjoy that I am, I started to ask where the comedy was coming from. How much of the humor rested on the assumption that friends don't decide to spend the rest of their lives together? Was it really that absurd?

———————

My interest in these questions was more than theoretical. I've long thrown myself into friendship with the fervor others reserve for romance. I've announced to people that I've had a "friend crush" on them (turns out, it's a great way to speed up the growth of a budding friendship). I've often joked that I'm a "friend pusher," because I take delight in introducing my friends to each other and watching them form a relationship of their own.

And then came M. We met in our midtwenties, a few months after I moved to a new city, and she stretched my understanding of the role a friendship could play in my life. A friend could be an essential part of my daily routines; we'd commune in her house for oatmeal and rib-crushing hugs before I made my way to the metro for my morning commute. A friend could ask me to be her plus-one at her office holiday party, proudly introducing me to everyone from entry-level coworkers to C-suite executives. A friend could make me feel so smitten that I deliberately limited how often I mentioned her to avoid sounding obsessed—the same self-censoring I'd done at the start of my relationship with my now-husband. A friend could electrify my life.

Having seen through M how expansive friendship could be, I wanted to find people who were ahead of us, who had already redrawn the borders of friendship, moving the lines further and further outward to encompass more space in each other's lives. By the time I came across that joke from the wedding officiant's speech, I had talked to many dozens of people who wanted to spend the rest of their lives with a friend (or friends). Actually, *wanted* is not quite the right way to put it. That implies an unrealized future. These friends had already been living side by side for years or decades and planned to do so indefinitely.

The first pair I spoke to was Andrew Bergman and Toly Rinberg;

Andrew's sister, who happened to be a friend of mine, had told me that Andrew and Toly were so close that she considered Toly her brother-in-law. In 2018, the four of us met for lunch in my office's cafeteria, and I asked Andrew and Toly about their friendship. My office turned out to be a fitting place to talk because the tone of our discussion felt mentor-like, as though I had invited a pair of more experienced coworkers for coffee to talk through their careers. I hadn't before spoken at length to people with the same type of friendship that I had stumbled into with M, let alone a pair of friends who were as committed to each other as they were.

Andrew and Toly had met fifteen years earlier, when Toly was the new kid at their high school in suburban New Jersey. His sparse social life consisted of hanging out with his brother and practicing martial arts in a community room next to the public library. A Super Bowl party that they both attended turned out to be their Rubicon crossing from acquaintances to friends; Toly joined Andrew's friend group, composed of about ten nerdy boys who played Ultimate Frisbee and frequented Hoagie Haven after school. Eventually, the two of them formed a one-on-one friendship.

They also had a three-way friendship with a classmate named David, who enlivened everyday hangouts with his spontaneity and zeal. Once, David realized there was no limit to what you could deep-fry, so he and Toly prepared batter, and the three of them deep-fried every edible item in Toly's kitchen. David also struggled with his mental health, and toward the end of high school and in college, Andrew and Toly, as they describe it, were his two "lifelines." David dropped out of college early into sophomore year and, while Toly was a junior, spent months sleeping on a mattress next to Toly's bed in his college apartment. He later stayed with Andrew. Hundreds of miles apart from each other at their respective colleges, Andrew and Toly regularly had calls, sometimes staying on the phone for hours, to talk about what was going on with their friend. David later died by suicide. Andrew and Toly made a pamphlet for his funeral, gave speeches to honor him, and gathered friends in the basement of Andrew's parents' house for a night of reminiscing and mourning. When they talk about David now, their voices don't drop into a somber register; instead, they marvel and chuckle when they call back memories of him. It helps that as they grieved, they had someone else who knew exactly what it was like to lose David.

After graduating from college in 2011, Andrew and Toly moved their lives in parallel. Looking to be helpful and, in part, inspired by David to think beyond conventional paths, they volunteered as software developers for the National Institute for Medical Research in Tanzania, living there together for seven months. Andrew says there was no one moment when he and Toly determined that their friendship went beyond what people typically mean by best friends. "Our commitment was almost more borne out by how we acted in moments where it could have fallen away," he says, especially during the two years they spent on opposite coasts. They spoke often and went on to become roommates in graduate school, where they studied soft matter physics in the same lab, and again when they cofounded a government transparency nonprofit. From living together to working together, they made deliberate decisions to organize their lives around each other. Andrew and Toly became a *we*.

Their closeness threw off some people who knew them. On a phone call when Andrew was about thirty years old, his mom, Lisa, asked him if he was gay. She said she wanted Andrew to know that if he and Toly were in a romantic relationship, she was fine with it. Though Andrew appreciated his mom's acceptance of a hypothetical same-sex romantic relationship, that's not what he and Toly had with each other. He thought he'd already made clear that he and Toly weren't romantically involved.

"Deep down inside," Lisa says, "I didn't think that it was a romantic relationship, because Andrew's not the type of person that would be shy about saying it was, if in fact it was." Andrew is also not the type of person to repress same-sex attraction, had he felt it. He and Toly regularly have marathon conversations in which they inspect their feelings and behavior with the fastidiousness of psychoanalysts. If he or Toly had sexual interest in the other, it would have come up.

Lisa says her confusion about the nature of Andrew and Toly's friendship "gnawed at me," but she retired her questions about it. She switched to asking Andrew if he was dating anyone. Andrew responded with a question of his own: Why was it so important to her that he was dating? She said she wanted him to have someone who could give him "emotional wholeness," someone he could go to if he had a problem or a hard decision to make. As a mother, she said, she would be happy to know there's somebody in her son's life who gives him that kind of fulfillment.

Andrew told her he already had all of that—with Toly.

"What do you mean?" Lisa asked.

Andrew described Toly as a "platonic life partner."

Lisa said, "I don't understand how your life partner can be someone who you aren't romantic with."

Andrew's friendship defied two widely held beliefs: that a partnership is, by definition, a romantic relationship, and that without a long-term romantic relationship, life is incomplete.

———

This is a book about friends who have become a *we*, despite having no scripts, no ceremonies, and precious few models to guide them toward long-term platonic commitment. These are friends who have moved together across states and continents. They've been their friend's primary caregiver through organ transplants and chemotherapy. They're co-parents, co-homeowners, and executors of each other's wills. They belong to a club that has no name or membership form, often unaware that there are others like them. They fall under the umbrella of what Eli Finkel, a psychology professor at Northwestern University, calls "other significant others." Having eschewed a more typical life setup, these friends confront hazards and make discoveries they wouldn't have otherwise.

People who haven't experienced a friendship like this firsthand may not even realize they've seen one before, although they've likely known others who've had one and can recognize it when it's pointed out. It was common for friends and acquaintances I told about this book to recall, as if an *aha* thought bubble had bloomed above their heads, an aunt or a grandmother who shared a house with a friend until the end of life. Doctors who worked with older patients told me that frequently the person at a dying patient's bedside is not a spouse or relative but a longtime, dear friend.

I started working on this book with the simple desire to bring attention to these friendships. My friendship with M made the world pulse with more possibilities for intimacy and support than before, and I wanted others to feel those possibilities for themselves. As I talked to people who had devoted, life-defining friendships, I heard stories like Andrew and Toly's, about how their loved ones sometimes reacted with confusion or suspicion. I began to see how these unusual relationships can also be a provocation—unsettling the set of societal tenets that circumscribe our intimate lives: That the central and most important person in one's life should be a romantic partner, and friends are the supporting cast. That romantic love is the real thing, and if people claim they feel strong platonic love, it must not *really* be platonic. That adults who raise kids together should be having sex with each other, and marriage deserves special treatment by the state.

Challenging these social norms is not new, nor are platonic partners the only dissidents. People who are feminists, queer, trans, of color, non-monogamous, single, asexual, aromantic, celibate, or who live communally have been questioning these ideas for decades, if not centuries. All have offered counterpoints to what Eleanor Wilkinson, a professor at the University of Southampton, calls *compulsory coupledom*: the notion that a long-term monogamous romantic relationship is necessary for a normal, successful adulthood. This is a riff on the feminist writer Adrienne Rich's influential concept of "compulsory heterosexuality"—the idea, enforced through social pressure and practical incentives, that the only normal and acceptable romantic relationship is between a man and a woman. Some of the first stories we hear as children instill compulsory coupledom, equating characters finding their "one true love" with living "happily ever after."

In a society governed by compulsory coupledom, those who aren't one half of a couple can feel excluded. Meg, an artist in her seventies who I got to know while working on this book, told me about the period when her friends married off and she was relegated to the "lunch slot." Dinner was reserved for their husbands. I've heard from single people a generation or more below Meg that they've felt others have demoted them, treated them like "an extra" or as immature—like a train that stalled before reaching the station of full adulthood. The privileging of romantic relationships, thoroughly documented by scholars, pervades not just our social norms but also the law; to give an example, Americans can extend health insurance and Social Security benefits to spouses but not to the closest of friends.

Just as compulsory heterosexuality disregards people's experiences of same-sex attraction, compulsory coupledom ignores the large number of people who aren't in a romantic unit. For the last few decades, the age of first marriage has steadily ticked upward, as young people look to financially establish themselves and feel certain about their compatibility with a partner before signing up for devotion until death. While some people are heading down the aisle later, others aren't getting married at all. Only about half of adults in the US ages twenty-five to fifty-four are currently married, down from 67 percent a few decades ago. At the same time, the share of adults in this age group who have never married has increased to nearly one-third. And marriage has practically become a status symbol, attainable primarily by those with more education and money: wealthier Americans are more likely to marry than those with lower incomes. Americans are forgoing more than marriage; many don't come home to a romantic partner at the end of the day. According to 2019 data from Pew, 38 percent of American adults are neither married nor cohabiting with a partner, up from 29 percent in 1990.

One response to these changes has been to lament them and attempt to turn back the clock. Some politicians and policymakers have made impassioned pleas to encourage marriage while the US government has spent hundreds of millions of dollars on marriage promotion with little to show for it. In general, we should be wary of paternalism, but in this case, we have grounds to be particularly skeptical: the idealized romantic relationship rests on shaky ground.

That instability comes, at least in part, from modern expectations of romantic partnerships. One man I interviewed observed that many people he knows have a "one-stop shopping" approach to romantic relationships: get your sexual partner, confidant, co-parent, housemate, and more, all in the same person. Prominent experts have recognized this pattern and are concerned about it. "When we channel all our intimate needs into one person," the psychotherapist Esther Perel writes, "we actually stand to make the relationship more vulnerable." Such totalizing expectations for romantic relationships can leave us with no shock absorber if a partner falls short in even one area. While we weaken friendships by expecting too little of them, we undermine romantic relationships by expecting too much of them.

Asking so much of one person looks even riskier when we realize that, most likely, we can't rely on one romantic partner for the entirety of our adult lives. By and large, marriage or a marriage-like relationship is a temporary status of adulthood. Few Americans enter a romantic relationship at age eighteen and stay in one continuously until death. They have stretches of singleness. They break up and divorce. They outlive partners; women are especially likely to survive their spouses: about one-third of American women over sixty-five are widowed. Meg, who had been consigned to the "lunch slot," married at fifty—around the time that many of her friends were getting divorced—and was widowed twenty years later. So far, she hasn't been married for more than two-thirds of her adult life.

Like Meg, many of us are spending a large part of our lives outside of marriage. The average marriage spans fewer of the years that are considered the prime of life—eighteen to fifty-five—than it did a few decades ago. In 1960, the average marriage encompassed twenty-nine of those thirty-seven years; in 2015, it was eighteen. As I read statistics on marriage, divorce, and surviving spouses, I was reminded of Susan Sontag's remark about the precarity of health: "Everyone who is born holds dual citizenship, in the kingdom of the well and in the kingdom of the sick." Most of us hold dual citizenship in the kingdom of the couple and the kingdom of the single. It's prudent for us to embrace forms of connection that exist beyond the dominion of romantic relationships.

———————

It can be confusing to live in the gulf between the life you have and the life you believe you're supposed to be living. In response to an article

I'd written for *The Atlantic* about friendships much like Andrew and Toly's, I got a flurry of responses from people who are familiar with that confusion. One email came from Paula Archey, who told me about her friend who surpasses the closeness of a best friend. Each time Paula had to designate an emergency contact, she struggled to find a label for their friendship and jotted down terms like "platonic life partner" and "my person." Paula divorced in her midthirties and, since then, had been searching for a new romantic relationship. She wrote, "Even though my person and I provide so many of the things for each other that are traditionally provided in a marriage-type relationship in our society, I've still felt the need to find a person to fill that marriage-type role." Reading stories of other friendships like hers was a "(much needed) slap in the face." Because Paula had absorbed the idea that a romantic partner makes you whole, she hadn't previously considered that she might be happy as-is, that she already had a relationship that sustained her. Eventually, she realized there wasn't a hole in her life that needed to be filled.

There's value in social practices like dating that help us bridge the chasm to other people's minds; by giving us a script to follow and shared expectations and priorities, they spare us the exhausting work of making every decision ourselves. But these practices, and society's messages about relationships, affect us in ways that we can overlook: they alter the possibilities we imagine for our lives. They can make it hard to understand what we want, or, like Paula, notice when we already have what we want. Even if we manage to discern our desires, as long as we think no one else longs for the same thing, we may simply end up feeling isolated. But from the reaction to *The Atlantic* article and working on this book, I've learned that many people either have or want a life that doesn't fit the one-stop-shop coupledom ideal and are eager to build a life with friends. They just don't know how many other people like them are out there.

It's been a professional preoccupation of mine to uncover mismatches like these, between perception and reality. By identifying our mistaken beliefs and the social rules that confine us, I hope we can forge deeper ties with others. This is no small matter at a time when Americans are experiencing a "friendship recession" and loneliness is pervasive enough that the US surgeon general declared it an epidemic. Study after study has found that lack of social connection ravages our health and happiness, and even political conservatives have been arguing that we need a broader set of relationships than the nuclear family provides. In the decades since the political scientist Robert Putnam published his groundbreaking book *Bowling Alone*, which chronicled the decline in Americans' engagement in community life, Americans have continued to withdraw from sources of social connection, as captured in trends ranging from falling church attendance to a drop in the number of friends Americans have. At the same time, depression and anxiety have grown among both adolescents and adults. It's uncontroversial to argue that many Americans need a thicker web of relationships. And yet, the cultural ideal continues to treat a single romantic relationship as the key to fulfillment.

Society neglects the possibilities for profound platonic connection, but the friends I profile in each chapter of *The Other Significant Others* insist upon them. Friendships, they show, can provide security and transform the people in them. They can contain the thrill and tenderness that most people only expect to find in relationships that involve sex.

Though there are many ways to pursue a meaningful life beyond romantic coupling, platonic partnerships deserve special attention because their close resemblance to romantic relationships offers valuable insights. Comparing these types of relationships exposes deep-seated assumptions about romantic partnerships, friendships, and family that might otherwise go unnoticed.

The chapters of the book, each built around a close-up view of one friendship, turn those assumptions into questions: Is sex essential to partnership? Must two people be (or have been) a couple to make suitable co-parents? Why do we recognize the loss of some types of relationships as devastating but not others? The first chapter of the book asks questions that emerged from my friendship with M and which laid my path to this project: What exactly *is* this kind of friendship, and what does it mean that people today find it difficult to understand it? The book starts with stories of people in their twenties and thirties, a period when many feel pressure to find a lasting romantic relationship if they want to unlock a full life. The chapters that follow explore how committed friendships bend and expand around the terrain of later life stages, from caregiving to retirement. The intimate portraits of friendships in this book are not a call to replace existing norms with a new imperative or a new hierarchy. Nor are they a how-to guide for platonic partnerships. Rather, these stories are an invitation to expand what options are open to us.

I've found that the unscripted nature of these friendships has advantages, and I write about those in this book, but I am not suggesting that everyone pawn their wedding rings, nor am I arguing that platonic partnerships are inherently superior to romantic relationships. Platonic partnerships aren't utopian, and romantic relationships can be tremendously fulfilling. But romantic coupledom isn't the setup that leads everyone to flourish, and for an increasing number of people—single, divorced, widowed, and more—a romantic relationship is not their life's centerpiece, whether by choice or circumstance. The question is whether people can pursue the relationships that matter to them with dignity and recognition by their society and legal system.

Like many people who have organized their lives around a romantic relationship and have encouraged others to do the same, Andrew's mom had good intentions. "I want both of my children to be happy," she told me. "To me, that emotional happiness would come from having a relationship"—a romantic relationship, she meant. Lisa was trying to nudge her son toward the form of happiness she knew well. But it's easy to mistake what is familiar for what is wise. Andrew and Toly found there are other relationships that could lead them to the same destination that Lisa wanted for her son, to a vista she hadn't known was there.

1

DEFINING THE RELATIONSHIP

Platonic love's possibilities, then and now

The hardest things to talk about are the ones we ourselves can't understand.

—ELENA FERRANTE

In 2017, five months after moving to Washington, D.C., I walked to the narrow back room of a bar called Lost & Found to celebrate the birthday of my roommate's best friend. The room was an industrial shoebox, its low ceiling, exposed brick wall, and concrete floor trapping the sounds of the crowded space and forcing us to shout. On the other side of the room was a person who, even from far away, I found magnetic. She didn't resemble the other D.C. young people at the bar on this Wednesday night, their blazers and button-downs not fitting quite right, like costumes for a performance of adulthood. In her pastel sleeveless blouse and snug pencil skirt, she had the posture of a dancer—if that dancer were also running a boardroom meeting—and expressive gestures. Later, I managed to pull her into conversation, and I noticed the clear diction and melody in her voice.

Slightly tipsy, I blurted out what could have been a pickup line: "You're a singer, aren't you?"

She was surprised I had detected that after only a few sentences of conversation. In fact, she sang as a soprano in two choirs.

Her name was M. Glasses of wine in hand, we talked about my amateur performing arts experience as a kid; how she came from a musical family and got an early start with piano and voice lessons. Our throats sore from raising our voices over the din of the bar, we left the party after a couple of hours and walked to the metro. During the four stops it took to get to our neighborhood, we discovered that we lived only a few blocks away from each other. After exchanging numbers, I left M off at her house and felt giddy as I walked to mine.

I quickly discovered that M has no chill. Or at least, she had no self-consciousness about showing enthusiasm. Soon after we parted that night, I got a voice memo from her. I would discover that M's voice memos were the audio equivalent of her emails to friends, smart and stream-of-consciousness. She had an ability to turn observations about the tiniest things into intriguing questions. Between us was a blizzard of ideas—from books and articles we were reading and details about the important people in our lives, toggling easily between the interpersonal, emotional, and intellectual.

Three days after we met, M invited me to a casual weekly gathering she held at her house that introduced me to what I would come to think of as her "extroverted introversion." M often brings friends together but might also opt to celebrate her birthday by taking herself to a movie, alone. At this gathering, she merged the two impulses by convening friends to talk over a meal she'd cooked for us and then, after lighting a candle, have us curl up in her living room and read our own books in silence.

It took us little time to introduce each other to the people and spaces that mattered to us. M became a regular enough presence at my office that she cracked jokes with the security guard. About a month after we met, M invited me to join her family at an outdoor jazz festival in D.C. We dropped by each other's homes with the effortless frequency that before then had only seemed possible on sitcoms.

It was all a magnificent surprise. I didn't expect to feel the exhilaration I found with M, because it didn't occur to me that those feelings could strike more than once. I met her two and a half years into a relationship with my now husband, whom I'll call Marco. I felt fortunate to have found a partner so young and assumed that I had made a trade: in exchange for finding my partner at twenty-two, I wouldn't get to feel what it's like to fall in love again—unless something went wrong between Marco and me. But here were those same feelings, just shorn of sexual desire.

In certain ways, M and Marco were similar: analytical, disciplined, charming. But while Marco was steady—his lows not very low at all, and his highs not off the charts—M had the dial turned up. She was an easy crier, and she couldn't contain the evidence; when her tears evaporated, rings of salt formed under her eyes. She gave such wise advice that therapists I went to disappointed me—it felt absurd to spend time and money talking to people whose insight was inferior to hers. Whereas Marco sought beauty by spending time outdoors, M looked to the stage.

The intensity of my friendship with her was without any real precedent. I'd had a best friend in elementary school, who moved away. I had another in middle school: we took acting and singing classes together and had sleepovers most weekends, making Easy Mac and recording goofy videos. I came to feel like a member of her extended family, but after we grew apart in high school, I tended to rely on several close friends, not a single person, and I never found someone who made me want to open up as I later would to M. In high school,

I struggled to talk about what was going on: that my mom had lost her job during the recession; my dad hadn't been working for years; my parents were functionally separated, and the main reason my mom stayed in the same home as my dad in New Jersey was the unaffordability of moving out now that she was unemployed. I couldn't talk about how despair could overtake my mom and how my dad, who had been such an adoring father to me, could scare me with his ire and bitterness toward my mom.

During my junior year, I became close to a girl named Sophia, who was a grade above me. I shared more with her than with other people, but I still couldn't broach some of my issues at home. Sophia also helped me put my finger on something I wanted, as she had a best friend that she spoke to all the time and could call at any hour. She and her friend were a recognized unit. I approached that kind of connection in graduate school, when I made a best friend, Anna, though we later moved to different cities. Then I met M, to whom I eventually became so close that the term *best friend* seemed inadequate.

On New Year's Eve in 2017, M and I cohosted a party at my house for about a dozen friends, some of whom were passing through town and didn't know the other guests. Like a poet who enjoys the creative constraints of rhyme scheme, M takes pleasure in devising structured social gatherings. M arranged for our friends (and she herself) to play music and led people through a writing exercise: a series of prompts to reflect on the past year and to look forward. She asked us: What vows do we want to renew to ourselves?

Her vow to herself was to ask for help more. "Every time you begin a new project, personal or professional, you should *start* by asking, *Who could help me with this?*" she said. My vow was meant to reduce the alienation I felt at my large office—where I felt reserved, far removed from my social self—by reaching out to a new person each month whom I wanted to know better. To be with M was to be pushed to grow, and I would later see this element of our friendship mirrored in the account of a couple's romantic relationship. One of the partners, on her blog, described a core principle in their relationship as "Mutually Assured Non Complacency."

Through M, I experienced a kind of vitality and besottedness in friendship that I hadn't had before. I relished it all. I wanted to understand how her mind worked, to mimic the exuberant way she moved through the world. And I felt privy to a secret: that it's possible to find the headiness and security that we associate with romantic relationships within a friendship.

"Secret" is hardly hyperbole, because as M and I got closer, we found that our friendship didn't have a ready-made label. We felt like a species that biologists had yet to classify. We weren't merely "friends." Even "best friend" felt like a downgrade; our commitment exceeded that of most best friends we knew. We would exchange voice memos multiple times per day and regularly bcc each other on important work emails. We introduced our friends to the other, and though we maintained our own ties, a network of mutual friends grew.

If I wanted someone else to get to know M, I'd ask her if I could extend an invitation to one of the parties she hosted every few months. At these parties, M's musically talented friends performed pieces that traversed centuries, genres, and continents, from nineteenth-century classical choral music to African children's songs to original folk songs. The setting was casual: dozens of us would sit cross-legged on the living room floor and a five-dollar bouquet from Safeway, M's décor splurge, would rest on the mantel. But she carefully choreographed the parties with a set list, hours of practice, and a strictly-adhered-to party end time. (At one party, a friend of M's gifted her a banner that read "Please leave by 9.") One of M's shticks as emcee was to explain that a language her parents speak has no exact translation for the word *singer*; there's a cultural expectation that everyone sings, so it would be odd for someone to describe themselves as "a singer" or say, "I'm not a singer," as people do in the United States. M carried that idea into the party. Toward the end of the night, she would break us into sections, directing us to sing a round together, or she'd lead us in a well-known song like "Seasons of Love." You could have the singing voice of a raccoon and still feel like you contributed to the dulcet tones.

She also cared for me as no other friend had, blending the ebullience of a fairy godmother with the occasional eat-your-vegetables entreaty of an actual mother. More than once, when I had a cold, she came over to my house with a tote bag full of lemons, fresh ginger, and black tea, which she turned into a concoction on the stove. She made me finish the steaming drink, even as I winced from the acidity and complained like a child. She talked me through family difficulties, sent me email reminders to find a therapist, and reduced the self-consciousness I felt when talking about sex. It would have been plenty if she simply made me comfortable discussing events and thoughts that I had previously kept hidden. But through her open-mindedness and spirit of exploration, M helped me ask myself questions I wouldn't have asked before and identify thoughts and feelings that I hadn't yet given the soil to grow.

I knew that I was her person, too. On a couple of nights when she was having a hard time, I went to her house and held her. I slept over, overheated by her faux shearling blanket. I saw how she worried about her family members and about her tower of student debt. She often struggled to balance her wonky, analytical interests with her creative ambitions as a musician and writer—she was like a house that would short-circuit if too many appliances were on at once; she had to choose which to turn on at any given time. We talked often about how she could keep these two essential parts of herself running.

Four months after we met, M ended a call between us by saying, "I love you." I lobbed back, "I love you, too," in an aw-shucks tone. I was sitting next to a stranger on an Amtrak train—a setting that made it hard for me to take in those words and earnestly say "I love you" back. I regretted that I couldn't muster more sincerity, because there was no question that I loved M.

A couple of days later, I tried to parse in my journal what it was that we had been building together. I didn't know how to think about our friendship, I wrote. And without a framework, I went on, "I don't have an easy way to describe our friendship to others, which feels crazy because our friendship has got to be the most important development since moving to D.C."

———————

I may not have had much personal precedent for a friendship like the one M and I developed, but the historical record reveals plenty.

On the floor of Merton College's chapel in Oxford, England, beneath stained glass windows that depict apostles, a flat, ten-foot-long brass monument marks the joint crypt of John Bloxham and John Whytton. The men stand side by side, garments draping down to their feet, each holding their hands in prayer as if they're a pair of saints. Why were they buried in this chapel—together—and memorialized as a pair? The most direct answer is that Whytton arranged for it to happen. He provided funds for the monument and the tomb after Bloxham died in 1387. He also asked to be buried with Bloxham.

After visiting this memorial and others like it, the British historian

Alan Bray considered a radical possibility: maybe they were evidence of a long-forgotten practice of same-sex marriage. After all, their design mimicked those for husbands and wives in medieval English churches. Other monuments to same-sex pairs included the marriage knot that appears on monuments for spouses. Some featured family shields, suggesting the merging of two lineages.

It took decades for Bray to arrive at a different conclusion, that these men had a type of relationship that is now foreign to us: a societally recognized, committed relationship built around platonic love. Intent on interpreting the past on its own terms, Bray determined that Europeans in earlier centuries had a different conception of friendship from our own. Friendship was not a private relationship, as it's now understood to be, but one of public significance, regularly honored in churches.

Bloxham and Whytton's path to their resting place in the chapel began around 1364, when they met as young men at Merton College. At the time, Whytton was likely a young scholar and Bloxham a fellow at the college. Their friendship spanned more than twenty years. Besides the fact that they were buried in a church, a detail in the tomb's monument elevates their friendship to a spiritual plane. The engraving of the name *Johannes* seems to identify Saint John the Baptist as the men's spiritual godfather, which would make Bloxham and Whytton spiritual brothers.

Bloxham and Whytton appear to have followed a practice that was common in medieval and early modern England, in which men were ritually turned into brothers and, afterward, were expected to support each other for the rest of their lives. Sworn brotherhood had deep roots. Monks in the fourth to seventh centuries would sometimes pair off, each member of the duo taking responsibility for the other's spiritual progress. In the sixth century, two monks from Syria, Symeon and John, had such a deep connection that they shared the same visions. Ultimately, they left the monastery they had joined in Jordan and became desert hermits together, but before they parted, the abbot kneeled, each man on either side, and prayed for them. The ritual between these two men, according to Claudia Rapp, a Byzantine scholar at the University of Vienna, was the inaugural act of *adelphopoiesis*—literally, the making of brothers.

For centuries in the East, these rituals took place in Christian churches: two friends would enter a church, place their hands on the Gospel, one on top of the other, and the priest would say prayers over them. After embracing, the men would be seen as "brothers" for the rest of their lives. Adelphopoiesis was practiced by monks and laypeople in the Byzantine Empire, and limited evidence suggests there were also sworn friendships between pairs of women and between women and men. Historians have found similar forms of brotherhood—known alternately as *wed brothers* or *blood brothers* and celebrated with a variety of rituals—throughout Europe, Asia, and the Middle East. Though men could enter into these relationships for instrumental reasons, such as to secure a strategic alliance between families, many men were driven to become brothers out of deep fondness for one another. Sworn brotherhood could exist alongside marriage. Sometimes men chose to be buried with their sworn brothers rather than their wives.

The very features that make such intense friendships seem out of place today were, at other times in history, seen as normal and laudable: the affection, devotion, and ritual they involve; the way friends operate as a unit; how the friends are integrated into each other's families of origin. One of the earliest pieces of written literature, *The Epic of Gilgamesh*, is a paean to an inseparable male friendship. The Old Testament features stories of extreme devotion among friends: David, the future king of Israel, bound himself by covenant to his friend Jonathan "because he loved him as his own soul." Ancient Greek and Roman thinkers used language much like this to describe friendship. In ancient Rome, a person might refer to a friend in terms that people would now find appropriate for a spouse, such as "half of my soul" or "the greater part of my soul."

In antiquity and the early modern period, family, friend, and spouse were not ranked in a clear hierarchy, and a friend could take on roles that we now assume would only go to a relative or spouse. This was true throughout the world. Friends in late medieval France and elsewhere in the Mediterranean could join their households in a legal contract known as *affrèrement* (roughly translated as "brotherment"). They promised to live together and share "*un pain, un vin, et une bourse*"—one bread, one wine, and one purse—and usually became each other's legal heir, withdrawing that right from blood relatives. Sworn brothers in China contributed to the dowry of a sworn brother's daughter, to the cost of a funeral in a sworn brother's family, and had mourning obligations when the sworn brother's parents died. This kind of relationship blurred the lines between friend and kin.

Though sworn brotherhood used the language of family, it resembled marriage. Both relationships involved rituals that created kin by promise rather than biology, publicly tying families together. Both were enacted before witnesses and sanctified by taking Holy Communion. In fact, these friendships were often referred to as "wedded brotherhoods"—in Middle English, *wed* meant a pledge or covenant and didn't exclusively refer to a "wedded" husband or wife. Men might speak to their friends using terms associated with marriage or kinship. The seventeenth-century English King James I and the first Duke of Buckingham referred to each other in their letters with a medley of terms, including "friend," "husbande," "wyfe," and "chylde," suggesting that their friendship blended each of these relationship types. Bright lines didn't separate marriage, family, and friendship from one another.

Today, friends cannot walk into a house of worship or clerk's office and "wed" each other, turning themselves into siblings in the eyes of the community. But it would be a mistake to assume that people have always organized relationships as we do now, with stark dividing lines and rankings. As incoherent as language like "wedded brotherhood" may seem to our eyes, Bray, the historian, writes, "The confusion lies not in these terms from the past but with us."

———

There was nothing new about the kind of closeness I found in my friendship with M, but the terms to describe it and rituals to commemorate it had disappeared. Without those forms of social recognition or awareness of the history I now know, I felt like she and I were surveying unmapped territory. One afternoon, a friend named Adam suggested a different way to think about my friendship with M. He asked me how my relationships with Marco and M differed. I had to sit with the question for a moment.

Marco and I had met at Oxford, where we were both in master's programs. He struck me as serious—our first conversation involved a discussion of the fall of the Soviet Union—so I was surprised to find that this bookish guy who wore a collared shirt as his casual attire made generous use of emojis in online messaging. Only months after we started dating, he conveyed to his dad how our relationship felt different from other ones he'd been in. Marco, who once considered pursuing an ambitious political career, told his dad that he could see himself instead standing in the wings, watching and supporting me. When he followed me to the United States to get a Ph.D., he was so concerned about making the best use of his time that he kept a spreadsheet tracking his activities in six-minute intervals, yet I'd learn that he can also sit with a friend's toddler and watch him uncap and re-cap markers, happily engrossed, for what seems to me like an eternity.

Marco isn't the type to use terms of endearment unless the purpose is to tease. He calls me "Barnacle," sometimes shortened to "Barney," because of the way I hug him and occasionally refuse to detach myself. (M, meanwhile, has hugged me tightly enough to make my back crack, and I once had to ask her not to hold my hand while walking around my office, which she had done unthinkingly.) Whereas I'm a geyser of affectionate words, true to his Dutch heritage, Marco shows affection through his actions.

Marco and M expressed themselves differently, but I felt that the fundamentals of my romantic relationship with Marco and my friendship with M were similar. The obvious distinction was that I had sex with Marco and didn't with M. My friend Adam told me that I was polyamorous—an assessment he felt comfortable making, as someone who had experience in polyamorous relationships. As he saw it, Marco and M were both partners to me; my partnership with M just didn't involve sex. The framing of polyamory didn't speak to me, though. I associated polyamory with sexual relationships, and I believed others did, too. What use would it be to describe myself as having polyamorous relationships with Marco and M if other people understood that to mean something it wasn't? Though Adam's suggestion didn't fix my nomenclature problem, his comment that I have two partners gave me outside validation that my friendship with M was significant, in some ways closer to a committed romantic relationship than a conventional friendship.

Up until that point, M had been a bigger day-to-day presence in my life than Marco was. He was getting his Ph.D. at a school that's a six-hour train ride away from D.C., and we saw each other every other weekend. Marco was glad I had found someone who quickly gave me a feeling of rootedness in my new city and whose company he enjoyed, too.

In October 2017, I proposed to Marco. I had conspired with a group of friends to host a dinner at my house, structured like many that Marco and I had been to in grad school and later hosted, in which everyone brought a short reading, to be read aloud and then discussed. After Marco kicked us off by reading an excerpt from a book about information theory, everyone else read a text—from an excerpt of Tina Fey's memoir to a transcription of a conversation with their grandmother—that related to love. Because Marco was so intently focused on each specific reading, even scribbling notes on a paper napkin, the theme flew right over his head. He was stunned when I proposed, and he said yes.

After pouring ourselves prosecco, the nine of us broke off into conversations. I found myself with the wife of a friend of Marco's, who asked me how the two of us had become so close, so quickly—but she wasn't referring to me and my new fiancé. She was talking to me and M. Both moony as we took turns narrating, we traced the trajectory of our friendship. We were deep into telling the story when I remembered that minutes ago, I had proposed to Marco. And this wasn't the only time I would be reminded of the way my relationship with M echoed the one that society would publicly recognize.

At my wedding in the Netherlands a year and a half later, M sang multiple songs. During our first dance, Marco and I aligned our *slow-quick-quick* foxtrot steps to the beats of M's rendition of "I Could

Write a Book," the jazz standard she had picked to perform at our engagement party. As a thank-you for singing and helping organize a surprise event during the wedding weekend, I gave her a framed photo of the two of us that had been taken before the ceremony. In it, I hold a bouquet in one hand and my other grips M's waist. M, who is seven inches taller than I am, tilts her head down, and our foreheads touch as we laugh.

A colleague saw this photo on M's desk and asked whether she had gotten married. It was a reasonable interpretation of the photo: besides the obvious intimacy between us, we were enclosed in an arch of lavender flowers, and I wore a lace gown while M had on a white summer dress printed with roses.

————

In earlier centuries, it was understood that women could feel just as deeply for their same-sex friends as for their husbands. Women sent locks of hair as gifts to their male suitors and female friends alike. In Jean-Jacques Rousseau's epistolary novel, *Julie, ou la nouvelle Héloïse,* the friendship between Claire and Julie exceeds the intensity of the connection between Claire and her fiancé. Claire writes to Julie that "next to my Julie [my fiancé] is nothing to me" and tells her fiancé so. Claire writes to Julie, "From our earliest years, my heart has been absorbed in yours . . . you alone took the place of everything for me, and I lived only to be your friend." Her fiancé wasn't threatened or put off by her passionate feelings for Claire; instead, he considered them an indication of her essential goodness, making him more drawn to her.

Such relationships weren't only the stuff of fiction. Sarah Stickney Ellis, the author of the most important nineteenth-century conduct book in England—think Emily Post, but Victorian—treated female friendships as the handmaiden of marriage. At the time, marriage was believed to join two creatures of opposing natures: man and woman. Ellis argued that intensifying the difference between men and women promoted love between spouses. Ellis shows how same-sex friendships can do this, writing, "In the circle of her private friends . . . [woman] learns to comprehend the deep mystery of that electric chain of feeling which ever vibrates through the heart of woman, and which man, with all his philosophy, can never understand." Women's friendships with one another put them in touch with a particularly feminine way of feeling, to marriage's benefit.

There was a dark side to the easy harmony between romantic friendships and marriage. It was rooted in gender inequality: women's economic dependence on men blunted the edge of any perceived threat a same-sex friendship could pose—most women needed to get married, no matter how ardently they felt toward their friends. Like Ellis, men wrote approvingly of women's "romantic friendships" in part because they believed that they served as training grounds for wifehood.

The possibility that a relationship with another woman could replace wedlock emerged in the late nineteenth century, when clerical jobs opened to women, as did coed universities and some prestige professions like medicine, creating more options for women to strike out on their own. During this time, pairs of women—typically well-off or well educated—lived together and supported each other in what were known as *Boston marriages*. The historian Susan Freeman describes these long-term relationships between two unmarried women as "a kind of cousin of romantic friendships." I think of them as a cool older cousin who gets to move freely, without a curfew, unlike the women in romantic friendships who ultimately had to live under a man's control. A nineteenth-century editor of the *Atlantic Monthly*, who knew a number of women in Boston marriages, called them "a union—there is no truer word for it."

A union is what comes to mind when I look at the Queen Anne house—located a few miles from my own—that was owned by two intellectual luminaries of Washington, D.C., Lucy Diggs Slowe and Mary Burrill. In 1922, they purchased this house on a hill when Slowe was the dean of women at Howard University and Burrill was a teacher and playwright. Collectively, they influenced the realms of education, politics, and the arts. Slowe helped found the first sorority for Black university women and, as assistant secretary of the Baltimore NAACP, fought for Black women in the suffrage movement. Writers of the Harlem Renaissance era looked to Burrill's work as a model, and in some cases, they were trained by her.

People treated the two women like a unified pair; friends would compose letters to Slowe with a mention to send their "love to Ms. Burrill." Slowe dedicated one of her poems "to my good friend MPB"—Burrill's initials—"whose sympathetic encouragement induced me to write these lines." Their house, where they lived together for about fifteen years, was a hub for students, educators, politicians, and activists. Grinnell College professor Tamara Beauboeuf-Lafontant, who wrote a biography of Slowe, believes Slowe and Burrill had an erotic relationship in Audre Lorde's understanding of the term: one that strengthens your resolve, feeds creativity, and gives you energy to change the world around you. Like many other women in these arrangements, theirs was a female universe, built around the intellectual and emotional lives of other women—in Slowe's and Burrill's cases, the lives of Black women.

After Slowe's death in 1937, Howard's registrar directed an obituary writer to Burrill, noting that she "has been a lifetime friend and companion of Miss Slowe and I am sure that there is no one who knows her life better than she." Another message read, "My heart aches for you, for I know you two loved each other as only sisters could. I know life will be sad and lonely without her sweet companionship." Burrill had copies of a eulogy for Slowe bound and distributed to her peers. In response to Howard's repeated mistreatment of Slowe (for instance, at one point, they wanted her to live in a house that faced the university dump), Burrill banned the president from having any official role in the funeral that was held at Howard. She got back at Howard by having Slowe's papers sent to Morgan State College. A fierce protector of Slowe's legacy, Burrill was.

———————

The question hovering in the background of stories like Slowe and Burrill's or medieval sworn brothers' is: Did these "friends" have sex? There's no doubt that some of them did. Scholars have uncovered evidence of sexual relationships between same-sex pairs. It's essential to acknowledge these cases, especially because mentions of sex between people of the same gender were, for a long time, deliberately erased from the historical record. To give one example, while looking through the diaries of the English landowner and diarist Anne Lister, an antiquary and Lister's heir decoded sexual references to her relationship with a woman. The antiquary suggested burning the whole lot of Lister's diaries. Scholars, even when they had evidence of sex, didn't acknowledge it.

But there's a risk of overcorrection. Contemporary ideas about sex and intimacy aren't easily portable across time. In his book on male friendships in eighteenth-century America, the historian Richard Godbeer notes that Americans during that period did not assume—as they do now—that "people who are in love with one another must want to have sex" with each other. The upshot is that friends' proclamations of fervent love did not necessarily imply sexual desire.

Because there wasn't an automatic link between sex and affection, it was considered normal and innocent for friends to gush. Around the turn of the twentieth century, when two students at a women's college became enamored of each other, they were declared "smashed." (In England, a similar relationship was known as a "rave.") As an 1873 letter about the phenomenon describes, "When a Vassar girl takes a shine to another, she straightaway enters upon a regular course of bouquet sendings, interspersed with tinted notes, mysterious packages . . . locks of hair perhaps, and many other tender tokens, until at last the object of her attentions is captured, the two become inseparable." Men in the eighteenth through early twentieth centuries had same-sex friendships that—in one historian's words—"verged on romance." Ardent declarations like the one made by printer Thomas B. Wait to his friend George Thatcher wouldn't have stood out as unusual at the time; in a letter he wrote in 1809, Wait described his heart problems to Thatcher and assured his friend that "this heart of mine, however feeble and how soon soever it may cease to move, its last pulsations shall vibrate for you." Men shared beds and expressed their feelings of fraternal love. Not only were forms of affection out in the open; the emotional intensity and physicality that we now associate almost exclusively with romantic relationships was then a hallmark of friendship.*

One risk of assuming that passion always translates into sexual attraction or consummation is that we can fail to see relationships for

---

* There's a rich area of historical scholarship exploring whether romantic friendships fall within queer lineages. See, for instance, Martha Vicinus's *Intimate Friends: Women Who Loved Women, 1778–1928.*

what they were. Bray, the British historian who spent decades trying to understand the meaning of shared tombs like Bloxham and Whytton's, had previously written a book about sex between men in Renaissance England. He had no interest in denying sex where it existed, but while working on his next book, *The Friend*, worried that narrowing our attention to sexuality could cause us to miss what was really going on in relationships from centuries ago. "The inability to conceive of relationships in other than sexual terms says something of contemporary poverty," Bray wrote. A laser focus on sexuality can also limit the questions we ask; Bray argued it can "obscure that wider frame" of inquiry.

Widening the frame allows us to see that today's discrete categories and hierarchies are neither innate nor universal: Marriage doesn't have to rank above friendship. Love doesn't automatically involve lust. Romantic and platonic feelings aren't always easy to distinguish.

And another: *sexual* is not the same as *erotic*. Columbia University professor Sharon Marcus traces how mainstream Victorian culture endorsed same-sex eroticism among girls and women but not sex between women. Girls were encouraged to idolize or caress their female dolls; wives were expected to take pleasure in looking at illustrations of women wearing the latest fashions. Marcus explains that women could speak in rapturous terms about other women without interpreting their desire as sexual, "precisely because Victorians saw lesbian sex almost nowhere." That's why, in 1874, a married twenty-five-year-old woman could unselfconsciously write this in her diary about women she had observed skating: "The beauty of the girls was something to make one scream with delight. The older I grow the more slave I am to beauty." Until lesbianism became a sexual identity—and a stigmatized one at that—women could openly enjoy the sensual pleasure and intense emotions they inspired in one another.

The distinction between the sexual and erotic, clearer in the past than it tends to be now, has helped me understand feelings in my own relationships. I had grown up thinking I was straight because I had crushes on boys, which ruled out being a lesbian; I hadn't considered that I could be bisexual, as I'd been told that bisexuality wasn't "real"—that people who claimed to be bi were lying either to others or themselves. After I realized that bisexuality was indeed real and a spot-on label for me, I looked back on earlier female friendships and wondered whether I felt queer desire in any of them. The answer was yes: whereas I'd previously interpreted my feelings about certain girls as envy for them, I now see sexual longing. But I didn't feel that way with all my friends, including M, who's also queer. My friendship with M has a different kind of charge, something not sexual but erotic in Audre Lorde's definition. M brings out a sense of aliveness in me. When we exchange what's on our minds, it's as if we're jointly creating a new way of seeing the world and ourselves. Between coming out and studying historical friendships, I came to understand that there are far more forms of desire, attraction, and connection than I had been made to believe.

———

Once M entered the picture, it took me little time to realize that it could be a boon to have deep relationships with more than one person. I appreciate being influenced by her as well as Marco. When we talk about a personal issue, Marco is liable to offer a different perspective from my own, while M will often reassure me that my feelings about the situation are warranted and comparable to ones she's had in the past. Both are helpful. Being so close to two people, I got to learn, by the osmosis of everyday conversation, about the subject of whatever political biography Marco was reading but also whatever new psychology concept M found eye-opening. I had two temperaments and life experiences to learn from, two main tributaries flowing into my mind. The occasions when the three of us walked in our neighborhood—sometimes M would hold one of my hands, Marco the other—felt decadent to me.

Early on, M and I craved a label for our relationship, primarily to help other people understand it—a term as firm and clear as *sister* or *supervisor* or *spouse*. Pop culture made me suspect that other people could use a term, too: there was the wacky, enamored bond between Ilana and Abbi in *Broad City*, the unwavering devotion between Cristina and Meredith in *Grey's Anatomy* (Cristina famously told Meredith, "You are my person"), and the abiding affection between Gayle King and Oprah Winfrey, who teared up during an interview when she said Gayle is "the mother I never had" and "the sister everybody would want. She is the friend that everybody deserves." As I spoke to people with friendships of similar depth and commitment, I found it both poignant and frustratingly inefficient that individual pairs of friends labored over finding language to describe who they were—from platonic soulmate to non-romantic life partner—and often didn't know that other relationships like theirs existed. The belief that their friendship was unique made their connection feel special but also could make them feel alone.

I thought shared language, maybe a term borrowed from the past like *romantic friendship*, would help people who had similar friendships today make sense of their own experience. Maybe a term could legitimize these friendships in the eyes of others and enrich people's imaginations for what a friendship could be. I decided on the term *platonic partnerships* to describe the relationships I write about in the book, but over time, I became less interested in trying to popularize a label. People might simply add a category to their relationship dictionary and move on, whereas my friendship with M had given me far more than a new flash card to memorize: it led me to probe received wisdom about relationships that I hadn't known needed fact-checking. Besides, our friendship would eventually change such that a label like platonic partner wouldn't be relevant to us. What outlasted my search for words were the questions that our friendship, and friendships like ours, had cracked open.

OTHER SIGNIFICANT OTHERS

Beyond "the one"

True Love in this differs from gold and clay,
That to divide is not to take away.

—PERCY BYSSHE SHELLEY

On an early date with a man she was getting to know, Kami West decided she'd better make one thing clear. Whatever came to pass between the two of them, Kami's number one person would always be her best friend, Kate Tillotson, or Tilly. She had been there before he had and "will be here after you," Kami said. "And if you think at any point that this isn't going to be my number one, you're wrong."

Kami and Tilly had met in 2007 at the United States Marine Corps boot camp in Parris Island, South Carolina. Though their uniforms turned the recruits into a blur of camouflage, Kami stood out as one of the tallest women in the platoon, and having spent almost ten years in the Young Marines, a youth leadership program, she was skilled and confident when it came to drills and commands. Tilly, on the other hand, was unassuming and quiet, but Kami soon sensed that she was a smart observer of other people and situations. She was a good person to have on your team.

A month into training, they were assigned to the same bunk and found they were more committed to the marines than most of their peers. Tilly had grown up in a military family and was homeschooled through frequent moves, until she entered a huge public high school in a Tulsa suburb. There, she ate lunch alone almost every day. Kami, who'd grown up in a small town outside Denver, had been bullied at her tiny high school and often wound up in fights; her teachers, it seemed, wrote her off as a student who would never amount to anything. Now, though, her drill instructors saw her as someone with leadership ability.

As they got to know each other over nighttime discussions, Tilly thought, *I click with you. Like some gooberness in me clicks with the gooberness in you. We must be friends.* They also discovered that Kami's mom had moved from Colorado to a suburb of Tulsa called Broken Arrow, close to where Tilly's parents lived. After graduating from boot camp, Kami and Tilly both landed in Oklahoma, and Tilly, after a fight with her parents, moved in with Kami for two weeks. They passed the time by driving around aimlessly in Kami's mom's black sedan, sunglasses on, Flo Rida and Beyoncé blaring out the rolled-down windows.

In the years since then, through relocations and romantic relationships and children and the pandemic, they've talked almost every day. "Tilly knows inside and out every detail, every secret, everything about me. Everything," Kami says. Whether or not Tilly was in a romantic relationship, Tilly would first go to Kami to talk about something tough—"consulting with the Oracle," as she calls it.

Kami had chosen to explain her closeness with Tilly to her date because it had become something of a problem for one of her past boyfriends. He had tried to discourage Kami from spending time with Tilly. He'd called Tilly a slut—an epithet Tilly found comical because her dating life had been in a prolonged drought. He blew up at Tilly when she made a joke that favorably compared Kami's butt to Kim Kardashian's. His controlling behavior escalated, which put a strain on the friendship. After Kami broke up with him, she vowed, "I will never ever, ever have that happen again because [Tilly] is so important to my life."

She hoped she could keep a romantic relationship from threatening the friendship through a head-on conversation about Tilly's number one status. But this date didn't quite get her message. He asked, "Eventually, I'll be your number one, right?"

————

Kami's date was operating on an assumption that ripples through American culture: that a romantic relationship comes first, and friendships should retreat in their wake. Hell, in the TV show *Friends*, friendship comes second: Rachel is forced to move out of the apartment she shared with her best friend, Monica, so that Monica's boyfriend could move in.

From our first encounter with Disney movies and rom-coms, we're taught to fantasize about finding our soulmate, who, in psychologist Bella DePaulo's words, we also expect to be our *sole* mate. A romantic partner is supposed to be the one-stop shop where we can meet the full spectrum of our practical and psychological needs. For a lot of people, that now includes the role of best friend. Whereas, in the past, the overlapping features of marriage and friendship equalized different types of relationships, the spouse-is-my-best-friend phenomenon feels like hoarding; spouses, who are already in a place of honor, get to claim the top title in another relationship category.

This privileging of romantic relationships can make them feel compulsory. Singleness might not carry the same stigma as it did just decades ago, especially for women. And yet, like Paula from the introduction, we may have internalized the message that we're missing something fundamental if we're not in a romantic relationship. Language like *my other half* suggests that you only graduate to being a full human once you have a romantic partner.

At the same time, the one-stop-shopping ideal sets unrealistic standards, setting the stage for disappointment. (Dating apps probably don't help, as they give the impression that someone better is only a swipe away.) These two relationship ideals can push in opposite directions: the urge to find our "other half" can lead us to jump into romantic relationships while the one-stop-shopping standard can lead us to give up on relationships too easily. Yet both reinforce the primacy of romantic connections. If we believe that a romantic partner will make us whole and be everything to us, it's logical for that relationship to come first.

Marriage hasn't always been under this pressure. In past centuries, people did not expect their spouse to be their passionate lover and best friend, all in one package. In fact, American and Western European marriages before the late eighteenth century bore more resemblance to government treaties than to *The Bachelor*. Among other things, marriage created political, economic, and military alliances and set out rights and obligations such as sex and property ownership.

This is not to say that people in the distant past, even those who wed for instrumental reasons, never experienced genuine romantic love. At least four thousand years ago, betrothed lovers wrote romantic poems. But until the mid-1800s, writes historian Stephanie Coontz, "love in marriage was seen as a bonus, not as a necessity." Indeed, if a suitor could offer a woman financial security but not much passion, she had to weigh whether pursuing love was worth starvation or social disapproval. In a letter to her niece, the novelist Jane Austen captured this dilemma. Though she insisted that "anything is to be preferred or endured rather than marrying without affection," she added a deflating reality check: "Single women have a dreadful propensity for being poor—which is one very strong argument in favor of Matrimony."

At the time Austen was writing, wives couldn't own property—rather, they were their husband's property. Husbands could beat their wives (as long as he didn't permanently injure or kill her in the process) and were entitled to sex with them whenever they pleased. It's little wonder that until the twentieth century, people generally had stronger emotional connections with their friends than their spouses.

Some Enlightenment thinkers, persuaded by ideals of equality and citizenship, came to believe that marriage should be a voluntary contract between husband and wife and that people should marry for love rather than for financial, familial, or religious reasons. By the mid-nineteenth century, a radical idea took hold: that love should be not merely a bonus but rather the *basis* for marriage. There's fervent debate among historians about the timing and cause of changes in marriage, particularly whether shifts in the economy altered marriage dynamics or whether shifts in marriage and family dynamics made the Industrial Revolution possible. And marriage did not change in the same way across all classes or in a straightforward line of progress.

Whatever the cause, marriage evolved from being a union designed to acquire useful in-laws or money to a private relationship between two people. The ideal of a "companionate marriage" became easier to achieve as women gained autonomy. In the mid-1800s, some US states started to unravel the rules of coverture—the legal idea that wives were subsumed (or "covered") under their husband's identity—that gave men authority over their wives. Still, only some people were allowed to use love as the basis for marriage. In the United States, laws denied marriage rights to enslaved Black Americans, interracial couples, and same-sex couples.

By the late twentieth century, the legal picture had changed. Divorce law didn't heavily favor men anymore, marital rape finally became illegal, and women could do such extravagant things as get a credit card in their own name. It was around this time that Americans began ratcheting up their expectations for spouses. Eli Finkel, a psychology professor at Northwestern University, calls the last several decades the era of the "self-expressive marriage." This form of coupledom demands not only love and companionship but also fulfillment of deep psychological needs. Finkel says we want our spouses to act like Michelangelo to our proverbial marble, to be the sculptor who reveals the best version of ourselves that's locked within the stone.

Some of these higher expectations are a welcome change from a time when wives had disconcertingly low standards. When Coontz interviewed women in the 1950s and '60s, they made remarks like, "Oh, it's a good enough marriage—he doesn't hit me." The bar is not that low these days, but expectations may have swung too far in the other direction, so extensive that they're hard for one person to satisfy. That doesn't stop spouses from trying. Having heard the relatively recent maxim that "marriage is hard work," spouses put in effort to maintain a successful relationship. In an essay analyzing prominent on-screen depictions of marriage, the *New York Times* cultural critic A. O. Scott writes, "In film and television, work and wedded bliss are now synonymous: the harder marriage is, the more romantic it seems."

Because couples must invest more time and have greater emotional skills to meet these lofty expectations, Finkel argues that "the best marriages today are better than the best marriages of earlier eras; indeed they are the best marriages that the world has ever known." But the same expectations that have launched the top sliver of marriages to supreme heights appear to be damaging the average marriage. The title of Finkel's book captures the stark divide: *The All-or-Nothing Marriage*. Over the last several decades, the proportion of spouses whose marriages aren't measuring up to expectations has grown. Fewer Americans report being "very happy" in their marriages. Finkel says the average marriage has worsened during this time because it's tough to meet such demanding requirements. By asking so much of one relationship, marriages today are like handblown glass: exquisite, but fragile.

The all-encompassing expectations for marriage can compromise relationships that sit outside matrimony's cocoon. The sociologists Naomi Gerstel and Natalia Sarkisian write that the common goal of finding a "soulmate," which is an aspiration that few people declared only decades ago, "means turning inward—pushing aside other relationships." Partners who see each other as soulmates pour their energy into each other, and that's time lost on friends and neighbors. In an analysis of large national surveys from the 1990s and early 2000s, Gerstel and Sarkisian found that married Americans were less likely than unmarried or divorced Americans to live with, visit, or call relatives. Married Americans socialized with neighbors or friends less than unmarried Americans, were far less likely to take care of aging parents than unmarried adult children, and were less politically involved. Gerstel and Sarkisian conclude that marriage, instead of being the cornerstone of community, as many politicians and experts claim, often strains community ties. Other researchers found that when wives believed that marriage is a relationship between soulmates—rather than a loving relationship that is also about forming a financial partnership and raising children—both the husband and wife were less likely to spend time volunteering. All this undivided attention that marriage demands, sociologists say, makes it a "greedy institution."

As Americans delay or forgo marriage, the tendrils of marital expectations have extended to nonmarital romantic relationships. Whether or not a romantic partnership has been formalized through marriage, the effect is the same: people who feel dissatisfied in their relationship may find it easier to blame themselves or their partner rather than faulty expectations. Even if the thought of deepening connections with friends or family members crosses their mind, it might not feel like a way to strengthen the marriage but instead like settling.

These standards don't just harm people who are actively dissatisfied. People who are currently in a rewarding romantic relationship may find, at some point, that having more than one person to lean on would enrich their lives. It's a safety net: if one person is your everything and the relationship ends, you stand to lose it all—your confidant, best friend, sexual partner, professional coach, and more—all at once.

Romantic partners today are supposed to occupy so much space in our lives that it's hard to imagine anyone rivaling them. But Kami and Tilly, through the abiding support their friendship provides, found that romantic relationships don't have to be all-consuming.

This is not to say it's always been uncomplicated. Their friendship faltered in 2008, after Kami came across MySpace messages between her then-fiancé and Tilly. She made an angry phone call to Tilly, who was on duty at her marine base, and Tilly hung up on Kami. They didn't talk for months. By the time Kami, who'd misunderstood the nature of the exchange, sent a Facebook message to apologize, Tilly had deployed to Iraq. They kept in touch after that, but it wasn't until 2010 that the two friends finally saw each other in person again.

So much had happened. Kami had given birth to a son, Kody, and was raising him on her own. Tilly was enamored of the toddler with white-blond hair but also worried for Kami—she had seen another single mother in the marines struggle. Kami had in fact been having a hard time at work. Kody had a low red blood cell count, and Kami was reprimanded when she had to miss work to take him to doctor's appointments and blood transfusions. Her situation wasn't like that of the marines' male leaders, who often had civilian wives at home to handle childcare issues. While she'd once hoped to be a career marine and work in the legal field, she found herself saddled with dull administrative work on a base in California.

Tilly, meanwhile, had wound up in a bad marriage. She'd had a courthouse wedding right before her deployment at nineteen. Now she was stationed in North Carolina and renting a house near the beach to get some distance from her husband. She was ready to end things with him.

Seeing each other in person brought their friendship back to life. Kami felt "an ocean wave of emotions again"—a dormant exuberance had resurfaced. Before Tilly left, they committed to staying in touch. They started texting, emailing, and calling all the time.

There were some things Tilly didn't say over the phone: that her efforts to repair her marriage hadn't worked, that PTSD had turned her sleep into a reel of nightmares. In 2012, she returned to Oklahoma, ashamed that she was getting a divorce and that she couldn't afford to stay in New York. Kami, in contrast, greeted Tilly's impending return with excitement. She forced Tilly to go out and have fun. They took Zumba classes and got drinks at the bar Kami loved for its *Cheers*-like atmosphere.

Tilly became a regular at day care and then preschool pickup. Kody would stand in the middle of the two women, holding each of their hands. Kami felt like "the seas parted" when they walked down the hallway past the child-size lockers. Eyeing Tilly, a teacher would ask, "Who is this?" It was too hard to explain the depth of their friendship to each inquirer, so they began to refer to themselves as "boot camp besties."

The term *boot camp besties* captures how the friendship started, but not how it had reached the level of intensity it now had. During those years in Oklahoma, the friendship entered a new category. Kami and Tilly were together constantly. Kami followed Tilly's suggestion to switch to a college that was closer to her; they took all the same classes so that they could share textbooks and save money.

Kami had recently ended her relationship with her controlling boyfriend, he of the humorless response to Tilly's Kim Kardashian joke, but that didn't leave her feeling empowered. Sitting around Tilly's fireplace, Kami said she saw herself living in a trailer and "working at a little store with my little son, and that's just going to be my life." She thought she wouldn't graduate from college, would never find a romantic partner, and would become worse off financially. Tilly told her, "The F it's going to be your life."

Tilly asked Kami to come up with a list of what she wanted in a partner and what she wouldn't put up with. After having been careful not to pressure Kami to leave her boyfriend, Tilly finally leveled with her friend. She emphasized that a partner "should bring something to the table" and welcome her son. Tilly, as Kami's friend, had already demonstrated what it would look like to do that. Tilly didn't mind that Kami couldn't go out drinking because she needed to take care of her son. When Kami worked at a bar, Tilly watched after Kody.

Kami, who had a history of romantic partners who didn't treat her particularly well, considers this conversation "a stepping stone for me, that I can be valued as a mother. I can be valued as a wife. I don't have to settle." She says, "I tell [Tilly] that all the time, like, 'Dude, you really taught me how to be okay with myself and how to set my standards high.'"

Although Kami's ranking talk did not go well the first time she raised it on a date, she kept with it. By saying that Tilly was her top priority, Kami was breaking with convention. "Our boyfriends, our significant others, and our husbands are supposed to be number one," Kami told me. "Our worlds are backwards."

Eventually, she started dating a man, Rawley Brenton, who reacted differently. He told Kami that he was sorry to hear what she'd gone through with her ex and how great it was that Tilly stuck with her. Tilly was immediately impressed by Rawley, the Brawny man incarnate with his plaid shirts and burly build. In particular, she noticed how much he cared for Kody. Rawley brought Kody around like the boy was his sidekick. If Rawley was repairing something, he'd walk Kody through what he was doing. The two of them developed inside jokes.

In 2014, Kami and Rawley had a daughter, Delilah, who was diagnosed with a rare genetic condition. The last semester of senior year, Kami dropped out of college because she was in the hospital with Delilah every week for days at a time.

Unable to go to school or work, Kami was cut off from other people. "I had no communication outside of my four walls unless someone came over," Kami says. She lost her friends because no one seemed to understand what it meant to have a child with special needs. The exception was Tilly. She was at the hospital with Kami all the time—sometimes simply to keep Kami company while she was on the phone for hours, battling with her health insurance. To save Kami fifty miles per day in driving, Tilly gave Kami the keys to her house, which was down the street from the half-day special needs school that Delilah attended. That way, Kami could nap or have some "normal adult time" with Tilly until she had to pick up her daughter at noon.

Kami and Tilly maintain two ideas that appear to be at odds: that their friendship raises their bar for relationships but also makes them ask less of a romantic partner. For many people, in a society that doesn't treat you like a full adult if you're not part of a couple, being in an imperfect romantic relationship can feel like a better bet than being in none at all. But Kami and Tilly's friendship releases them from these unpleasant bargains. Because they have each other, they don't need to worry that if they're not in a romantic relationship, no one will be involved in the intricacies of their lives. And because their friendship already provides so much, they don't think it's necessary to find everything in one partner. Tilly considers a romantic relationship to be supplemental—"the cherry on the cake." Referring to herself and Kami, she explained, "We're the cake."

By asking less of a romantic partner, you risk lowering the bar too much; there's no clear line that marks where reasonable expectations end and settling begins. But Kami and Tilly's friendship hasn't diminished their standards for romantic relationships. It's fine-tuned them. Kami and Tilly can cut through the morass of expectations and figure out what they consider most important.

On the whole, a diverse relationship portfolio makes for more satisfying romantic relationships. A 2015 study led by psychologist Elaine Cheung found that people who disperse their emotional needs across multiple relationships are happier than those who concentrate their needs in fewer. For a 2018 study, researchers measured the levels of the stress hormone cortisol in married people. They found that spouses who felt satisfied with the degree of social support they had outside of marriage experienced less physiological stress from day-to-day marital conflicts than those who weren't as satisfied with their support network. To strengthen marriage, Finkel, the psychology professor, recommends that people have OSOs—other significant others.

The idea of distributing the load also underpins ethical non-monogamy—the practice of consensually forming nonexclusive romantic relationships. Some advocates of ethical non-monogamy argue that many people enjoy a better relationship with a primary partner when the pressures on that relationship are reduced by an outside one.

In this setup, prospective partners must sidestep the typical trajectory for romantic relationships—what's been called "the relationship escalator." This term refers to the expectation that a couple in a "serious" relationship should ramp up their commitment and entwinement, becoming exclusive and accumulating roles of confidant, roommate, co-homeowner, co-parent, caregiver, default plus-one. Like an escalator, these expectations have a momentum of their own.

Because the idea of the all-inclusive romantic relationship is so ingrained, trying to work out other terms can be tricky. Andrew Bergman and Toly Rinberg, whom I wrote about in the introduction, found themselves struggling to explain the depth of their friendship to potential romantic partners and ultimately resorted to non-monogamy as a model.

While dating a woman in 2019, Toly spoke openly about who Andrew was to him: Andrew had been his best friend since high school, his roommate for years, and a partner in his intellectual and political development. A few months into the relationship, she invited Toly to breakfast. Sitting at an outdoor patio in Somerville, Massachusetts, she told him she'd been describing his friendship with Andrew to her therapist, who responded, "It kind of sounds like they're married." She thought, *Yeah!* Toly wasn't pleased with the therapist's characterization—"*That's* the language you have to use to describe it?" he says as he relays the story to me.

That morning, she ended things with Toly. She implied that she wanted a romantic partner who would be more involved in her life—"a companion." Toly was disappointed, but he understood it was probably for the best.

By then, he and Andrew had a history of breaching other people's expectations of friendship. The head of the lab where Andrew and Toly worked as Ph.D. students asked other lab members if the two of them were romantically involved. Well before Toly's breakup, Andrew's mom had the nagging question of whether her son and Toly were in a romantic relationship. Something about Andrew and Toly's friendship wasn't computing for the people around them.

They made major life decisions with each other in mind, a level of dedication that is unusual even for the closest of friends. About a year into his Ph.D. in applied physics at Stanford, Toly applied to transfer to Harvard, where he would be able to work in the same lab as Andrew. Because he was transferring from one elite school to another, Toly could explain the move as a decision to go where the research was more exciting. He had genuine enthusiasm about the work he'd get to do at Andrew's lab, but he was also compelled to move because it would mean he and Andrew would be in the same place for years. After Donald Trump was elected president in 2016, Toly and Andrew both took leave from graduate school to start a government transparency nonprofit in Washington, D.C. They felt their time in D.C., where they built the organization from their seventh-floor sublet, leveled up their friendship. Andrew says their move was "a different kind of commitment because we're changing our lives, and we're changing it together."

When they eventually returned to school and got involved in labor organizing and the scientific field of carbon dioxide removal, they would learn that Toly, whose quietness people equated with kindness, was sometimes better positioned than gregarious, barnstorming Andrew to communicate their shared ideas. Toly brought his skills as an implementer to translate Andrew's out-there ideas into reality. They have trouble parsing whether they began working together more because they were becoming closer friends or if their growing closeness as friends naturally led them toward joint projects.

Though Andrew and Toly didn't feel the need to define the friendship for themselves, they thought they should find a way to make the friendship more comprehensible to others. The breakup at the café was part of a pattern in which, three to six months into a romantic relationship, a woman would want to occupy a larger share of Andrew's or Toly's lives than either was willing to give. Andrew and Toly didn't hide how important their friendship was and that it would continue to be their priority, and yet that idea took a long time for the women they dated to fully understand. It was like Andrew and Toly's friendship was a UV light, not a color on the visible spectrum; no matter how much information their girlfriends had about it, they couldn't see it and only started to grasp its power once they felt burned.

As averse as Toly was to the therapist's marriage comparison, it at least put his friendship with Andrew on par with a romantic relationship, much like how I felt affirmed when my friend told me I was practicing polyamory with M and Marco. To avoid confusion with future romantic partners, Andrew and Toly needed to convey just this, that they were as devoted to each other as are people in long-term romantic relationships. They found an existing framework—non-monogamy—and tried on the label for size. Though neither of them felt drawn to having more than one romantic partner, they decided to tell potential dates that they were nonmonogamous, so that women wouldn't be caught off guard by the friendship's significance in their lives.

In February 2020, Andrew worried about the risk of this decision as he got ready to meet up with a woman in his labor union, Nevena.

Maybe she would consider non-monogamy a nonstarter, he thought. About an hour into their conversation at the bar, the topic of non-monogamy came up organically. It turned out that Nevena was excited about approaching relationships in this way, too.

Toly felt less comfortable with the label. Because his relationship with Andrew isn't romantic, he didn't want to unnecessarily limit his dating pool to people who were okay with non-monogamy. He thought he could describe his friendship with Andrew on an early date, and perhaps someone who wanted a monogamous romantic relationship would still be on board. But Andrew was skeptical that women who expected exclusivity would accept their friendship. "*This* is how many [monogamous] people think they're okay with it," he says to me, his hands held apart wider than his shoulders. "*This* is how many actually are"—now, his hands are about as wide apart as his neck. Toly eventually agreed, and the two of them started referring to each other as a "partner"—the same term Andrew and Nevena used for each other. Toly used these updated terms to explain his friendship with Andrew during a date in 2021. The woman he was starting to see said she was relieved to hear that Toly prioritized his friendship with Andrew; she also deeply cared about her community.

Through their respective romantic relationships, Toly says, they're "learning to rely on other relationships as a way to buffer and find things that we can't get from each other." In one sense, the non-monogamy framework encourages them to ask less of the friendship, but in other ways, it encourages them to ask more. On occasions when Toly has felt let down—whether it's Andrew leaving his sweaty running clothes on the living room chair or not sending an important text he promised he would—he's told Andrew that he wasn't acting like a good partner. The word *partner*, originally meant for others, reminds them that they can expect a lot from each other.

Their DIY conception of "partner" has its limits, though. It isn't a term they use in academic or professional contexts; then they'd have to give caveats or explain what they mean by the more specific but lengthier term *platonic life partner*. Though Toly will gladly answer questions people have about the friendship, he prefers not to volunteer information about it. Because he's averse to drawing attention to himself or implying that he's special, Toly allows his friendship to be misunderstood in everyday settings. He and Andrew don't have the privilege that a monogamous couple does: to carry out their relationship without constant explanation.

———————

Years after asking if her son was gay, Andrew's mom, Lisa, found herself in a similar conversation but, this time, on a different side. On a Zoom call, friends of Lisa's were all talking about their kids getting married; it felt competitive to her as, one by one, the women relayed a traditional marker of success their kids had attained. When Andrew came up in conversation, one woman insinuated that he was romantically involved with Toly. Lisa said her son and Toly have a different kind of close relationship. She directly pushed back on her friend's assumption that closeness between two people must mean there's something romantic at work.

The belief, in the West, that same-sex intimacy necessarily involves sexual desire gained traction a couple of centuries ago. A pamphlet titled *Satan's Harvest Home*, published in 1749 in London, claimed that men who greeted each other with a kiss—at that point, still a ubiquitous greeting—were set on the path to Sodom. Disgust toward sodomy in eighteenth-century England swelled, and authorities rounded up accused sodomites in mass arrests and executions. With the specter of sex now hanging over men's physical interactions, it made sense for them to withdraw from one another. By the late 1780s in England, kissing had been replaced by the handshake.

Same-sex intimacy held on longer for men in the United States but began to recede from public view by the nineteenth century. At the turn of the twentieth century, a more aggressive form of masculinity—embodied in Theodore Roosevelt—eclipsed the sentimental masculinity that preceded it, in which a man could tell his male friend, without fear of judgment, that his heart's "last pulsations shall vibrate for you." Modernization was weakening the dominance of men who were at the middle and lower end of the economic spectrum: men stuck doing wage labor lost the autonomy they once had through self-employment. Men's power relative to women was rockier, too, as women were making (sometimes successful) demands for economic and political participation. A muscular form of masculinity could act as a kind of compensation for men's losses. The category of homosexuality—along with the stigma attached to it—emerged around this time. If a man expressed love for a male friend, his intention could be misread as sexual.

In *Gay New York*, the historian George Chauncey details how same-sex intercourse between men hadn't been hidden in the late nineteenth and early twentieth centuries, but, around the 1930s, became the target of heightened hostility. By the mid-twentieth century, the connection between sexual behavior and identity had changed. No longer could someone have a same-sex sexual encounter without risk of being branded with the new label of "homosexual." It's the difference between saying you live in New York and describing yourself as "a New Yorker." One is a potentially temporary fact; the other is a description of your essence as a person. Heterosexuality and homosexuality hardened into opposing categories; the former linked with normality, the latter associated with physical disease; a euphemism for homosexuality was "morbid."

Intimacy between women was eventually sexualized and stigmatized, too, though not as widely criminalized or severely punished as sodomy was. During the turn of the twentieth century, influential books by sexologists such as Havelock Ellis helped reframe women's passion for one another as deviant. All same-sex ardor—even when the woman in question didn't crave sexual intercourse with other women—seemed to qualify as "inversion," as in, her desires or behavior were upside down, more like a man's than a woman's. A woman whom Ellis identified as a "true invert" simply describes her avid, chaste love for her friends. But after picking up a copy of another sexologist's book, she questioned her affection. The book had taught her that "feelings like mine were 'unnatural and depraved' and 'under the ban of society.'" Women were now scrutinizing themselves for feelings that had been perfectly condoned all their lives. Sigmund Freud, whose influence went on to surpass that of other sexologists, framed homosexuality as a kind of arrested development.

One flash point in Britain was the government's censorship of *The Well of Loneliness*, a 1928 novel that portrayed a lesbian relationship and became the subject of a highly publicized obscenity trial. The medical journal *The Lancet* found the novel troubling enough to issue a critique: "The fallacy of the book lies in the failure to recognize that strong attachments between members of the same sex occur as a phase of normal development." The novel didn't depict women's attachments to one another as fleeting, and therein lay its threat. While women who'd had only an adolescent dalliance with same-sex love could still become a man's wife, adult women who had a loving same-sex relationship might not. "Romantic friendships," "smashes," and the like had lost their innocence. The draining of intimacy from same-sex friendships coincided with rising expectations for emotional connection in marriage. Marriage was like a man on the subway with spread legs: it left little room for anyone else. If friendships wanted to fit, they needed to shrink.

———————

In 2022, after spending much of the pandemic in Washington State, Tilly moved into Kami's house in Broken Arrow, ready to restart life in Oklahoma. I visited them that summer, and as we sat and talked in the kitchen, there was a palpable contentment between Tilly and Kami. When they're telling a story, it can feel like watching an improv sketch; like actors, they *yes-and* each other's accounts and have the theatrics of performers. Tilly pantomimes as she explains things and slips into a shrill voice to channel the words of someone who's annoyed her. Kami bellows when she says something she thinks is funny or outrageous. Kami, who's used to being "in mom mode 24–7," says her friend allows her to be "2007 Kami"—the one who rolled down the car windows while listening to music and talked with Tilly about "funny shit." Tilly says being with Kami means she gets to exist "in a world outside of expectations."

Though Tilly was animated in conversation, she'd be the first to say that she's not a hugger or emotionally open. She didn't want to share much about her romantic partner, a former marine who suffers from chronic pain, but, years into their relationship, she had a besotted smile when she talked about how she loves him.

As best I could tell, there are at least three Kamis: exhausted Kami, wild child Kami, and don't-mess-with-me Kami. The first was the easiest to notice. One night, her daughter kept her up; the next night, it was a family emergency. Her exhaustion lived in her lumbering movements as she carried a full laundry basket into the living room or in the way she mechanically cut a breakfast burrito into small pieces for Delilah. She wore the same bubble gum–pink sweatpants two days in a row. But every so often, her eyebrows arched and her toothy grin appeared, and I could imagine her taking pleasure in breaking rules or throwing back drinks at a bar.

While I sat with Kami at her dining table to ask questions, Tilly roved in the background, preparing a snack for Delilah, disciplining her, and rocking her on her lap in a leather armchair. She moved with the authority and confidence of someone whom Delilah trusted. A few months earlier, when Kami returned home from her niece's graduation, she walked into a house that had been deep cleaned by Tilly. (Kami described the pre-cleaning state of the house as "if a tornado had a tornado.") Until Tilly stayed with them, Kami hadn't understood how much help she and Rawley needed.

When I asked Tilly about what appeared to be an imbalance in hardship and need in their friendship, Tilly challenged the assumption baked into my question. "The friendship isn't based on whether or not I get something," she said. "It's more, does this feel right?" She said it would be one thing if she felt used. "But for me it's like, oh no, I just want to pour more in your cup because I have lots in my cup," she said.

And Kami looks after her in subtler ways. After I talked at length with Tilly about her experience in Iraq and then, not long after that, raised a subject she found sensitive, Kami asked Tilly to "do her a favor." The favor required Tilly to leave the house to run an errand. It took me several minutes—plus confirmation from Kami—to pick up on what Kami was really doing: giving Tilly an excuse to retreat. It was a form of care.

Besides the platonic nature of their tie, there's an important difference between their friendship and many romantic relationships: their friendship has room for connections of similar intensity. In the spring of 2015, Tilly asked Kami if she could "do me a solid and help my friend out" by letting her friend live with Kami. The friend was Ziraya, a single mom of two who wanted to move to Oklahoma; she was the same friend who had given Tilly a sense of how hard life as a single parent in the marines could be. Tilly said she'd take full responsibility if the arrangement didn't work out. Kami had no trouble making the decision. She told Tilly, "Heck yeah. I trust you. I trust your judgment. Bring her down." Kami knew that Ziraya was going to face a difficult transition from being in the military to learning how to be a mother in the civilian world. She wanted to surround Ziraya with the support that she and Tilly could give her.

Tilly's main concern was whether everyone would get along; she thought it was a lot of kids for one house. As it turned out, in the nine or so months that they all lived together, Ziraya's son and Kody, who were the same age, became best friends. Tilly wasn't worried about the friendship between Kami and Ziraya overshadowing what she had with her boot camp bestie. "I was more excited that this friend was going to supplement what I already had with Kami."

When the pandemic hit in 2020, Kami had far more stress to manage than usual. Rawley would get home late because business surged at the building supply company where he works; Kami felt like she was "single mommying it." The kids couldn't attend school. While Kody begged to go back, Delilah, without the regular distance from Kami that school imposed, experienced even greater separation anxiety than usual. Kami would lift her leg to walk out of the room, and Delilah would yelp at Kami for not taking her hand. In the early months of the pandemic, getting out of the house wasn't much of an option. She worried about Delilah's safety—if her daughter caught COVID, her health would be at serious risk. It didn't help that their neighbors weren't especially cautious. Kami would go shopping at Walmart and be the only person wearing a mask.

Tilly stayed with Kami for a few days in May 2020 before heading to an island in Washington State, where her parents had moved. During those days, Tilly saw how Kami's life had become a tangle of noise and need. She bought Kami a pair of AirPods as a sanity device; they could drown out the noise that flowed through Kami's one-floor open-concept house.

Kami and Tilly called each other every day until they realized that the monotony wrought by the pandemic had robbed their lives of plot. There weren't enough new things going on to report in daily calls. "When the three of us talked six months into the pandemic," Kami said, as far as she's concerned, it was "Day 8,326 in quarantine, and we're still doing the same damn thing"—drawing out the word *same* for dramatic effect. Tilly added, "Same kids are yelling in the background." They both laughed.

Over in Washington, Tilly wasn't suffering like Kami was. She felt fit for the first time in years, having lost nearly one hundred pounds. She found serenity in the Pacific Northwest's majestic scenery. But she was hesitant to share every positive development when Kami's life was backsliding. Tilly also found some pleasures hard to fully experience without her friend around. With Kami far away, she said, "It feels like there's not seasoning in the house." As she drove up Hurricane Ridge in Olympic National Park, pine trees shooting out of the mist, Tilly felt an urge to turn to Kami and exclaim, "Colorado!"—Kami's home state, the land of mountains she adores.

Kami's difficulties have given her an unexpected outlook. She has an acute awareness of what it means to not be able to move through the world freely, which makes her all the more encouraging of Tilly to enjoy her freedom. "I feel like I have a gypsy heart. I would just get up and go if I could," Kami told me. Not being able to do so "puts my heart into perspective for other people," she said; "If they can do it, tell them to go do it, because I can't."

Kami believes Tilly's support has reduced her stress and, in turn, left her with less stress to thrust onto her relationship with Rawley. Getting coffee with Tilly or hanging out with her perks Kami up. With Tilly as her "venting partner," she doesn't have to put everything on Rawley. Kami explained, "Before my partner gets home, and Tilly's off work, I'm like, 'Girl, guess what happened today.'" Tilly jumped in to say, "And you can hear the child screaming in the background. 'Whee!'"

> Kami: She takes so much off Rawley's plate because . . . I'll be angry, and I'll be upset like, "This insurance company," or "This therapy group," or "My child just hit me or spat on me, and I am going to—I'm moving out! I'm done!"
> Tilly: I'm burning the house down!
> Kami: Yeah. So by the time Rawley gets home, I'm just like, "Oh, hey," and he's like, "Hi, how are you today?" I'm like, "A lot of crap, but everything's golden now."

When Kami feels better, Rawley ends up with a calmer partner. This is consistent with what I've heard from other platonic partners, that the friendship makes them more patient, and steadier in their romantic relationships. (Conventional friendships have spillover benefits for romantic partners, though any individual friendship probably does to a lesser degree than one platonic partnership.) Tilly's romantic partner benefits from Tilly's brightened mood and support from Kami. Each relationship takes pressure off the other.

Kami and Tilly have learned through practice what relationship experts argue: though the current romantic ideal dictates that one person should provide everything, relying a little less on one relationship can in fact lead to a sturdier bond.

There are trade-offs: as the saying goes in polyamory communities, love is infinite but time is not. Tilly thinks that she probably talks less to her sisters because she already has go-to people in the form of Kami and her romantic partner. Their romantic partners might also learn less of the play-by-play of their lives because Kami and Tilly have each other as a first stop. But the equilibrium they've reached seems to work for them.

Tilly describes her friendship with Kami as "a trust bank, so we deposit trust, and that piggy bank is fat." Just as she doesn't expect her romantic partner to single-handedly fulfill her, "I also know I can't get everything from Kami. That's not Kami's job. And if I do that to Kami, I'm going to ultimately end up disappointed because people are human, and humans mess up all the time." She thinks it's too much to ask one person—whether a romantic partner or a friend—to meet every need. "I can't expect my best friend to be the wisest person on any particular issue," she says.

Indeed, having an all-in-one best friend or romantic partner would run counter to the expansive notion of family on display in Broken Arrow. Tilly uses the word *framily*—a portmanteau of *friend* and *family*—to refer to the close people in her life. She and Kami often make the five-minute drive to Kami's parents' house and lounge in the sunroom, a place to laugh and talk while smoke swirls from their Newports. Next to Kami's dining room table, a large pot holds a plant that belongs to Tilly's family. They put their beloved "Vern the Fern" in Kami's charge nearly a decade ago because their cats kept nipping at it.

In the kitchen, Tilly opens the pantry door, revealing a flyer that reads "Vote for Lawrence" for "Family Draft 2022." Lawrence is Ziraya's brother, who moved to Oklahoma and immediately jibed with

Rawley. Years ago, Tilly told Kody that there's a family draft—like the NFL or NBA draft. He believed that you could lobby to be drafted to a family you wanted to join. When Tilly started living with Kami, she printed "Vote for Tilly" flyers and planted them in unexpected places—the inside of a toilet seat, in an Amazon envelope. Once, Kody opened a textbook at school to find a flyer promoting Tilly. His friends were confused, and he brushed off their question by saying it was a family joke.

Now, Lawrence was in on the game, advertising his love of dance and music. Of all the skills to advertise, dancing is a fitting one. Witnessing Kami and Tilly's friendship can feel like watching two people practiced at bringing their movements in sync with each other. But they're capable of more than a partner dance. They'd be ready to break out into a Scottish ceilidh or a formal dance from long ago, in which dancers weave in and out, link up with multiple people, assemble and reassemble into new forms.

More people means more moving parts—for some people's tastes, just the idea is dizzying, with too many opportunities for collisions. But with more than one partner, there's more than one person to tend to you if you fall, to teach you a new way to spin.

WHAT'S SEX GOT TO DO WITH IT?

Partnership reconsidered

> Sometimes it seems that we live together in a future
> that only we believe in or understand ... Can it be that
> the love between us is so bizarre? I love you. This is not
> romantic love.
>
> —ANDREA DWORKIN

Call a group of people "privileged," and you're all but guaranteed to inspire dissent. Couples in romantic relationships are an exception. They enjoy the benefits of their elevated status—they're viewed as more mature, stable, and happy than single people—without the label of "privilege." Far from outraged denial, daytime talk shows and movies perpetuate the uncontested assumption that romantic relationships make life whole. But friendship, in American culture, doesn't possess that life-completing power.

Yet people I've spoken to who have platonic partnerships report levels of commitment, love, and fulfillment that rival the most devoted romantic relationships. Both types of relationships are voluntary relationships, not ones you're born into. In platonic and romantic partnerships alike, "best friend" is a label partners often use to describe each other. When my friend Adam asked what the difference was between my relationships with Marco and M, all I could come up with was sex: I had sex with Marco but not with M, and M and I weren't attracted to each other in that way. Others have shared with me the same intuition about what separates romantic relationships from even the closest of friendships. A dinner guest once asked me, "Isn't a romantic relationship just friendship plus sex?" According to that equation, sex is what triggers a state change, from *just* friends to *more than friends*.

Since Stacey Reimann met a woman named Grace in college, the two of them have spent countless hours thinking about the boundaries between different kinds of relationships. But as a freshman, Grace wouldn't have predicted that Stacey would shake up her beliefs about relationships, or really, anything. At the time, she couldn't picture Stacey as someone she'd even want to talk to. When she first saw him, her internal GPS told her to turn the other way.

She had spotted him across the room at a party for the University of Chicago's student newspaper, where they both worked. He exuded masculinity; she guessed, correctly, that he belonged to a frat. One of Grace's friends would later compare Stacey to Marlon Brando— though Stacey has a more chiseled jawline, higher cheekbones, and blue eyes. Grace had a less flattering comparison; he reminded her of the lacrosse players she did her best to dodge at her high school in suburban New Jersey. She was the kind of teenager who, when a bomb threat required that everyone evacuate the hotel where she was staying, ran back into the building to get her backpack; she didn't want to lose her homework. Seeing Stacey at the editor in chief's apartment, she all but rolled her eyes, thinking, *I don't really want to talk to that beautiful frat bro over there.* She had expected college to be an escape from guys like him.

A few weeks later, Stacey and Grace met again at a student career event. They were placed at the same table that gathered students with interests in journalism, media, and the arts—evidently, Stacey and Grace had similar career aspirations. Grace thought she would do work related to the visual arts, maybe at a gallery, and Stacey was drawn to the film industry. But Grace still wasn't interested in him; in time, she wouldn't even remember that they'd had a conversation that day.

During her sophomore year, Grace ran into Stacey for the third time. She was still recovering from a breakup the previous spring. It had been her first serious relationship: Grace and her ex-boyfriend had talked about the kids they wanted, the dogs they'd have, the kind of house they'd live in, and the trips they'd take. Despite experiencing what she describes as "a crazy amount of mad love," she'd broken up with him because the relationship felt suffocating. She'd hoped her college years would introduce her to a range of new people and new experiences; this single obsessive relationship left no room for the exploration she wanted. Though she'd initiated the split, her despair afterward was so overwhelming that when she returned to campus that fall, she didn't unpack her boxes for weeks. She wasn't sure she'd be well enough to stay for the whole term.

Determined to make friends and occupy herself with something other than dark thoughts, Grace turned her life into a variety show. She auditioned for an a cappella group; it went so badly that she laughed herself out of the room. Though she's not especially girlie or social, she joined a sorority. She signed up for the university's Institute of Politics despite having neither knowledge of nor interest in politics, and during her second term there, she was tasked with leading a team of students who provided administrative support to the institute's fellows. Stacey, the dandelion that kept sprouting on her lawn unbidden, was a member of her team. She tried to create team cohesion by organizing outings to get milkshakes or take a fellow out to dinner at the local diner. Getting to know Stacey was practically a line in her job description. To her surprise, she liked being around him.

Next thing she knew, Stacey was assigned to be her editor on a video project she was working on for the paper. He asked Grace to teach him about film photography, and Grace, who didn't sleep much, met Stacey in the dead of night that winter, in the darkroom, to develop photos. She discovered she liked to (playfully) boss him around.

Grace told her friend Caroline about a boy she was spending a lot of time with, in the darkroom and elsewhere. She was so interested in him as a person, intellectually and artistically. They had great conversations. Their night sessions in the darkroom felt romantic—but was that just situational? It was hard to figure out the line between platonic and romantic. Then again, one of Grace's friends commented that the sexual tension between her and Stacey was palpable.

Stacey started showing up at the coffee shop where Grace worked. It didn't matter who walked up to the counter or whose table she was serving; Grace seemed to have a joke or connection with everyone there. The energy she brought to everyday interactions was something he strived for himself. To Stacey, simply observing Grace chatting with customers was intoxicating.

In the Reimann family canon are videos of Stacey dancing to Ricky Martin songs at age three or four, too young to know that he was bouncing his hips to the music of a queer icon or even to know what the term *queer* meant. But now as he watches, he sees a kid having a solo queer dance party. His dancing, like other childhood behaviors— how he gravitated toward girls, exclusively wore pink goggles while swimming, and chose a bright pink shirt to wear for his fifth-grade graduation—were met with approval by family and peers. That approval evaporated when Stacey's family moved from the Atlanta suburbs to Birmingham, Alabama, and he started middle school. After his first practice on the swim team, he understood that if he wanted to fit in, he couldn't wear his pink goggles. Also in middle school, he heard a girl say, "Some people say my boyfriend has a high voice, but then I can always say Stacey has a higher voice." Stacey didn't want to embarrass his own girlfriend, so he trained himself to lower the pitch of his voice.

He retained this deepened voice even when he started dating a boy in sixth grade. The boy's father found out and instructed them to go to church. There, Stacey was taught that the devil was testing him. He dedicated himself to becoming more religious. He attended Bible study before school and read the Bible before going to sleep. But three years later, he realized that he still would have chosen to date the boy, had it been an option, and decided on a new mission: to get out of Alabama. He became more ambitious as a student and a soccer player—if he excelled in both, he would better his chances of getting scholarships to out-of-state colleges. The irony did not escape Stacey that, to free himself from the heterosexual masculine norms of Alabama, he devoted himself to an activity that required him to become more stereotypically masculine.

———

There's a stock question to ask queer people about their sexuality: *When did you first realize you were gay?* But when Lisa Diamond was interviewing sexual minority women as a psychology graduate student in the late 1990s, she asked them a different question: *Who were the three people you felt most attracted to in your life?* Over and over, women described an emotionally involved and encompassing friendship. One woman said, "Our relationship was so intense it was nearly spiritual." Their stories reminded Lisa of her best friend from high school, with whom she analyzed avant-garde films and scoured used bookstores for confessional poetry.

Along with the rest of their English class at an all-girls high school in Los Angeles, Lisa and her best friend read Virginia Woolf's novel *Mrs. Dalloway.* The book's main character, Clarissa, experiences a giddy love for one of her friends, going "cold with excitement" when she's getting ready to see the friend, and then she's overcome by the knowledge that the friend is nearby, saying to herself, "She is beneath this roof . . . She is beneath this roof!"

During a class discussion of the *Mrs. Dalloway* scene, Lisa and her best friend said, "That's what we feel!" (Decades later, as Lisa recounts the story to me, she mimics her teenage self by declaring those words in a screeching voice.) It was the first time the two of them had seen a depiction of a friendship as adoring as their own.

Their classmates had a different interpretation of the scene: clearly, the students said, the characters were lesbians. Lisa and her friend shot back that the characters weren't lesbians because friends can feel what the characters did. "It's a normal thing to feel!" they said. By the time class ended, Lisa and her friend understood that they'd come off as weird, as if all the students were having the same thought: *What a coincidence. The two girls who are attached at the hip didn't think the characters were lesbians.*

When Lisa went off to college, a roommate asked her which boyfriend made her the mixtape she was playing. Lisa corrected her roommate: her best friend, not some guy, was the person who'd spent hours assembling the mixtape. Lisa's roommate then observed that the tape was filled with love songs. "Well, that's how strongly we love each other," Lisa told her. Later in college, Lisa came out as a lesbian, but her feelings for her best friend had always been platonic.

So as Lisa heard the women in her graduate school study talk about their category-defying friendships, she knew what they had experienced. She decided to follow up with the women. Of the eighty women she interviewed who were lesbian, bisexual, or didn't label their sexual orientation, seventy said they'd had a platonic friendship as emotionally intense as a romantic relationship. These "passionate friendships," as Lisa called them, were far more likely than conventional friendships to include thoughts and behaviors associated with romantic relationships, including inseparability, cuddling, hand-holding, and preoccupation. For some of the women, the friendships were laced with sexual desire. But for a lot of them—as in Lisa's case—the friendship dwelled in what Lisa describes as an "in-between world": it was too involved to be a standard friendship, but their passion couldn't be explained by suppressed sexual longing.

The women Lisa interviewed didn't know other people had similar relationships, now or throughout history. If they'd combed through academic research, they wouldn't have found much either. The article Lisa published in 2000 is one of the few scholarly papers that exist on contemporary passionate friendships. Though Lisa's interviews showed her that this type of friendship was common, many of the women she spoke to considered it unique or even abnormal.

———

When Stacey had to figure out who to ask to be his date to his fraternity formal during his sophomore winter, there was no question but that he would ask Grace. She was his favorite person to be around.

They had been seeing each other all the time, in a way that's effortless in communal environments like college or summer camp.

Grace was excited to spend a whole night talking to Stacey and thought they might kiss or hook up. She arrived at Stacey's apartment for a dinner that he and the other two men in the friend group had arranged for their dates. The guys set the table and wrote a menu on a chalkboard, as if they weren't merely eating Mediterranean takeout but dining at a restaurant. From there, they took an Uber to an underground club in downtown Chicago. Grace wasn't impressed by the pretentious feel of the club—you have to pay to enter a square at the club's center while everyone else stands around the roped-off square, looking at the people who paid more. Despite drinking and dancing a lot, she and Stacey were too self-aware to really let loose. Grace recalls they were "basically psychoanalyzing it the entire time we're there and enjoying it, but not enjoying it." Their joint critique of the space felt to her like flirty banter.

The night proceeded with a mix of extravagance and sloppiness. When Kanye West's song "Famous" came on, Stacey and Grace snuck into the roped-off square without paying and danced. Soon after, they left the club, taking an Uber with one of the other couples. The Uber pulled over at one point so the guy could get out and throw up. His date stayed with him, and Stacey and Grace returned to campus. As they got closer, it seemed more and more likely to her that something would happen with Stacey.

They walked into Grace's residence hall, a stately brick building divided into about one hundred single dorm rooms. Students joked that you navigate the building using the quotes on the walls, painted every year by orientation week staff. Outside Grace's room on the third floor, Stacey paused to read a quote by the Roman philosopher and emperor Marcus Aurelius, painted in a rainbow of colors, starting in red and ending in purple: "Wait for it patiently—annihilation or metamorphosis."

Grace opened the door to her room, which matched the brooding style of her photography with its black and maroon décor, and they sat on her twin bed. Feeling that they were on the verge of a kiss, Stacey said he wanted to tell Grace something: he was dating a man whom he'd met through his job at the admissions office, a recent graduate who'd since moved to Boston. In the three months since they'd started dating, Stacey had never mentioned the relationship to anyone. Stacey thought the other members of his friend group from the admissions office would support his coming out—most of them were queer themselves—but that it could be messy to explain who his boyfriend was. These friends considered each other chosen family, and dating someone within the group could destabilize their unit. Stacey also didn't feel ready to come out to nine people at once. Making things more complicated, he didn't know how he'd label his sexual orientation. Though he'd thought he was gay, having sex with a man hadn't made everything snap into place as he had expected. Stacey told Grace about his confusion and said, "I think we just need to be friends."

Grace was taken aback—she hadn't thought this was where the conversation was going. And she was disappointed. They'd spent the night dancing in a club full of horny college students. It had felt like a date. But she quickly pivoted; she realized the weight of what Stacey was saying and what an enormous moment this was for him.

She cradled him in her bed as he cried. Now that he'd told her, he felt he'd soon enough be out to everyone, a step he wasn't sure he was ready to take. And he was worried she would feel that he'd led her on. But some of his tears were happy ones. Stacey embraces signs from the world whenever he senses them, and the Aurelius quote rendered in rainbow colors struck him as a sign that it was time to be open about who he was. In Grace, he'd found the right person to tell. Stacey observes that "this demon that was in me for twenty years, I was comfortable giving to this person that I met three months ago"—Grace, that is—"versus anyone else in my life." Looking back, he thought that he cried, in part, because "I felt like who I wanted to be my whole life that night and it felt like a precursor of a good life to come."

———————

As it happens, Lisa was also an undergraduate at the University of Chicago when she came out as a lesbian. People then asked her whether her high school friendship made her realize she was gay. She said no— she hadn't been sexually attracted to her friend (and her friend is heterosexual). Lisa found that pattern held for many of the friendships she studied. Though the women she interviewed were attracted to women, often, the friend they shared an intimate connection with identified as straight. Nevertheless, the passion in the friendship was mutual: the friends wrote letters to each other, cuddled, spent all their time together. Lisa spoke to a small number of straight women for this study and for future research, and many of them also answered the "top three attractions" question by talking about an emotionally intense friendship with a woman. Lisa says passionate friendships are less useful for predicting sexual orientation and are "more indicative of our . . . broad human capacity for love and attachment, which doesn't necessarily go along with sexuality."

The difference between love and sexuality became central to Lisa's work as a psychologist. Now a professor at the University of Utah, Lisa has found, as have other scholars, that lust and love are associated with different pathways and chemicals in the brain. Their work finds that androgens and estrogens influence sexual desire, whereas people in love get a drip of oxytocin, dopamine, and other neurochemicals that make them feel motivated and rewarded. Prominent psychologists argue that lust and love serve different evolutionary functions: that lust drives us to reproduce and, in doing so, continue the onward march of our genes, whereas love encourages us to cultivate a lasting bond that feels safe and rewarding—what's called an "attachment" relationship. It's a bond we first experience as vulnerable infants, when we need to stay close to a caregiver to survive. Lisa is among the researchers who believe this biological system that originally evolved for infant survival was repurposed: to motivate a pair of adults to stay together for the long haul.*

Some researchers see attachment as the second stage of romantic love, the first being infatuation, which keeps us around the person long enough for feelings of attachment to kick in. (These are generalities: not everyone begins romantic love in a heightened state; some feel security and calm from the start and may prefer steady love to the unpredictable highs and lows of passion.) Lisa calls time, togetherness, and touch the "magic ingredients" of attachment. Though sexual desire can encourage lovers to spend large amounts of time together, she says sex isn't essential for attachment to happen.

Based on research that shows lust and love have distinct biological processes and purposes, Lisa went on to argue that sexual orientation only orients sexual attraction, not love. One clue came from the passionate friendships she studied: most never became sexual. She

---

* Philosopher Carrie Jenkins is an example of a researcher who has a skeptical take on a purely biological explanation of romantic love. In her book *What Love Is*, she analyzes the same body of research I described above and concludes that romantic love has a "dual nature": biology influences our experience of romantic love, but so do our social expectations of it.

got additional support for the idea in her follow-up interviews with the women. In the ten years since Lisa first interviewed these women, many of them fell in love with someone they shouldn't have been attracted to based on their stated sexual orientation; lesbians fell in love with men; heterosexual women fell in love with women. Rather than assume these women were wrong about their sexual orientation, Lisa took their experience as evidence that love and sex don't always follow the same track. But these drives can reinforce each other; for some women, love may have sparked sexual desire for someone they wouldn't ordinarily have felt sexually attracted to.

Beyond Lisa's research and neurobiological studies by other scholars, there's evidence that love and sexual desire don't always coincide. In a study from 1979, 61 percent of women and 35 percent of men reported having experienced love without a desire for sex. Thirty years later, 76 percent of the people who responded to a survey agreed with the statement that "true love can exist without a radiant/active sex life." A study from the 1980s of young people likewise found that infatuation—often understood as a key part of romantic love—need not involve sexual desire. If they were inextricable, children who haven't gone through puberty shouldn't be able to experience infatuation. But children's physical maturity didn't make a difference when the kids in the study, ages four to eighteen, rated the extent to which they agreed with statements about someone they'd had a crush on, such as, "I am always thinking about [my crush]" and "I want [my crush] to know me, what I am thinking, what scares me, what I am wishing for." Those results might come as little surprise to anyone who's had a childhood crush or obsessive friendship. Lisa recalled a recent occasion when she joined her friend for a playdate between the friend's seven-year-old daughter and the daughter's best friend. At the end of the playdate, the mothers had to grab the girls by their legs to physically separate them, as if they were two ends of a rope in tug-of-war. As dramatic as the scene seemed, this wasn't unusual; the mother of the best friend, while pulling her daughter, said in resignation, "Here we go again." These enamored friends, to Lisa, represented "the human brain learning to connect and learning to seek security and other people."

Lisa now sees attachment written all over her high school friendship. The way she felt soothed by the smell of her friend's rose-scented lotion—"That is a hundred percent attachment," Lisa says, not fundamentally different from a parent who feels comforted by the scent of their newborn. The *Mrs. Dalloway* scene resonated with Lisa because the character, in exclaiming, "She is beneath this roof!" was delighting in the mere presence of her friend. "That feeling of cherishing and being cherished actually has nothing to do with sex," Lisa says. "It has to do with the infant-caregiver attachment system. That is what all humans want, is to feel that someone else puts them first. And although in our modern context, that's usually a sexual partner, the attachment system doesn't give a flying fig" about sex.

———————

The morning after the formal, Grace texted some friends a tongue-in-cheek reference to the graphic memoir *Persepolis*, in which the main character's ex-boyfriend thanks her for helping him realize he's gay. Grace laughed with her friends about this turn of events. But unlike in the *Persepolis* story, Stacey and Grace's incompatible sexual orientations didn't get in the way of their closeness. After that night, they made a habit of speaking to each other every day.

They were each other's guests for whatever events landed on their calendars. Other people started to notice how enmeshed they were. At a party, a woman with whom Stacey had hooked up at a formal they'd gone to together asked, "Are you and Grace a thing?" Stacey escaped the conversation without giving a clear answer.

For a long time, Stacey and Grace didn't have a label for their friendship, though once Stacey had come out to the whole soccer team, he jokingly began to refer to Grace as his girlfriend. He laughed when his teammates would ask if Stacey's girlfriend, well established as a superfan of the team, was coming to the next game.

Eventually, he found less tongue-in-cheek ways to characterize the relationship. The year after they graduated, the team competed in the Division III Final Four in North Carolina, and Stacey wanted to support his close friend who was on the team. Grace joined as well. She flew across the country and spent time with Stacey's family, who were eager to stop at Chick-fil-A because Grace had never been to the chain restaurant before. She ordered nuggets without fries, not realizing that this was what Stacey always ordered. Stacey and Grace noticed little commonalties like this—perhaps latching on to any semblance of a cosmic sign, as Stacey is inclined to do—but they also noticed less probable overlaps. Their moods seemed synchronized, as though part of the same weather pattern. Even when they no longer lived in the same city, they'd get sick at the same time. They started to say they were the "same soul" or "same person." It was the kind of inexplicable connection that many people hope to find.

Before Stacey entered Grace's life, there was Grace's other best friend, Caroline. Grace and Caroline had met in 2014, in a Facebook group for students who had been admitted to the University of Chicago but weren't sure if they would go. Both were torn between UChicago and Georgetown, and they traded long, stream-of-consciousness messages about their uncertainty. Caroline's indecision was at odds with the poise beyond her years that she usually projected, and she felt "really buoyed by seeing another person who I felt was similar to me who was struggling with the same things."

They met in person on move-in day. Grace climbed out of her parents' car and walked toward Caroline to hug her, but then tripped and fell, skinning her knees so badly that she ripped her jeans. Caroline would come to see this moment of clumsiness as "classic Grace." During their junior year, Caroline woke up to a series of wild texts about how Grace sprained her elbow while trying to hurdle a construction sawhorse in the middle of the night.

Caroline didn't share Grace's chaotic energy. She earned the nickname "Mama Carol" because she'd be the person to arrive at a cabin weekend with friends packed with a cooler that had all the necessary groceries, spices, and a well-balanced meal plan. (Stacey and Grace were more likely to have backpacks stuffed with dirty laundry and one cell phone charger between them.) Caroline's blend of analytical thinking and selflessness naturally steered her toward a career in public service, which she'd known she'd wanted to pursue since she was in high school.

Caroline and Grace saw themselves in each other, having come from suburban, close-knit, supportive families, and in college, their sense of kinship grew as they endured formative crises together. After a brutal winter in their first year and feeling frustrated by students in their dorm who, Caroline says, "got off on being miserable," she and Grace both talked to their advisers about transferring to Georgetown, though they both ultimately decided to stay at UChicago. Later that year, Caroline helped Grace get through her breakup, and Grace helped Caroline navigate confusing and disappointing romantic relationships that dotted her college years. Caroline says Grace is "a soulmate kind of friend." She thinks Grace is endlessly interesting and admires her commitment to the important people in her life.

Grace describes Caroline as "a piece of me in another body." Though Grace generally shares the same personal details with Caroline and Stacey, she expects them to react differently. She says that Caroline, "like Stace, is always eager to support any of my crazy dreams or ideas but, compared to Stace, is perhaps a bit more of a realist." If Grace decided she wanted to quit journalism to pursue her art full-time, Caroline would be the one to make sure Grace had a plan to support herself financially.

At the beginning of their senior year, Stacey and Caroline realized they had moved into neighboring brownstones; hers was a unit shared with five other women that they would dub "the Nunnery." Stacey had eight soccer players for housemates. In front of both homes, there's a stone path and a tree, forming a canopy, and they had a shared backyard. Grace would come for a two-for-one visit, staying over at Stacey's house and eating breakfast at Caroline's, or the reverse. As a birthday gift for one of the women who lived in the Nunnery, Stacey made a drawing of the two brownstones. The image of those adjacent houses would become an emblem of the community of friends Stacey, Grace, and Caroline wanted to build their adult lives around. Caroline adopted a mantra that two of her older friends had coined: "Chicago by thirty-five." It gave their friends license to scatter, if necessary, to build their careers and pursue education but called on them to eventually move to the same block or neighborhood. Caroline's friends had more than sentimental reasons for a shared setup: because people in their circle tended toward public service (read: unlucrative) careers, they didn't think they could afford to live alone or raise children with only one other person's income. A community could spread costs and caregiving and restore the pleasures of the interconnected social worlds they had in college.

Caroline and Stacey found each other in their shared backyard when they'd discovered they'd both gotten Fulbright fellowships to teach English in Spain. After running into each other's arms in what Caroline describes as a "life-affirming embrace," they joked that if they ever wanted to have a friend-wedding for the two of them, it would have to be in the backyard, because, in that moment, they felt like they had entered a larger commitment to be in each other's lives. Stacey spent a year teaching English in a small town in Spain; Caroline ended up just a train ride away in Madrid, and because they traveled together every few weeks, Caroline thought about Stacey as her "medium-distance boyfriend." Grace spent the fall working at a newspaper in India and then bounced from New York to D.C. to Chicago for journalism jobs. While Stacey was in Spain, he and Grace constantly texted and sent photos and voice memos over WhatsApp, as did Caroline and Grace, filling in the pieces of each other's lives from afar. Their friendship was now a party of three.

———

When Stacey was in high school, sex only came up in conversation in the form of warnings: Don't have sex before marriage. Sex is dangerous. In college, however, sex strutted onto center stage. Students bonded by talking about their sexual escapades. Stacey says, "That whiplash was confusing—to not talk about it and then to *only* talk about it." Coming from an environment where sex was repressed, he found the open discussion of sex liberating—at least for a little while.

Stacey's enthusiasm petered out once he came to believe that straight, cis men set the terms for sex. His soccer teammates were no exception. They talked about sex they'd had or wanted with women and often gossiped about who was dating whom. They teased Stacey for having made friends with members of the women's soccer team, insinuating that he wanted to sleep with them, never guessing what he was most drawn to: a female friend-group dynamic he envied.

His teammates' jokes not only assumed a sexual interest in women but also a general desire for sex that Stacey didn't feel. Over the course of his college years, though he developed romantic connections with different men, he continued to have little interest in sex. He came up with explanations: he was in a transitional phase after being closeted for so long; he needed to purge himself of Catholic guilt; maybe he wasn't so attracted to this or that particular guy. Several of his relationships were long-distance ones, and when a man he was dating would visit, he'd cram their trips with activities and make plans to get cheese fondue or some other lavish meal to keep them from being in bed together; he knew any GI discomfort would be a turnoff.

In Spain, Stacey revealed to a close friend that he wasn't sexually interested in men. His friend had been having similar questions about the role of sex in her life. It was the first time Stacey had heard anyone say they'd felt as he did. Validated after this conversation, Stacey decided to tell a guy he was just getting to know that while he wanted to be emotionally close with him, he wasn't ready to invite a more physical component, that he was exploring asexuality. The guy responded with empathy and agreed that it didn't make sense to continue developing a relationship.

Despite the compassionate response, Stacey felt broken afterward. He didn't understand why he so clearly felt drawn to men yet didn't want to have sex with them. When Stacey had come out as gay, he said, one "door had closed, and then there was this other door that I'd seen open with this light coming in." But once he started to accept that he might be asexual, "then that door was closing, too. And it was me sitting in front of these two closed doors."

———————

People who are asexual, also known as *aces*, are often made to feel that they're broken. Angela Chen, the author of *Ace: What Asexuality Reveals About Desire, Society, and the Meaning of Sex*, writes that aces get the message that they're "made in the shape of a human, but with faulty wiring and something lost, something fundamental to a good life." A 2020 study of sexual minorities found that asexual respondents felt more stigma than queer men and women who aren't asexual. People who used to be sexually active are similarly treated as if there's something wrong with them. Ubiquitous advertisements for drugs like Viagra pressure men to maintain virility through old age. These judgments and pressures are examples of compulsory sexuality at work, a set of assumptions that promote the idea that sex is a crucial part of a "normal," satisfying life and that not wanting sex is unnatural. Consider it a link in the same chain as compulsory coupledom.

There's no shortage of arguments supporting the notion that sex is essential to a full life. Sex can be seen as a great unifier, making two people one—and then, potentially, creating new life. It can foster intimacy; it's vulnerable to be naked and make someone privy to your desires and unbridled expressions of pleasure. Within religious contexts, sex is typically a sacred act.

In the modern imagination, sex does even more than all of this. Sex is supposed to help us figure out who we are. In his classic four-volume study, *The History of Sexuality*, the philosopher Michel Foucault identifies the nineteenth century as a turning point in the West, when sex stopped being an activity that, first and foremost, secured a person's place in society through marriage and family ties. The kind of sex someone had—particularly whether it was considered acceptable or unacceptable—came to shape their identity and perceived moral worth. Foucault found it ironic that people believed sexuality was key to liberation because, in his view, sex is invariably entangled with power and social norms. Try to toss out one set of norms and you'll end up adopting another. Or you'll have a mix of old and new, as happened with the sex positivity movement in the late twentieth century. It sought to remove the stigma around certain forms of sex, yet it maintained the connection between sex and the self. Sex was to be a site of self-discovery, self-expression, self-actualization.

While sex can foster these forms of meaning and growth, it doesn't for all people at all times. Sex isn't always a profound union. Therapists point out that some sexual encounters, whether casual or within a committed relationship, may be more about producing pleasure than "making love"—let alone making life. Sex may be one medium for intimacy, but it's certainly not the only one, or the ultimate one. This is what I heard from a wide range of people I interviewed—people who are in happy romantic relationships; single people; religious Christians; polyamorous people; people who don't enjoy sex; people who enjoy sex so much that they decided to become porn actors. John Stoltenberg, who had a category-defying relationship with the writer Andrea Dworkin, put it best when he quipped: "Orgasm is deeply centering. It's also pretty ephemeral. It comes and it goes."

Alongside the dominant cultural message that conflates sex and intimacy, there's at least one tacit acknowledgment that they can be distinct. The concept of an "emotional affair" suggests that a nonsexual connection can become so close that it rivals, even threatens, a sexual relationship. Just as partners can differ in how much sex they want, they can also differ in their appetites for intimacy, sometimes seeking it outside their exclusive romantic relationship. The existence of the term "emotional affair" highlights how different people meet core needs from different places.

Although sex can help people develop a sense of who they are, even forming a major part of their identity, it is by no means the only route to self-discovery; art is a form of exploration, expression, and pleasure, yet American society doesn't demand that everyone stand in front of an easel every week to be seen as a full human.

———————

Stacey wound up coming out to his parents twice, once in college and again years later, at their house in rural Alabama. Its screened-in porch, a room that's neither fully inside nor outside, has been the site of every intimate family discussion he can recall. One summer night in 2020, when his dad was out of town, the sun was setting and insects murmuring as Stacey sat down for dinner with his mom. It would be his last night in Alabama before taking a roundabout journey to his new home, New York City. The morning and afternoon had brought a series of stings, as Stacey felt aware of his mom's unease with his queer identity, and he responded by saying things he knew would upset her. He proposed having dinner on the porch to defuse the tension.

Stacey's mom didn't understand why her son was describing himself as "queer" when three years earlier, as a college junior, he'd told her he was gay. The reason, Stacey explained that night, was that he was asexual. He didn't enjoy sex, and when he pursued relationships, he would talk openly with potential partners so they'd know he wasn't looking for sex.

When he came out as gay to his conservative parents years earlier, he'd felt on the defensive, batting away their assumptions about gay people. In contrast, the conversation with his mom on the screen porch felt like they were gently playing catch, curious and open with each other. His mom told him, "It's so great that your generation has the vocabulary to articulate what they want." When she was growing up, she got the message that she was supposed to want sex once she hit marriage, or in some cases, all the time. She didn't have a string of questions for Stacey, as he thought she might. He exhaled deeply throughout the conversation.

About a week later, Stacey's dad called. Stacey's mom had filled him in, he said, and he understood that Stacey didn't want a partner. In that moment, Stacey realized that the discussion with his mom hadn't gone as he'd thought it had—or at least the meaning had become jumbled somewhere along the line. "I think sex and partnership has been so tied together that some assumptions were made that I don't even want a partner," he told me. (It's not just his parents who assume this: one question on the Frequently Asked Questions page for the Asexual Visibility and Education Network is, "I just don't see how asexuals can be close to anyone. How can you have a relationship without sex?") Stacey suggested to his dad that they find time to talk in person. Then he could give another session in the birds and the bees series he'd been inadvertently putting on for his parents. On a Sunday-morning bike ride through Alabama's hilly backroads, Stacey, repeating lines from the lesson plans he developed while teaching sex ed to students in Spain, explained to his dad that sex isn't necessary to have a partnership. His dad seemed to get it. Stacey told Grace about how elated he felt after the conversation.

Stacey's observation about sex and partnership applied to his relationship with Grace. Over time, the two of them figured out that they had built a partnership. As their postgraduate years went on, they noticed they were doing something different from their peers. Their friends from college were making decisions about where to live based on their boyfriends or girlfriends and spent their scarce vacation time with their romantic partners rather than friends. Not so for Stacey and Grace. They got on planes to see each other and spent holidays together. They prioritized each other. As Grace puts it, they became each other's "primary person."

Everyday decisions reinforced their role as each other's primary person. When Stacey explained that he finished the book he'd been telling Grace all about and that it made him cry on a long car ride home, she said they should talk about it that night. This conversation and others like it are what couples do over dinner after work: they debrief. Partnerships rely on the intermingling of the mundane and the intimate; it's both by knowing the ordinary and private details that partners can have an up-to-date, high-definition picture of the other's life. Stacey and Grace had been sharing the full range of thoughts and feelings throughout college, so Grace would have found it surprising if they stopped being involved in each other's lives in this way. Caroline has been in a serious romantic relationship since the end of college (with a man she met through an event that Grace's mom hosted) and sometimes wonders if she's being left out of a meaningful friendship because Stacey and Grace are pursuing a certain kind of connection together. But when the "anxiety portion" of her mind quiets, she realizes that she admires and wants to support what Stacey and Grace have. The three of them are still intent on making "Chicago by thirty-five" happen.

About six months after the birds and the bees talk with his dad, Stacey picked up Chen's book and came to understand asexuality as a spectrum—some people experience sexual attraction infrequently, others never. People also differ in how they respond to sexual acts: some aces are indifferent to sex, some are repulsed, some find sex pleasant. He learned about different types of attraction and realized that what he thought was sexual attraction to men might have been a different kind of pull—to be physical in certain ways, such as kissing and holding hands, which aces refer to as "sensual attraction."

What he appreciated about the book and has found the most rewarding aspect of exploring asexuality is its role as a conversation starter. He's learned to ask, *What does sex mean to you? What do you want sex to look like in your life?* It's a way of thinking about sex that he didn't encounter growing up in an environment that condemned nonmarital, non-straight sex. It also didn't come up in his young adulthood, in what he felt was a hypersexual environment, where he thought sex positivity became tantamount to *the more sex the better.*

Instead of asking himself why he wasn't more interested in sex, he arrived at a different question: *If sex isn't the thing that's going to be moving my life and my relationships forward, what is?* He found an answer in his relationship with Grace. He realized that he and Grace prioritized their relationship and supported each other. "That is exactly what I'm looking for in a partner. We have it. It's there. I'm ready and I'm interested in: how do we center that? What does that look like?" Through the ace community, Stacey had been introduced to the idea of queerplatonic partnerships—a type of committed friendship that doesn't have all the trappings of a conventional romantic and sexual relationship. Maybe that's what he could have with Grace.

For the three months leading up to November 2020, Stacey worked on a US Senate campaign in Alabama, and after the election, like a lot of people working in politics, he felt totaled. To reset, he was going to spend time with Grace, who was rising through the ranks as a newspaper reporter. Together, they took long bike rides around Chicago. Grace was interested in moving to another part of the city, so she and Stacey visited an artsy neighborhood that she didn't know well. While riding, they pointed out streets where they could see themselves living, and "Chicago by thirty-five" began to feel less dreamy, more real. They debriefed over Ethiopian food, discussing what features they'd ideally want in a neighborhood for this future community of friends: proximity to Lake Michigan, a diverse public high school nearby. Stacey says on the trip—during which he, Grace, and Grace's cat slept in the same bed for three weeks—"I realized how special living with her could be, and how good we would be at it."

Stacey had been spending more time thinking about what he wanted his life to look like as he got older. Back when he thought of himself as gay but didn't yet identify as ace, he envisioned having a family with a male partner, with Grace living next door. Now that he knew he was on the ace spectrum, he "had to reimagine everything." Maybe Grace should be his co-parent. He and Grace discussed taking steps expected of romantic partners: living together, raising children, having a wedding. They saw this plan as a fallback; if they didn't find romantic partners, maybe they could fill these roles in each other's lives.

The following summer, sitting across the table at a bar with drinks in hand, Stacey raised these questions with more urgency. He wanted to know if they were actually going to do it. He wanted to commemorate their partnership, maybe have a friend-wedding before loved ones or even get legally married. It was a proposal to bring definition to their undefined relationship.

Grace was taken aback. She told him that she wasn't sure.

As Grace has wrestled with whether she could make the primary relationship in her life her friendship with Stacey rather than a romantic relationship, she has thought about a passage from the novel *A Little Life*. Two characters in the book, Jude and Willem, have a relationship that blurs the lines between friendship, partnership, and romance. Willem thinks about a moment from *The Odyssey* when Odysseus returns to Ithaca and has to ask whether it's home; Odysseus is so disoriented he doesn't recognize his own country. As Grace interprets it, Willem has found home in his unclassifiable relationship with Jude, but he can't quite see it. Grace wonders if she has also found home—that is, a grounding life partner in Stacey—but isn't embracing it. She's felt haunted by this idea. Is Stacey her Ithaca?

For Stacey, romantic love is epitomized in a scene in the movie *Eternal Sunshine of the Spotless Mind*. At nighttime on Valentine's Day, the two protagonists look up at the stars and tease each other while lying hip to hip on a frozen lake. The hazardousness of walking onto a frozen lake mirrors a romantic relationship in his mind. He says, "Being in partnership feels like a choice to invite risk and mess into two people's connection together and deciding to go for it anyway."

The two of them actually found themselves on a frozen lake one winter, while on a camping trip in Indiana, which they'd inadvertently planned for Valentine's Day. Stacey felt a sense of romance as they huddled under layers of blankets and sleeping bags to keep each other warm and gazed up at the stars. To him, romance is about commitment, vulnerability, and deeply knowing someone—a definition that lines up with psychologists' conception of "companionate love." Whatever Grace's understanding of romance is, it doesn't quite line up with Stacey's. She tells me, "I can easily say I love Stace, but I think I mean it differently"—differently from the infatuated way she loved her college ex-boyfriend.

A lot had changed since that Valentine's Day weekend trip: Caroline had moved from Wisconsin to D.C.; Grace considered reviving a relationship with her college ex; Stacey began to understand that they're genderqueer (from here on in, I'll use they/them pronouns for Stacey; Stacey asked that I write about their earlier life with he/him pronouns). But, years later, as we sit in Caroline's apartment in D.C., which she shares with her partner, Andrew, all of them are still sorting through their definitions of romance. Grace and Stacey have driven down in advance of the New Year's Eve party that Caroline is hosting tonight to ring in 2023. When I ask them if their thoughts about romance have evolved, Grace ventures that romance entails some degree of mystery. Stacey has an opposite instinct—that a defining quality of romance is certainty: knowing you're the people for each other now and in the future. I toss the question to Caroline, who winds through the apartment in a gold sequin wrap dress, lighting tapered candles and plating appetizers for the party. She reminds us of her history of having a hard time distinguishing between platonic and romantic feelings for friends. The idea that garners the most agreement is Stacey's suggestion that romance is about celebrating intimacy—dressing up and making time to honor how important you are to each other. Though you can celebrate an individual person through an event like a birthday party, romance is distinctly about celebrating the relationship.

As they go back and forth, I think of similar conversations I'd recently found myself in with friends. We had tried to define what a romantic relationship is and concluded that it's a slippery term that isn't based in some immutable essence. Instead, it fits the philosopher Ludwig Wittgenstein's concept of a "family resemblance." Think of a family portrait where people don't look identical but widow's peaks and dimples suggest a biological relationship between them. Likewise, romantic relationships have overlapping qualities but don't need to tick all the same boxes to belong to the same category. Some romantic relationships course with sexual passion while others enjoy the steadiness of companionate love. Some romantic partners are each other's closest confidants while others have a relative or friend in that role. Despite these differences, they're all societally recognized as romantic relationships.

Around 9:30 p.m., friends of Caroline, Andrew, Stacey, and Grace start to file into the apartment for the party, and even before they've had time to take off their jackets, which are slick with rain, Grace ambushes them with the question, "How do you define romance?" One guest says he used to believe that romantic relationships amounted to friendship plus sex, but he doesn't anymore. He describes himself as "a big R romantic," but says, the odd thing is, he's found romantic relationships don't live up to his ideal whereas his friendships often do.

I know firsthand how friendships can be inflected with romance. The infatuation I felt for M was much like what I felt for Marco early in our relationship—what the polyamorous community calls New Relationship Energy, or NRE. NRE describes the ecstatic early days of a relationship, when a new partner is captivating and the world seems aglow. Even after that heady early period in our friendship, M and I have remained affectionate and have celebrated the anniversary of our friendship with flowers and matching necklaces. As Chen argues in *Ace*, "there is overlap and no clean separation" between romantic love and platonic love. You could say romantic relationships and platonic partnerships, too, bear a family resemblance.*

Though it's tough to pin down what romance even means, people seem to have strong ideas about what role romantic relationships should play in a person's life. Recently, Grace's friend had the two of them do an exercise that the friend had learned in her social work master's program. They mapped their "social atom," drawing bubbles on the page; the size of the circles and their distance from the center represented the space each person takes up in their lives and how close they are. Grace's friend commented that Grace had an overwhelming

---

* Even though I'm intentionally destabilizing the categories of "romantic" and "platonic," I still use the terms "romantic relationship" and "platonic partnership" in the book for clarity. I hope our understanding evolves to recognize the diversity within and overlap between relationship types.

number of close relationships and asked her how she could ever have space for a romantic partner. Grace's friend wasn't in a romantic relationship either, but on her page, she'd drawn a circle to indicate the space that she'd make for that potential addition to her life. Grace is interested in some kind of relationship that would fulfill her sexual desires (she's trying—she'd just been on an ill-fated date with someone who turned out to be an alien conspiracy theorist), but she doesn't want to "pop a bubble" on her map to do so. She thinks whoever was involved in that aspect of her life wouldn't occupy the kind of space romantic partners are expected to; they wouldn't be the first person she called if something happened. Maybe they could be the second, after Stacey or Caroline.

Grace was a bit offended by her friend's reaction to the map of her social life. She thought there was another conclusion to draw: *Look at all my people. I have so much love in my life.* When her friend asked her how she could have room for a romantic partner, Grace said, "I don't know, but I'm happy. Isn't that the main goal?"

Stacey used to think that because they weren't having sex, they weren't experiencing full intimacy with someone; sex, they assumed, would add another layer or depth to the emotional intimacy they felt. They've stopped discrediting the forms of closeness that would now fit their definition of intimacy: "the space to feel comfortable in one's body to dream, to explore thoughts and feelings that come up in life with somebody." It's not that Stacey thinks physical connection is irrelevant to intimacy—their closest relationships involve cuddling and bed-sharing. Instead, Stacey thinks there are numerous forms of physical connection and people will differ in which types feel more intimate to them. Stacey says, "There isn't a hierarchy of 'sex is more intimate than cuddling than dancing than massaging.'"

Stacey and Grace still describe themselves as "same soul." While Stacey was visiting Grace in Chicago, Grace was working on an investigative article and couldn't decide whether to lay out the facts in chronological order or to alternate the perspectives of her sources. Stacey was busy reading in another room, then put their book down and walked in to say they needed to talk to Grace about something: the novel they were reading was powerful because of how it alternated between the perspectives of different characters. Grace thought, of course that's what Stacey was reading, because she was thinking about that exact form of storytelling. Grace says, "It's this bizarre, same-soul feeling of just like, no matter where you are in the world, [having] the same experience, the same emotions or thoughts." She says, "It's hard to mark where one person begins and the other ends."

Stacey doesn't treat their special connection as a reason to develop a universe for their friendship, isolated from others. They say, "I think the beauty that I see with Grace in my life specifically is I wouldn't want to be with somebody where I just feel like, *oh, we're a same soul and we're just going to do that.* It's like, what parts of your soul will then connect to other parts of other people's souls? And for me, that's going to build a community that I think we both dream of." In other words, because Stacey and Grace have such similar taste, their relationship makes it possible to build deep ties to other people who will mesh well together.

Along with their "same soul" connection, Stacey and Grace's partnership is, at its core, about finding someone to do life with, a teammate who tempers life's everyday drudgeries. When I talk to friends who are single, this is what they seem to crave most from a romantic relationship; to the extent they miss sex, they can satisfy that need far more easily—there's Tinder for that.

Romantic relationships may only bear a family resemblance to one another, but there's a common factor that I think explains their privileged status today—a time when romantic relationships often don't carry religious significance or lead to children. That factor is the value of having a long-term teammate. When Caroline's partner, Andrew, explained what he thinks makes a relationship "romantic," without realizing it, he quickly switched the terms of the conversation from "romantic" to "partnership." He shared how he adores his best friends from childhood, is in contact with them every day, and can turn to them for support, but he said, "None of that is partnership." What makes his relationship with Caroline distinct is how easily the two of them can glide between different modes. He says, "In a relationship, at any point you can take it from 'What are we having for lunch?' to 'I was really feeling this way about something today.'" A partner is someone who is there for all of it, for the long term.

This is the idea underlying the wedding vows *to have and to hold, for better, for worse, in sickness and in health*. And this, most reliably, is the moment in wedding ceremonies when I've seen brides and grooms start to get choked up. At the wedding I officiated, the groom explained in his vows how, when he was recovering from ankle surgery, his soon-to-be wife brought him a baking tray, and they folded wonton dumplings, which she'd prepared by re-creating his mother's recipe. "As we sat there eating dumplings that night," the groom said, "I could see a whole future for us together."

Stacey has stopped thinking of sex as the defining factor for who will make up the "us" when they picture their future. Though Stacey initially felt like asexuality closed a door for them, it simultaneously swung open another one, leading to a room that inspired imagination and curiosity. Stacey started to notice that American culture encourages people to carve out a large segment of their lives for their romantic partner—to make them the dominant bubble in their social atom. And it's assumed that romantic partners are having sex with each other. Stacey became interested in understanding "What space do we give to the people that we're not doing that with? What space do we give to the ideas of raising children together, or the ideas of attending each other's family's funerals or living together?" With Grace, Stacey says, "the space feels endless."

BE YOUR OWN MAN

Navigating masculinity and intimacy

To be nobody-but-yourself—in a world which is doing
its best, night and day, to make you everybody else—
means to fight the hardest battle which any human being can fight.

—E. E. CUMMINGS

When I first saw Nick Galluccio on Zoom as part of a webinar in
2020, I found it hard to imagine him as a norm-breaker. Call it stereo-
typing, but what I saw was a guy who wanted to blend in. In a black
Adidas cap and beige hoodie, he spoke in the passive voice, giving the
impression that he wasn't the protagonist in his own story. I found
myself surprised when Nick broke out with tender, sincere comments
about his friend and fellow Christian youth pastor Art Pereira, as if he
were an actor reading lines for another character. When I asked Nick
why he found it so easy to open up to Art the first time they had tea
together as college students in 2013, a smile wiped across his face, and
he said, "Art is just the best guy."

The superficial details I noticed about Nick, maybe by sheer coincidence, hinted at fundamental aspects of his personality. Until his
midtwenties, the loudest voice in Nick's head told him not to deviate

from the conservative norms he grew up with. Nick and his four siblings got the message that living with a romantic partner before marriage was shameful and that gay people deserved whatever ill fate came their way. Sometimes what his family professed was veiled as a "pursuit of Christian values," but sometimes they just seemed concerned with image maintenance, worried that other people might disapprove.

Image maintenance motivated how Nick's family treated Art: with distance. Art was gay, and Nick's parents were apparently concerned that other people, if they learned about their son's close, devoted friendship with Art, would think the two of them were secretly gay lovers. Whereas women Nick dated for only a few months were invited to spend time with Nick's family around the holidays, Art was not.

Nick's parents were the rare people who weren't immediately enamored of Art. His warm smile, outlined by his trim beard, gives him a teddy bear quality that makes it easy to imagine him enclosing you in a tight hug or stroking your arm as you weep. It wasn't uncommon for people to tell Art their life stories when they met him and cry within the first hour. In the course of two years, Art had hosted more than six hundred tea dates on the floor of his dorm room at the small Christian college in New York where he and Nick met. As Nick sipped tea from Art's stone set during their first long conversation, he sensed that Art was invested in getting to know him, and he shared more than he normally would—sometimes in tears—about how lonely he felt, his difficult transition as a transfer student at their college, the fights he and his girlfriend were having.

Art and Nick had been asked to give the webinar because they had thought far more than most people about friendship and, more notably, acted on those thoughts: the two of them had committed to living as a family unit; they considered each other brothers. Ten days before the webinar, they had moved in together. It was an unusual setup for anyone, but especially for a pair of youth pastors who work in conservative congregations. The target audience of the webinar was gay Christians who follow conservative sexual ethics. To the hundred or so people who logged on, Art and Nick talked about the spiritual significance of friendship in Christianity and hoped to give them an image of what a rich life oriented around friendship could be, especially a friendship that traverses a gay-straight divide. It was one thing to live out their decision quietly, in private, another to broadcast it. After a quarter century of being preoccupied with image maintenance, Nick was working to care less about what other people think.

———————

In 2016, four years before the webinar, Nick broke up with his college girlfriend, and Art felt compelled to look inward. He noticed Nick was torn up about his ex-girlfriend for months. Art then thought about how his male friends described their feelings toward women—falling head over heels, having an intense desire to be with them. More often, Art felt that way with guys he was close to. He asked himself, "Do I not actually like women?"

It wasn't a new question for him. Art first sensed he was gay when he was eleven years old. Since then, he'd done what he was told: for eight years, he prayed to become straight. He went to conversion therapy. When he was fifteen, his Christian therapist told him to watch straight porn to nudge along the conversion, never mind that viewing porn was against Christian teachings.

By adulthood, Art identified as straight, someone who was "ex-gay." He had briefly been engaged to a woman. Now, at twenty-four, he was dating a woman. Art thought the questions about his sexuality were settled, but here they were flickering, the bulbs not quite out.

If he was going to admit this to anyone, it was going to be Nick. Art considered Nick his best friend. When they'd barely known each other, Art felt comfortable talking to Nick about the recent death of his dad and opened up to him about how they'd gotten into an argument right before he died. Art sensed that Nick didn't have a judgmental bone in him; he wanted the best for the people around him.

Now several years into their friendship, they had started celebrating the anniversary of becoming friends, a.k.a. their "brotherversary." The two of them had a weekly routine of staying over at each other's places on Thursday nights and spending Friday mornings drinking coffee, playing board games, and talking. Nick had even given Art a closet in his apartment to store his things.

On one of those Thursday nights in 2017, Art sat on Nick's couch with his duffel bag in the corner of the room. He said that he thought he was gay. After that admission, Art, in his own words, "instantly freaked out." He frantically packed his duffel bag and told Nick he was going home, convinced that Nick would feel uncomfortable with him sleeping over. Growing up, Art had been told that if other men knew you were gay, they wouldn't want to be close to you.

To Nick, it seemed like a scene out of a movie, when the spouse stuffs a suitcase and declares they want a divorce. Nick coaxed Art to sit back down and told him that whatever happened, they were going to figure it out. He persuaded Art to stay the night.

Nick had temporarily calmed him, but a question loomed over Art: What would he do about his sexuality in light of everything he had learned as a Christian? He booked a cabin at a retreat center in the woods of Pennsylvania. For three days, he sat with his journal and Bible and prayed. Analyzing the Bible, he couldn't find support for the progressive Christian interpretation that permits marriage and sex between people of the same gender.

As upsetting as that conclusion was, Art couldn't conceive of shedding his faith. He'd had a divine encounter as a sixteen-year-old that changed his life. Sitting in the corner of a dirty church basement, as part of a youth retreat that his parents had paid him to attend (otherwise, he wouldn't have agreed to go), Art cussed out God, telling him, "The options are either that you fucked up when you made me or that you fucked up your church." Then Art heard God tell him, "You're gay, and also I love you, and also I want you to walk with me, so let's figure this out together." When Art woke up the next day, he felt happy to be alive for the first time in years and stopped self-harming, which had been his habit several times a week. This was the year he decided to become a Christian, not just trudge to the church where his parents had found home among other Spanish- and Portuguese-speaking immigrants.

Living without Jesus was a nonstarter for Art; "The spiritual loneliness would be devastating," he says. He'd also lose his basic, grounding sense of reality. Art believes Christianity is "not just good, but it's true. And so even in the ways it's uncomfortable, it's the only thing that is solid and real." He tells me about a moment from the New Testament, when Jesus preached unpopular things and, afterward, watched his following dwindle. Jesus then asked the disciples if they wanted to leave as well. Peter responded, "Lord, to whom shall we go? You have the words of eternal life." Art says, "Abandoning Christianity felt like that." To whom shall he go?

Art figured out a way to reconcile his sexuality and religion: he would be celibate.

"Nothing seemed worse to me than celibacy," Art says. He didn't think the big sacrifice was giving up sex. The sacrifice was never having "a default person to come home to," someone who would hand him a mug of tea after a hard day and who knew when his plane landed. Because he is drawn to deep social connections, Art felt it was a "cosmic cruelty" to be called to a life of celibacy. He, Nick, and two close friends who referred to themselves as "the Amoeba" had recently taken personality tests, and Art's results blared that he was meant to share his life with others.

One evening, after a bad day at work, Art returned to his mom's empty house, where he was living. It felt like a preview of his life ahead: alone after a hard day. Having once expected that he'd be married with three kids by age twenty-eight, Art couldn't imagine living as a single person for the long term in a way that felt satisfying. He called Nick from his mom's kitchen, his voice hollow. Art was just twenty-five years old, and he told Nick, "I can't do this for another twenty-five years."

Nick said, "I want to be part of the reason that you want to live past fifty."

There had to be another option for Art besides unrelenting aloneness, Nick said, and he felt responsible for figuring out what that was. "This is not your problem. This is *our* problem," Nick told Art. Together, they prayed—on the couch where Nick would squeeze Art's shoulder as Art cried, or over the car's Bluetooth speakers when Art called Nick while driving at night. Nick also prayed on his own, saying he believed God was good—could He show them what a good life for Art looked like?

Nick believed he had been put into Art's life as a friend, and he felt God was calling him to help Art have "an abundant and full life." About six months after Art decided on celibacy, Nick proposed that they live together. Hearing this idea, Art felt a flicker of hope. But he immediately extinguished it because, Art says, "it felt too big to count on." Art told Nick that he didn't need to make such a generous offer. Nick didn't budge.

Ideas about the kind of home they might buy floated into their casual conversation. Maybe they'd purchase land and build a duplex. While driving around Art's neighborhood, Nick mused, "If we did live together, how cool would it be for me to get home from work and you're grilling in the backyard?" A few months after Nick started making these sorts of comments, Art told him they had to stop the daydreaming—unless Nick really meant it. Art later told me, the arrangement "sounded fantastic. It sounded relieving. And also, if it went wrong, nothing would hurt me more." Nick reassured Art that he had thought seriously about living together and was becoming even surer that it was what he wanted.

In 2019, Art ran the numbers on his windfall of credit card points, which he'd earned after opening a new card, and realized he had enough to cover two round-trip flights to Hawaii. Art couldn't wait to share his good fortune with Nick, and after the two of them caught up at Nick's apartment, Art told him the news. Whatever excitement Nick might have felt about a subsidized vacation was trounced by concern. He worried that other people would think he and Art were going on a romantic getaway.

This is the contradiction of Nick: a person who, on the one hand, identifies attention avoidance as a defining part of his personality; and on the other, he eagerly decided to build his life with a gay male friend even though he's a leader in a conservative religious community.

Nick's reaction exacerbated Art's doubt. Though Nick had been the one to suggest that he and Art live with each other, Art wasn't sure he could trust that plan. *If you're scared of going on a vacation with me,* Art thought, *I don't know that I feel really confident in your ability to buy*

a house, because what are people going to think of us when we do that?
Besides, Art thought some people inevitably would assume they were
romantic partners. Few Americans are used to seeing male friends as
close as they are. Often, the first question Art gets after he's come out
to someone as gay is, "Is Nick gay, too?" It's as if people have a rule
in their head: any man who spends a lot of time with a gay guy must
himself be gay. Art might not have read so much into this moment if
several similar situations hadn't just happened in close succession—
incidents where Nick openly worried that other people would think
he was gay.

The sociologist Eric Anderson calls the fear of being perceived as
gay "homohysteria." The inclusion of *hysteria* makes the term sound
provocative, maybe uncomfortably so, but the concept is valuable. It
helps explain why men like Nick constrain their behavior—avoiding
activities, people, or organizations that could mark them as gay. A
society can have high levels of homophobia—defined as the hatred
or prejudice against gay, lesbian, or bisexual people—without men
feeling like they must shore up their straightness. It only makes sense
for men to adjust their behavior if homosexuality is also believed to be
prevalent; then, there's grounds to worry that other people might think
they're gay and that being labeled as gay could carry consequences. A
turning point in homohysteria in the United States, according to Anderson, was the sexologist Alfred Kinsey's blockbuster study on men's
sexual practices. The study, released in 1948, claimed that 10 percent
of the population was homosexual. Around this time, men began to
keep emotional and physical distance from one another.

Though homophobia has waned in the last few decades, American
men still, by and large, aren't supposed to get too cozy with other
men if they want to fit in. By adolescence, boys learn that their rep-
ertoire for physical affection with each other is limited to back slaps

and side hugs. They're trained to act competitively within their male friendships, and they're expected to bond over activities, not shared intimacies. Working on this book, I saw how men's friendships get scrutinized differently from women's. When I'd tell people about Andrew and Toly, the physicist friends who are straight men, I'd get questions about whether they're *really* straight. People didn't react that way when I'd tell the stories of straight female friends. The subtext was: if a man is too close to other men, his straightness is suspect.

Art was freed from these worries over what people might assume about his sexuality because, he says, "as a gay man, I'm not really trying to fit stereotypical views of masculinity anyway. If someone looks at me and thinks I'm gay, they're just accurate. But for Nick, he wants to be perceived as who he is, which I think he deserves to be."

Though Art knew that Nick was subject to a rigid form of masculinity, he had little patience for Nick's ambient homohysteria and wasn't content to let Nick dictate how they acted in their friendship; Art would then have to censor behaviors that came naturally to him. He was particularly averse to placating the intolerance of Nick's family. Finally released from having to hide his sexuality, Art didn't want to "straighten up" when Nick's parents came around to their future home. Art says, "Because I've spent twenty-seven years of my life downplaying my sexuality and a pretty significant part of myself, I was really fearful that by choosing to tie myself up with Nick, I was choosing to live in fear of what people think of me, because that's how he was doing things." He didn't want other people to determine how they carried out their friendship.

Art encouraged Nick to care less about other people's potential judgments. When Nick would pull back from Art because he found some form of physical affection weird, Art would point out that Nick's perception of what's normal between friends is culturally specific. Art is Brazilian American, and it's normal for Brazilian men to kiss each other on the cheek or put their arms around each other. There, these actions aren't coded as gay.

American ideas of what's normal between male friends isn't based on something universal about men. Male friends in Korea engage in "skinship," a term that refers to nonsexual physical affection—music videos for K-pop bands offer plenty of examples. After George W. Bush and Crown Prince Abdullah of Saudi Arabia held hands while taking a stroll together in 2005, American news outlets informed their domestic audiences that it's common in Arab cultures for men to hold hands. The same is true in India and various countries across Africa. High levels of gender segregation in these societies mean that people often form their most intimate relationships with people of the same gender. Some of these same societies condemn homosexuality, but because it's treated as an aberration, sometimes even associated with the West, men don't need to constantly prove that they're straight. In countries such as Uganda, where physical affection between men is disappearing, scholars and writers link the change to the incursion of Western values.

Up until the early twentieth century in the United States and Europe, you'd have no trouble spotting physical affection between men. In 1851, a young engineer named James Blake described staying up late the night before parting from his friend because "our hearts were full of that true friendship which could not find utterance by words, we laid our heads upon each other's bosom and wept, it may be unmanly to weep, but I care not, the spirit was touched." What crossed the line of manliness for Blake wasn't laying his head on another man's bosom but weeping. In *Picturing Men*, a study of thousands of ordinary photographs of men taken between the 1850s and 1950s, California State University, Fullerton professor John Ibson shows how men of all races, classes, and regions openly engaged in physical intimacy with other men. Common poses included sitting on each other's laps, holding hands, or resting their head on the other man's shoulder. Physical closeness was once a prime feature of male friendship.

As Nick began to examine his intuitions, he started to believe that his discomfort wasn't always an accurate signal that something was wrong. But this new idea was disorienting. How could Nick know what he wanted if he'd been raised in a culture that denied him experiences such as emotional connection with other men? It's a culture in which it's common enough for men to be emotionally shut off that there's a clinical term for what they're experiencing: *normative male alexithymia*. Psychologists think some men have such trouble putting their feelings into words because of the way they are socialized to be tough and stoic.

About a year after Art accepted that he was gay, Nick began to wonder if he was also attracted to men. He was becoming more comfortable in close friendships—"But am I supposed to?" he asked himself. On a hike in a state park in Kentucky, Nick told Art that he thought he might be gay. Art ran through questions to detect desire for men, such as: Did Nick ever want to kiss a man? Was he attracted to Art? No and no. As far as Art could tell, nothing pointed in the direction of same-sex attraction, so he asked Nick what made him think he could be gay. Nick said he liked it when Art hugged him, and he missed Art when he was gone for a week. "Oh, that's just intimacy," Art said. "That's just loving someone, being close to someone."

Nick had equated emotional intimacy with sexual attraction; he hadn't known that it was possible to experience emotional intimacy in a platonic context—he'd only ever done so with a girlfriend. Even though American men in the past openly expressed love for their same-sex friends, today, straight men look elsewhere for intimacy.

Researchers found that while many heterosexual women felt more emotional intimacy with their female best friend than with a male romantic partner, that was generally not the case for heterosexual men. Their romantic partner was more likely to be their chief source of emotional intimacy.

In a survey from 2021, men were about half as likely as women to report having recently received emotional support from a friend, and married men were significantly more likely than married women to say their spouse is the first person they talk to when they have a problem. Men shy away from verbally affirming their friendships; about half of women said they told a friend they loved them within the past week, compared to one-quarter of men. Andrew Reiner, the author of a book about masculinity, concluded that the nearly two hundred boys and men he interviewed tended to rely on male friends to solve specific problems that were unlikely to inspire judgment—what he called "targeted transparency." These men and boys worried that their friends wouldn't want to discuss their emotionally laden issues, or they didn't want to "burden" others with their problems. If they sought emotional support, they generally turned to their romantic partners or female friends—forcing women to provide care for men that men aren't giving to one another. One writer called the tendency for straight men to hoist all their emotional needs on their female romantic partners "emotional gold digging."

On that Zoom event, Nick described a dynamic he used to have with Art: "For me as a straight person, it's been so easy . . . for me to go, 'Well, I'm uncomfortable, so you need to change because I'm in the majority.'" Nick said he now knows there are multiple reasons that could explain his discomfort. Maybe "it's a good and healthy boundary, but maybe there's homophobia or perception issues or intimacy issues that I've just grown up with," he said. Turning to

Art, Nick said, "Just because I'm uncomfortable doesn't mean you're wrong."

————————

It is a truth universally acknowledged, that a couple locked down together during the pandemic quickly committed or collapsed. In their friendship, Art and Nick did the former.

Art was living alone when he read Facebook posts from friends who are based abroad about stay-at-home orders in Italy. Talking on the phone, Art and Nick decided that being together was nonnegotiable. They already felt like they were functioning as a household—the operative term in the early stretch of the COVID pandemic, when your in-person world consisted of the people you lived with, not necessarily the people you were related to.

In the summer of 2020, Nick pointed out that they would soon be looking down the barrel of a winter alone; he thought it was time to move forward with living together. As they searched for an apartment, their Odd Couple contrasts came to the fore. Craft supplies and knickknacks crowd Art's room. Because he hates silence, he'll play ocean sounds when he takes a bath. Growing up in a house that was constantly filled with guests, he caught the bug for hosting. In contrast, Nick tries not to acquire things and needs to be fully alone to rest well. He wanted doors and walls between them when they lived together, so he insisted on an apartment that had a third bedroom or second living room.

Their limited budget and unusual needs made for a stressful search, but they eventually found a two-floor apartment with a wraparound terrace—a design feature that would become their home's namesake. The kitchen had space to set up a coffee bar, which they would use together for Friday morning coffee, a ritual they considered practically sacred.

If the story of their first few months living together in the Terrace were an epic, it would be told as three trials. The first trial was Nick's romantic life. Around the same time that they moved into the apartment, Nick began dating a woman.

They'd been through this type of test before. Early in Art and Nick's friendship, Nick regularly flaked on Art and showed up egregiously late because his college girlfriend, with whom he had a volatile relationship, always came first. Even when Art confronted him, Nick defended his behavior. Nick changed course after their breakup, setting reminders on his watch so he wouldn't keep Art waiting. He signed up for counseling when Art complained that Nick was making him do too much emotional work. In the years since his college relationship ended, Nick decided that it was a deal-breaker if a woman didn't accept the friendship because, he says, "I feel strongly that Art being in my life actually provides the healthiest hope of a marriage that I could have." Nick thinks Art pushes him to grow and points out issues he isn't self-aware enough to observe in himself. They began to joke that Art gets to go on Nick's first dates—not literally, but Nick will certainly mention him early on. When they met with Art's pastor, seeking a friendship version of premarital counseling, Art asked if it was possible for the friendship to work with Nick's future marriage. The pastor's response was encouraging: "It is as possible as you are committed to it," he said.

Weeks after moving into the Terrace, Nick and his new girlfriend had planned a date that Nick viewed as a gauge of how his friendship with Art would coexist with his romantic relationship. The three of them were set to have lunch at the apartment. The morning of the date, Art told Nick that his mom had COVID and was coughing blood; his stepdad was in the hospital for COVID. Despite the news, Nick ran out to get groceries because his girlfriend was going to arrive soon. They all had lunch for an hour, and then Nick and his girlfriend went out together. Nick didn't ask Art if he should stay rather than keep the one-on-one portion of the plans. Art didn't request that of Nick because he thought it was too much to ask if Nick didn't volunteer the idea. Instead, Art told Nick he would need support when Nick came home. Nick told Art to keep him updated and said they'd spend time together when he returned.

Art expected Nick to get back by 8:00 p.m. at the latest because Nick goes to bed early; Art compared Nick after 9:00 p.m. to a computer that's been turned off. When Nick got back after 9:00 p.m., he was surprised to find Art in bed—he thought they were going to hang out. Art told him to go to sleep; he didn't care at this point. Nick hadn't responded to Art's text that things had gotten worse with his family. Exactly what Art had feared had happened: a girlfriend had entered the picture, and Nick disappeared.

Nick felt blindsided by Art's reaction that night. He thought Art had given him his blessing to go on the date. In time, he came to believe he should have taken proactive steps to tend to the friendship rather than expect Art to ask for what he needed again and again.

As much as the right thing to do was clear in retrospect, Nick found the idea of canceling on his girlfriend hard to seriously entertain in the moment. The two of them had already had a fight about Nick's friendship taking precedence over their nascent romantic relationship. Prioritizing Art might have further incensed her. She later spent an hour and a half questioning Nick about the friendship. She brought up comments Art and Nick made during the webinar, including Art's remark that Nick was cute—the kind of banter that populates their everyday conversation. Nick's girlfriend felt there was too much room for attraction in their friendship. The discussion made Nick feel like he was "on trial."

After the date, Art and Nick had a series of conversations on their couch late at night. Art said they hadn't known what the friendship would cost Nick when they decided on this life together. In tears, Art told Nick that he couldn't be the reason that Nick didn't get married and have a family. Not for the first time, Art suggested they go their separate ways.

Nick told him, "I need you to stop bringing that up, because it hurts me every time." Nick didn't feel like it was an option not to continue to build a life with Art. Whereas Art describes himself as "quick to commit, but I'll rethink a lot," he says, Nick is "slow to commit, but once he's committed, he's never stepping back out."

It wasn't as if Nick felt hamstrung. He said the best version of his life has Art in it. "Yeah, I might miss marriage because of you," Nick told Art, "but a marriage without you wouldn't be a better option." He was also more optimistic than Art that things would work out. Nick thought it was a matter of how the two types of relationships would mesh, not if.

Art's suggestion that they step back from the friendship was motivated by more than guilt and selflessness. He wasn't sure if Nick had it in him simultaneously to sustain a romantic relationship and care about Art. Art felt Nick had dropped the ball repeatedly while he was in this romantic relationship, "and so part of it was like, man, if this is what it's going to be like if you're going to have someone in your life, I can't do that to myself."

―――――――

The second trial was called into session even before their move-in day in October 2020. Art felt national politics seeping into their new household. Across the country, Black Lives Matter supporters flooded the streets to protest police misconduct. The election was weeks away, and Art thought his livelihood was on the line because of President Trump's immigration policies. A DACA recipient, Art was advised by his lawyer to stop saving for retirement and divert that money to a fund he could tap into if he had to leave the country. Art worried that Nick, who is conflict-averse and whose family supports Trump, would think of the election as *just* politics. That's how some other people close to Art justified their indifference to policies he found distressing. Art felt his whole life was political, and he wasn't sure he'd be able to fully be himself around a straight white man. He told Nick this, saying it would be an issue if he had to code-switch in his own house to adapt to white, heterosexual norms. Nick suggested that Art stop code-switching, and they could see what happened. The main difference for Art was that he communicated with more physicality. Nick decided he could get used to it.

"As a gay Latino—and a very specific sort of gay person who's religious—I feel like I'm very misunderstood a lot of the time," Art says. But Nick "just gets it, even though he's none of the things I am: he's a straight, white guy from an upper-middle-class community . . . But I feel really known by him. I feel really understood. I have to explain myself very little when he's around." On November 7, 2020, Nick was standing in the kitchen when he learned that Joe Biden was declared the president-elect. He clutched Art and cried in relief.

About a month later, Art's life would transform for reasons that had nothing to do with the election. Art's denomination and the Evangelical internet caught wind of the same webinar that upset Nick's girlfriend, along with some tweets Art wrote about difficult experiences gay people have had in the church.

Though the local church that employed Art had no problem either with his friendship with Nick or his sexual orientation—he was allowed to be out at work—his denomination at large banned gay people from ministry regardless of whether they pursued a same-sex romantic relationship. Art says, "So I went from a really great job, out for the first time in my life, getting to hold my sexuality and faith together in a way I'd never gotten to, liking my church, feeling known at my church for the first time—to just being hunted pretty aggressively."

Evangelical blogs denounced Art, implying that their friendship was nonsexual only for now. One read, "Essentially, Art and Nick have a backdoor homosexual marriage without sex," and went on to argue, "We are not meant to live with our friends all of our lives." He was accused of being a danger to children. "Kind of every worst thing you've ever imagined religious people say about gay people was what happened," Art says. Art eventually resigned.

Anyone facing this kind of public scrutiny would probably have been disturbed by it, but for a pastor, whose role is intrinsically linked to good character, it was especially demeaning. While Art's job hung in the balance, he began to doubt his morality. He'd get home and ask Nick, "Am I a danger to my students?" Art says, "What was really helpful was having people like Nick who were like, 'Hey, hold on, that's not what we believe. That's not what we value. That's not what we see in scripture.'"

About a year after all of this happened, Nick, Art, and I sit at their kitchen table, Nick wearing a gray athletic T-shirt that reminds me he wakes up at 4:45 each morning to go to the gym and uses a kitchen scale to weigh all his food, the better to reach his training goals. Art had prepared a snack for those of us without training goals: halved figs topped with fresh basil and coarse salt. While Art recounts this unsettling period, the rings on his fingers catching the light as he talks with his hands, Nick stares into the distance with an intense gaze. Art asks him, "You okay, Bub?"—a variation of "Bubba," Art's pet name for Nick. In a flat tone, Nick says, "Yeah." Watching Art under pressure from his denomination, Nick says, was "super difficult. That was a difficult season." He pauses for a few seconds. He says he felt "totally powerless and unable to change anything except to sit and grieve with it."

Art had no good options. His interpretation of what the Bible says about gay people is a tiny overlapping sliver in the Venn diagram of conservative and progressive Christianity: that gay sex and marriage aren't permissible, but, Art says, "I also see the Bible inviting gay people into a really beautiful life and Jesus being really loving toward gay folks." (Though Art doesn't believe his reading of Christianity permits same-sex marriage, he thinks the government should allow it.) If Art switched to a church that was openly affirming of queer people, he would be working in a place that taught things about scripture that he didn't believe. He's also found these spaces to be unkind to people like him. His stepdad, who follows a more liberal form of Christianity, was upset when he learned Art was celibate and spent hours trying to persuade him to get a boyfriend. Whereas Art views celibacy as a decision made through deep thought and prayer, congregants in these places treat him like he's repressed or oppressed. "Sometimes more progressive folks want to rescue me from myself," Art says. "And I don't need to be rescued from myself."

When Nick started dating Morgan in the summer of 2021, what felt remarkable to him were all the things he didn't have to explain. Morgan immediately seemed to understand his friendship with Art.

Morgan's approach to friendship was part of the reason they were introduced. One of Nick's friends in the Amoeba knew Morgan and thought she and Nick might connect over their shared experience with devoted friendships. Unlike Art and Nick, who made the conscious decision to form a committed friendship, she had stumbled into hers. After college, Morgan returned to her hometown in rural Illinois and ended up in a bedbug-infested apartment. When the lease ended, she bounced between friends' homes until a couple at church to whom she had become close suggested she move into their home temporarily. Several months into living with the couple and their three- and seven-year-old children, Morgan realized they weren't only roommates. These people she saw at the end of every day felt like family.

In 2020, one of these family members got a job at a church in New Jersey. The couple didn't push Morgan to relocate with them but let her know she was welcome to do so. Morgan decided to move. She landed a job in New Jersey, and the couple turned the office of their new house into a bedroom for Morgan.

In his relationship with his ex-girlfriend, Nick felt he was in the interrogation chair, constantly having to justify the amount of time he was spending with Art. But Morgan didn't press him. She had her own commitments to friends and was relieved that she didn't have to defend them. Whereas, in past romantic relationships, Nick "often felt like my friendship with Art and dating relationship pulled against one another," with Morgan, the physics were different. These relationships, he says, are "actually working towards supporting one another."

When I've fallen into conversations about the idea of having more than one anchoring person in your life, like Art and Nick do, people sometimes balk at how complicated it seems. Morgan readily admits there are times when her living situation is exhausting "because family's exhausting. Caring for people is exhausting. It's not always easy, and it's not always fun," she says. "But for the most part, it is.

And so it makes those moments that are hard—the five percent of the time that it is difficult—it does make it very, very, very much worth it."

Like Kami and Tilly from chapter 2, Nick and Art both enthuse about what they gain by having another important person in their lives. "You have no idea how much of a gift this is," Nick says. "Each of us feels like we have an extra teammate." If Morgan is having a hard time, Art can support Nick in supporting Morgan. Art gets more care in return. As Art reeled from the public uprising in his denomination, Morgan constantly checked in with him, sent him DoorDash gift cards to make sure he had something to eat that night, and made him laugh.

Whereas Art had once worried about what would happen when Nick got married, now he can't wait. It means he'll get to "live with two of my favorite people." Art knows that Nick is slow-paced in relationships, so he chooses his words carefully when he talks to his friend about Morgan. "If it were up to me," Art says, "we would've proposed at Christmas. I would have told him, 'Bro, for Christmas, you're getting her a ring. That's what's happening. Go do it.'"

When I talk to Art on a summer day in 2022, he mentions that he's taking over Nick's date night with Morgan because Nick is out of town; he and Morgan will get dinner and hang out. Not long before, she texted Art a picture of a jade velvet couch. She asked him if they could buy the couch when she marries Nick. Art said, "Absolutely, we can."

While other people reserve Valentine's Day for their romantic partner, Art and Nick treat it as a day to honor their brotherhood. On Valentine's Day in 2020, Nick cooked dinner and bought tickets to a movie that he and Art had been wanting to see. Nick says, "It's one of the ways I'm practicing the whole, I understand this can look romantic, but I also need to not care, because I care about this person more." Art says there's been a "night-and-day difference" between the Nick who feared being clocked as gay and the Nick he knows now. He can't imagine the Hawaii incident happening today. When I bring up the Hawaii flights to Nick, he groans. He's embarrassed by his reaction three years earlier.

Art and Nick have come up with a framework that has helped Nick decipher why things feel uncomfortable to him. The two of them ask: *What is moral? What is cultural? What is personal?* Nick used to be unnerved when a man touched him, so Art pointed out that there's no moral stricture in the Bible against affection between men; men in the early church greeted one another with a kiss, and one verse describes John lying on Jesus's bosom. To unravel the source of Nick's discomfort with certain kinds of touch, Art brought up the distinct norms in American culture and the culture of Nick's family. Whereas Art grew up around Brazilians who readily showed physical affection toward their friends, Nick was raised in a household, much like other American families, that didn't model physical affection between men; Nick can't remember the last time he hugged his dad. He realized some forms of touch are unpleasant for him because he easily experiences sensory overload. After reflecting on these three questions, Nick figured out what he prefers: he's happy for Art to rest his hand on him as long as Art doesn't move his hand. This process takes effort. "A lot of my actions are lagging indicators of growing up with my family," Nick says. "Changing the way I've thought about things for twenty-six years . . . that doesn't happen overnight."

Art started using this same framework in his job. After resigning from his post as a youth pastor, he began working for Revoice, an organization that supports gay celibate Christians—the same one that ran the now-infamous webinar. Part of his job entails helping pastors in conservative congregations make their churches more welcoming to people who identify as LGBTQ+. He shows pastors that a lot of what they espouse from the pulpit are personal or cultural values, not anything commanded in the Bible. Art gets a kick out of bringing up the John-on-Jesus's-bosom example. In an arch tone, he tells me, "They don't know what to do with the fact that their savior's cuddling a man."

With one hand on the steering wheel, Art drives along a New Jersey highway to drop me off at the train station. It's just the two of us, and I say that someone could look at his friendship with Nick and think it must have been exhausting for Art to spend years shooing the monster of homohysteria from under Nick's bed. Their friendship has a dynamic that contravenes advice in a recent book on friendship: the friend with more privilege is responsible for putting in work to understand the less privileged friend's life experience. Art says it hasn't been that simple for them. He tells me that Nick has given up some of his straight privilege by openly making a lifelong commitment to a gay man. The same witch hunt that targeted Art came for Nick, too. People contacted Nick's church, calling for him to be disciplined. Evangelical blogs condemned Nick as well. Art says, "One of my big things is if you're willing to experience homophobia for a queer person, then, cool, ask me any question you want."

Though Art thinks, in general, the person with more privilege should make the effort to learn on their own, people like Art can step in to assist "the people who prove that they're doing the work." He expects Nick to learn basic ideas about homophobia through books or conversations with other queer people, but he wants Nick to learn some things from him "because I'm the gay person he has to live everyday life with."

As Art has made queer friends in recent years, he's found ease around them, like they're speaking the same language in how they express themselves. But he adds that Nick has learned to translate this dimension of his identity: "Do my queer friends know queerness better than he does? Sure. Does anyone know me as well as Nick does? No."

———————

Through his close friendship with Art, Nick has dodged the fate of many of his male peers. Americans have fewer close friends than just decades ago, and men are faring worse than women. In 1990, more than half of men reported having at least six close friends. In 2021, only about a quarter of men could say the same. Fifteen percent of men report having no close friendships—a fivefold increase from 1990. (Talking about baby boomer men, the stand-up comedian John Mulaney joked on *Saturday Night Live*, "Your dad has no friends. If you think your dad has friends, you're wrong. Your mom has friends, and they have husbands. Those are not your dad's friends.")

Having fewer close friends is associated with loneliness, and loneliness is linked to a variety pack of negative health outcomes, from high blood pressure to depression to cognitive decline. Compared to women who lose their husbands, men who lose their spouses experience a much more pronounced and long-lasting spike in loneliness and depression; they're more likely than women to die by suicide. Researchers attribute these differences to women having more diverse systems of social support.

The impoverishment of contemporary male friendship would have taken men in the past by surprise. They presented themselves as uniquely able to achieve platonic heights; women supposedly lacked the character or social position to do so. In his famous essay "On Friendship," the sixteenth-century philosopher Michel de Montaigne described women's fervent nature—"a rash and wavering fire"—as incompatible with the even temperament required in "true friendship." American men in the colonial period and beyond aspired to live up to the paragon of fraternal love in the story of David and Jonathan, who made sacrifices for each other and whose connection is described in the Bible in these terms: "The soul of Jonathan was knit to the soul of David, and Jonathan loved him as his own soul." In eighteenth-century American polite society, materials such as letter-writing manuals advised men to bring open emotional expression into their friendships. Intimacy in male friendship was not something to be ashamed of. It was the measure of a man.

Despite the nationwide drop in the number of men's close friendships, there's some sign that more men, especially those in younger generations, will get to experience friendships that approach the closeness of Nick and Art's. Homophobia has declined over the last few decades, and with less stigma attached to being gay, researchers have found that homohysteria has eroded, too. Men in a small study of British college students who had "bromances" described feeling deep emotional intimacy within these friendships, comfort with same-sex physical intimacy, such as cuddling, and lack of concern that people will think they are gay. Other studies of young men show that emotional intimacy and physical affection are increasingly possible in male friendships now because, compared to earlier decades, there are more shades of acceptable masculinity.

———

As can happen in any long-term relationship, whether romantic or platonic, the scales between Art and Nick have adjusted over time. Art had once felt an unspoken power dynamic, with Nick holding the power because Art would have Nick whereas "he was going to have a normal life plus me." He also felt indebted to Nick because "early into our relationship, it felt like Nick was saving me from loneliness," Art says. But he doesn't feel that way anymore. He has other options—he has friends and job opportunities in California—but he's made the affirmative choice to stay in New Jersey with Nick.

Nick feels he has a partner he needs, too. A major project of adulthood is figuring out what's in your personal user manual—what you like and don't, what your values are, what you need to flourish—and the friendship has helped Nick learn what's in his. He's no longer relying on the culture around him to provide an (often inaccurate) shortcut to those answers.

Art and Nick find pleasure in the everyday facets of shared living: the extra coffee Nick leaves in the pot for Art, the Pixar quotes Nick drops into conversation, the comforting predictability Nick feels in knowing that Art will be crocheting on the couch when he gets home from the gym. Art says, "I have a companion in a very real and full sense. My life is very not alone." They don't even need to be in the same place for Art to feel this way. Art says, "There's just a sense of knowing a person, and they're so integrated into your life, so even when they're not around, life feels full."

They've come to understand each other so well that when Nick was having a bad day, Art knew exactly what would take his mind off things: Art called Nick from Walmart and asked if he should pick up coffee there. A coffee snob, Nick burst out laughing—an instant mood boost.

Life also feels more fun. Art does not, in his nature, like small talk or fun. "I want everyone to tell me their trauma and, like, cry with me," he says, his tone deadpan but the sentiment genuine. Nick has helped him see that it's possible to feel connected with people without having soul-baring conversations with them. Art and Nick have blended friendship behaviors that are stereotyped to belong to one gender or another; they find closeness both through activities and dialogue.

With his newfound appreciation for fun, Art has embraced their house rule, "We're never too cool for anything." If something brings a person delight, Nick and Art are going to be delighted with them. They have leaned into this spirit with a custom-made straw doormat and pins printed with the words *The Terrace*. This rule is an outgrowth of Nick's attitude of relishing the joy of the people around him. Nick and Art think Nick is better able to show this side of himself because he's become attuned to his own feelings and has shed concern about other's judgments. Nick says that the friendship has made him pursue integrity, "specifically, being the same person everywhere that I am instead of different people in different places." That pursuit has spilled over into his romantic relationship. One of the things Morgan loves best about Nick is his guileless enthusiasm. She says he doesn't care if someone thinks his cheerleader-like ways of showing support are cheesy; that's just who he is.

While Nick's penchant for delight has shaped the spirit of their apartment, Art has brought his vision to the décor. When he moved into the apartment, he hauled in forty houseplants. Now the apartment has more than sixty. Art can't help but offer a plant analogy when he's reflecting on his friendship with Nick. "Ivy plants will always follow whatever trellis you give them," he says. "But if they don't have a trellis, they look for light."

He continues, "I think that a lot of us follow a societal trellis that is not actually ideal for who we are and what helps us thrive . . . Because there was no trellis, we got to create a relationship and a life that is really uniquely beautiful for us. I really like the life I have. It is way better than it would've been if I had just gone and gotten my husband or wife and two dogs and three kids or whatever."

Forging a path without a standard-issue relationship structure has, at times, been painful for Art and Nick. They didn't have language or books to guide them through tough conversations as devoted friends or the issues their unusual friendship created. Nick had trouble reconciling his previous romantic relationship and his friendship. He attributes some of those difficulties to the "societal trellis failing us and failing the type of friendship we want to have."

Nick says, "We needed to dismantle that trellis to pursue something better."

5

FUNCTIONAL FAMILIES

From friends to co-parents

Friendship is an upstart category, for it to usurp the place of kinship or even intrude upon it is an impertinence.

—ELSIE CLEWS PARSONS

On a spring night in 2009, Lynda Collins and Natasha Bakht sat down for dinner at one of their haunts in Ottawa's Chinatown. The dinner felt like several others they'd had before—they ordered salt-and-pepper shrimp and their other three favorite dishes—until Lynda realized that something about her friend was off.

"What's going on with you?" she asked.

Natasha sniffled. Her eyes were red and watering. She said she had seasonal allergies but refused Lynda's offer of a Claritin. Natasha wanted to evade Lynda's follow-up question. But by this point, her limited lying capacity was running on empty.

"Okay, fine! I'm pregnant," Natasha said.

"You're *what*?" Lynda said.

Natasha was suffering through allergies because she didn't want to take medication while pregnant. She'd realized that, at thirty-six and not in a relationship, she didn't want to rush one or miss the window for parenthood because she hadn't found a partner. After getting two rounds of anonymous donor sperm at her local fertility clinic, Natasha became pregnant.

Lynda blurted out, "I'd like to apply for the position of birth coach"—the person who would join Natasha for prenatal classes, be present during the delivery, and help navigate any issues in between. It was like her to make this sort of offer—impulsive and generous, driven by the wonder she feels for the world around her. Lynda considered birth a magical moment and thought this was a once-in-a-lifetime opportunity to see someone through the experience. She also knew she wanted to have kids and was interested in getting a close-up look at what pregnancy might be like for herself. As if she were drafting a cover letter, Lynda enumerated her qualifications: She had lived with a midwife for three years, who gave her an informal course about pregnancy. She operated well in crises. She lived near Natasha and made the case that Natasha should have someone in her same city to rely on, not just friends and family who lived hours away.

Natasha met Lynda's spontaneous proposal with deliberation. Lynda was offering to be a kind of birth sidekick, who would join Natasha over the next several months and in the delivery room. It was an intimate role to welcome anyone into, and though Natasha was fond of Lynda, they weren't at the level of best friends. They had met a few years earlier when Natasha was involved in hiring Lynda as a fellow law professor at the University of Ottawa. As soon as Natasha got to know Lynda, whom she found funny yet earnest, she could see the two of them becoming close. Though they were colleagues, they worked in different fields—Natasha in human rights law and Lynda in environmental law—so they weren't tempted to resort to shop talk. Wandering through the farmers' market on a fall day, they talked about the guy Lynda had a crush on but who didn't seem like he'd be a romantic partner of hers anytime soon and the lives they'd led before moving to Ottawa, including the different parts of the world Natasha had seen while touring as a professional dancer. To Lynda, Natasha seemed brilliant, her mind and dancer's body agile in equal measure. When Natasha and Lynda were together, time vanished. Six or seven hours would pass without them realizing how long they'd spent together.

After about a week of reflection, Natasha realized that Lynda was the kind of person who would be there for her. She could trust her. Natasha called Lynda to say she accepted her offer to be a birth coach. Natasha didn't have grand plans for Lynda's role. She figured Lynda would have an interesting experience supporting her during this transformative moment. Maybe Lynda would be an involved auntie in her future child's life.

When Natasha told her mom that she was planning to have a child, her mom said, "Unmarried girls don't have babies."

"I don't really think I'm a girl," Natasha said. "I'm thirty-six. I'm a law professor."

Natasha, in deciding to have a child on her own, had joined the growing number of people building families outside the nuclear model. In Canada, where she lives, two-parent families are on the decline, and now close to 20 percent of children younger than fifteen live in a single-parent household. The same trends hold in the United States, where the proportion of children living with two parents of any marital status dropped from 85 percent in 1968 to 70 percent in 2020. It's also become common for children to grow up in families with complex and fluid structures. *Blended families*, *stepparents*, and *half siblings* are now ordinary terms in the vocabulary of families. There's no longer one "typical" family form in the United States.

Politicians and public figures have declared their distress over the growing societal drift away from the "traditional family." Senator Marco Rubio, in a 2022 video, said, "We must make it possible for single-income households to raise a family," and called on Americans to "demand the same sense of urgency to prevent the traditional family from going under that we display when big businesses are at risk of going under." Much of the rallying around the nuclear family has come from the Right, but not all of it. In a 2008 speech at one of Chicago's largest Black churches, Barack Obama described the difficulty he faced growing up without a father in the house. He told the crowd, "Too many fathers are MIA, too many fathers are AWOL, missing from too many lives and too many homes . . . And the foundations of our families are weaker because of it." Proponents of the nuclear family tend to argue that this particular family structure provides unrivaled stability, enhances children's development, honors religious teachings, strengthens the country—or a combination of these.

Natasha's mom was attached to conventional ideas about how to form a family even though she had defied her own culture's orthodoxies about marriage: as a young Hindu woman in India, she married a Muslim man. Her disapproval of single motherhood receded once Natasha got pregnant and, in its place, came concern for her future grandchild and her daughter's health. Living nearly three hundred miles away, Natasha's mom was reassured by Lynda's support for her daughter. The friends attended weekly prenatal courses together, the only pair who weren't the target audience for the instructions *Moms over here, dads over there*, or comments intended to be comforting, like, "At least you're doing this with the person you love most in all the world." When the teacher made that remark to the class, Lynda jokingly apologized to Natasha for not being the love of her life but promised to do her best anyway. To keep in touch, Lynda, a longtime conscientious objector to cell phones, started carrying one around. Late in the pregnancy, Natasha's dad moved from Toronto into his daughter's Ottawa apartment, and the three spent many evenings watching tennis on TV and eating Häagen-Dazs, which Natasha consistently craved. Natasha's dad and Lynda like to say they put on a lot of baby weight during that period.

About a week before her due date, Natasha's dad joined her for a routine doctor's appointment. The ultrasound technician couldn't feel the baby move, so she sent Natasha to the hospital to induce labor and monitor the baby. Natasha called Lynda and told her she needed to get there immediately. Lynda dashed out of the lecture she was teaching and drove, in her words, "like a maniac" across the city through rush-hour traffic. At the hospital, she relieved Natasha's father, who, Natasha says, is "such a wonderful, wonderful man, but he is not great when his kids are in any sort of trouble or pain." The doula concerned herself with comforting Natasha's dad while Lynda and Natasha spoke with the doctor. They learned that Natasha would have to get an emergency C-section. Natasha immediately started crying, worried about whether her baby would be okay.

Lynda joined Natasha in the operating room. Still under the haze of anesthesia, Natasha heard the surgeon say that there was a "true knot" in the umbilical cord. The surgeon offered to show Lynda the baby; she was the first person to hold him after he was born. What should have been a thrilling moment was instead unnerving. The baby was gray. Lynda worried he wouldn't live. Once he was cleaned up, Lynda thought, "he was this beautiful, glowing, vibrant, little love bomb," and "immediately, I had a major tidal wave of love and probably hormones." The boy, who weighed less than five pounds, was shuttled to the neonatal intensive care unit.

After spending three days in the hospital with Natasha and the baby, who was now named Elaan, Lynda helped them settle into Natasha's apartment. The trio slept in Natasha's bed, with an alarm set for every three and a half hours to feed Elaan.

The next day, Natasha's mother, brother, and best friend arrived from Toronto, ready to take over. When Lynda closed the door to Natasha's apartment to leave, she started crying.

"It was very jarring," Lynda says, to be on the outside after days of being involved in round-the-clock care for Elaan, who'd already captured her heart. "The reality set in that I'm *not* this key person in this baby's life." She decided she had to let go, at least a little.

But then she didn't. Lynda used the keys she had to Natasha's apartment to come over every day for the first month. She tried to make sure she wasn't intruding, but when she'd suggest heading home, Natasha's family would tell her to stay for dinner. The next month, Natasha moved in with her parents in Toronto, where she'd spend the remainder of her maternity leave, and Lynda showed up every few weeks. During those visits, she slept in Natasha's old bedroom. Natasha's parents took to calling it "Lynda's room."

Lynda was too enamored of Elaan to be so far away from him. She says, "Although it was nice to get updates on the phone, sometimes I just wanted to give him a cuddle and look into his beautiful eyes." Lynda would decide spur-of-the-moment to get in the car at 5:00 a.m. and make the four-hour drive to Toronto. Once, she hopped in her car on a day when Natasha's parents were both going to be out of the house. Natasha had been worried about taking care of Elaan without anyone's help, so she'd asked a friend to come by that day. The friend had canceled last minute. Then Lynda pulled into the driveway unannounced. Natasha thought, *Oh, thank God!* Lynda wasn't only good company, as her other friends were. In caring for Elaan, Lynda had nearly mystical powers. Elaan suffered from what they believed was colic, and she figured out that music soothed him. "Auntie Lyndy," as she became known, sang and hummed constantly, to the point where she had to teach herself how to make music on the in-breath; if she paused to take a breath, Elaan would start to cry.

At one point during that first year, Natasha's mom came over to her daughter's room to speak to her. Her mom said, "I think Lynda should be Elaan's godmother."

"Okay, but we don't really do that," Natasha said. "That's not really part of our tradition."

"But you know she's more than an auntie," her mom said. "She just has such a special relationship with him."

Her mom wasn't belittling aunties. Aunties were fixtures in her life and in Natasha's. Because the relatives of Natasha's parents were back home in India, the other South Asian immigrants they befriended in Toronto became like family, and Natasha grew up referring to people who weren't technically related to her as "auntie" or "cousin." It's a common experience in immigrant communities to build family-like ties with people from shared ethnicities or nationalities. Natasha expected to raise her son in this sort of social world—teeming with caregivers. Natasha's upbringing made her understand intuitively something that nearly any anthropologist would claim: biology isn't necessary for kinship.

Today, people tend to associate parenthood with genetic ties, but Yale Law School professor Doug NeJaime says that's a modern invention. For much of American history, marriage—not biology—determined who a parent was in the eyes of the law. If a married woman gave birth to a child, the law recognized two parents: the woman was the legal mother and her husband was the legal father—even if he wasn't genetically related to the child. The man's marital bond to the mother made him the father. Children born outside of marriage, deemed "illegitimate," were stigmatized and deprived of legal rights. They were known in the law as *filius nullius*—literally, a child of no one. As legal strangers to their biological mother and biological father, they weren't entitled to inheritance rights and financial support. They didn't even have the right to carry their father's last name.

In the nineteenth and early twentieth centuries, some states passed legal reforms that relieved discrimination against "illegitimate" children. But it wasn't until 1968 that the Supreme Court ruled that children conceived outside of wedlock had a constitutional right to be treated equally to children conceived within marriage. The court reasoned that children shouldn't suffer because of their parents' marital status. Soon, the court went a step further, extending rights to unmarried fathers in the 1972 landmark case *Stanley v. Illinois*. The court wrote that "familial bonds" operating outside of marriage are "often as warm, enduring, and important as those arising within a more formally organized family unit." Now, as long as the father took on parenting responsibilities, biology trumped marital status.

The expansion of legal rights coincided with seismic shifts in the nation's demographics. No longer was marriage the sole acceptable arrangement for starting a family. By the 1970s, the number of single people and unmarried partners with children had risen. As rates of divorce and remarriage climbed, family structures grew increasingly complex; the labels of *mother*, *father*, and *children* didn't suffice to capture the diversity of familial relationships. Across the country, state laws started catching up with reality, making it easier for stepparents to adopt their spouse's children.

When assisted reproductive technologies (ART) arrived in the late twentieth century, as new technology often does, it both unlocked possibilities and introduced thorny legal questions. Couples with fertility issues, unmarried women, and LGBTQ couples could now form families with the help of egg donation, surrogacy, in vitro fertilization, and—as Natasha did—sperm banks. Around the same time that these technologies took off, it was a mark of progress that courts used biology, not marital status, to define parenthood. But as ART expanded the means of reproduction, this biology-based approach became increasingly outdated. If a couple conceived a child with the help of anonymous sperm donation, it wouldn't make much sense for the court to deem the sperm donor the father rather than the partner who intended to raise the child from the beginning.

The courts began to shift again. In 1994, a California appellate court heard a case that could have been the plot of a soap opera: A man's ex-wife revealed he wasn't the biological father of the four-year-old boy he had treated as his child, and the ex-wife wanted to assign paternity rights to another man she believed was the biological father. The court ruled against the woman, and her ex-husband remained the boy's legal parent. The court determined that biology isn't a sufficient condition for paternity rights, quoting an earlier case in which the judges put forward a thought experiment: What if a man had lived with a child, treated the child as his son or daughter, and bonded with the child? "This social relationship," the judges wrote, "is much more important, to the child at least, than a biological relationship of actual paternity."

For LGBTQ and feminist activists, this new legal understanding of parental rights was especially relevant. ART sparked what came to be known as a "lesbian baby boom" in the 1980s and '90s, and as is true for their straight counterparts, some of these lesbian couples broke up. But unlike different-sex couples, these women didn't have access to custody laws or the neat ties of biological connection that would have guaranteed parental status for both partners. As far as the law was concerned, the nonbiological mother was a stranger to the child. The biological mother, if she wanted to, could shut out her ex from the child's life. In these custody cases, the courts couldn't turn to their tried-and-true approaches to sort out disputes around parental rights—leaning on marriage, biology, or gender. Instead, LGBTQ activists successfully advocated for parents to be legally recognized based on intent or conduct: Did the couple intend to have the child and raise the child together? Did the person conduct herself as a parent?

Public opinion mirrored the rulings in these cases. A 1989 survey found that only 22 percent of respondents defined a family solely in terms of blood, marriage, or adoption, while the overwhelming majority—74 percent—embraced a broader definition: any group whose members loved and cared for one another. The law and the public acknowledged that behavior—not marriage, not genetics, and increasingly, not gender—was the crux of familial relationships.

If you're sitting in a courtroom facing the possibility of being denied child custody (or shelling out child support), the label *parent* undeniably matters. But the desire for accurate terms can recede behind life's demands, as it did for Natasha and Lynda.

"We probably started parenting long before we called it that," Natasha says. "We were probably too busy living our lives to really be analyzing it."

They sang to Elaan, often songs that Lynda wrote and played on the guitar. "Yes, my world feels better / You're around," the lyrics of one song go. "You're the notes to my music, the silence, the light, and the sound." They joked with Elaan, whose short black hair sweeps across his forehead, a miniature version of Natasha's haircut. It wasn't hard to get his toothy smile to wipe across his face or launch him into giggles. When they'd finally put Elaan to bed, despite their exhaustion, they'd obsess over a photo of him in an adorable outfit that friends had given him as a gift or reminisce about something he'd done that day.

Language may have also taken a back seat because Lynda and Natasha were preoccupied with caring for Elaan. Several months after Elaan's birth, they realized that what they'd believed to be colic was cerebral irritability—a symptom of cerebral palsy. Lynda's mother, a brain rehabilitation doctor, noticed that Elaan's small repetitive eye movements were, in fact, seizures. It was during this first year that Natasha took Elaan to get an MRI and made an appointment with a neurologist. She didn't want to bring her parents to the appointment because she feared they'd find it upsetting. When Lynda learned that Natasha planned to go alone, she asked to join.

The neurologist diagnosed Elaan with a type of brain injury called *paraventricular leukomalacia.* He explained that large areas of Elaan's brain were gone, likely related to the knot in the umbilical cord. Elaan would have significant impairment in every domain. Until this point, Natasha had been operating on a compressed time horizon, just trying to get from one hour to the next. Now the doctor was forcing her to look at the prospects for her son's development over the course of his life. On the drive home, Natasha stirred with shock and worry. She asked Lynda, "What kind of life is he going to have?"

"He's going to have a wonderful life," Lynda said. "We're going to make sure of that." For thirty years, Lynda had watched her mother, as a rehabilitation doctor, help people with brain injuries lead meaningful lives. Lynda also didn't feel devastated by the diagnosis because she had come into the appointment with grim expectations; she had feared that Elaan's condition was life-threatening. The news from the doctor was a relief.

Lynda told Natasha that now that they knew Elaan was going to live, they could focus on giving him the best possible life. And Lynda made an observation that helped Natasha realize something her shock had clouded. "You know him," Lynda said. "You know what makes him laugh. You know what he hates." The test results, she pointed out, hadn't changed that. For Natasha, Lynda's optimism was a welcome contrast to the grave tones and *sorrys* they would hear from doctors over the years as Elaan's diagnoses stacked up.

During these appointments, Lynda's unusual role often became apparent. Doctors would want to know who Lynda was and why she was pulling them into a detailed discussion of the benefits and draw-backs of the proposed treatments. When Lynda was asked at Elaan's appointments, "Who is he to you?" she found it odd to refer to him as "my friend's kid." Though the doctors were respectful, they had no ob-ligation to listen to her, a legal stranger to Elaan. Lynda's friends asked if she was certain she wanted to be so involved in Elaan's life when she had no rights. "What if Natasha decides to move to Fiji?" they asked. "Or you two have a falling-out?"

It took until Elaan was five years old and Lynda turned forty for her to consider pursuing the title of parent. By then, a coworker's passing comment had made her realize she was already parenting. When Lynda mentioned that she, Natasha, and Elaan all had a cold, the colleague told her, "I hope you and your family feel better soon." Lynda thought, *Wow, I have a family. It's a miracle.* But that wasn't enough to get Lynda to think of herself as Elaan's mother; she was still contemplating having a child of her own through sperm donation or adoption. On a walk in a national park, Lynda was struck with a thought: *Why would I adopt a stranger when I could adopt Elaan? Who I really want to mother is Elaan, and that's what I've been doing.* Elaan also happened to be a child with high needs. He, in Lynda's words, "needed two—or as many—parents as he could get."

She decided to ask Natasha if she could be his second parent. One evening, the women were on the floor of Natasha's apartment, Elaan sitting between them as they fed him. Lynda asked if Natasha would be open to her legally adopting Elaan.

"It wasn't like the birth coach moment when I thought, *Let me sleep on it,*" Natasha says. "It was just like, *Oh, right. That makes perfect sense. Why hadn't I thought of that?*" If Lynda had the legal status of parent— and the symbolic meaning of that word—that would simply reflect the reality of their years of co-parenting.

They enlisted a former law school classmate of Natasha's, Marta Siemiarczuk. As a family lawyer, she was used to serving clients whose families were splintering, so she was eager to support people who were building a family. But Marta, who initially assumed the women were a couple, soon realized that the friends would face hurdles to adoption. Had the women been married to each other, Lynda could have followed the straightforward process of stepparent adoption. But because they weren't related, the law dictated that if Lynda adopted Elaan, Natasha had to forfeit her legal rights as a mother. (If they had been in America, they would have faced comparable legal challenges in about one-third of US states, where unmarried partners aren't formally allowed to get a second-parent adoption.) The women considered mounting a constitutional challenge to the law; they believed it was discriminatory because Lynda's marital status prevented her from adopting Elaan. But constitutional challenges are expensive and lengthy. Natasha and Lynda were concerned about saving money for Elaan's care, which was becoming more expensive.

They found another route: a declaration of parentage, which grants the same rights and obligations that Lynda would have gotten through adoption. To get approval, they had to show it was in Elaan's best interest for Lynda to be recognized as his parent. They collected affidavits from relatives, friends, pediatricians, staff at Elaan's school, and people in their community, which amounted to odes to Lynda's parenting abilities. One of Elaan's doctors wrote that "Lynda has a remarkably astute way of reading Elaan's expressions and behaviours." His school principal observed that Elaan "clearly derives joy, love and a sense of security from Lynda's presence in his life."

The women weren't just marshaling evidence that Elaan and Lynda had a loving relationship. They were challenging an idea implied by the law: that two people must be in (or have been in) a romantic relationship to be parents.

As a legal scholar, Lynda wondered, "How could we have such an irrational test for parenthood?" Speaking to me a decade into caring for Elaan, Lynda says, "Romance is wonderful, but I'm not sure it has anything to do with parenting." What she thinks makes romantic partners great co-parents is "more of that core of what we have—that core of mutual respect and love and compatibility. Alignment in your values."

Thinkers on the political center and Right have made a version of this argument. Richard V. Reeves, a senior fellow at the Brookings Institution, writes that "romantic marriage . . . remains largely a figment of our Hollywood-fueled imaginations, and sub-optimal for children." W. Bradford Wilcox, the director of the National Marriage Project at the University of Virginia, has argued that romance isn't a necessary condition for child-rearing. The notion that marriage's primary purpose is to build an intense romantic or emotional connection, he believes, leads to more instability in the relationship and therefore for children. Wilcox's reason: spouses can justify dissolving the relationship if they don't feel emotionally satisfied; it's a relatively easy out. Wilcox calls for a shift away from the "soulmate model of marriage," which emerged in the 1970s (or what psychologist Eli Finkel, in chapter 2, called the "self-expressive marriage"). In an article cow-ritten with Alysse ElHage, Wilcox advocates for an older, "family-first" model, which, he writes, provides an environment that "will be stronger, more stable, and more likely to offer a secure harbor for children." His motivation for reducing the significance of romantic love differs from Natasha and Lynda's. A vocal proponent of the nuclear family, Wilcox hopes to encourage marriage and prevent divorce and single parenthood. In contrast, Natasha and Lynda want societal and legal recognition for whatever family forms provide a loving home for children. They also want to affirm nonnuclear family structures that are disproportionately found outside of the white middle and upper classes. But they all align in arguing that abiding commitment is the central tenet in defining family.

The reality on the ground is that when the curtain opens on parenthood, romance often exits the stage. To state the obvious: children are exhaustion factories. Even lovers who once couldn't keep their hands off each other may find that kids snuff the fire from their romantic relationship. This sentiment saturates popular media. A podcast about families has an episode titled "Is There Sex After Kids?"—the title itself implies that the default answer is *no*. This episode, and other media content like it, focuses on how parents miss their former sexual and romantic connection to their partner. Though stories like these acknowledge the ubiquity of waning passion, they don't suggest that parents who are marooned on a libidinal desert island are now incapable of taking care of their kids together.

Sacha Coupet, a professor at Loyola Law School, argues that American family law puts misplaced emphasis on sexual love—or what she categorizes as *eros*. She asserts that what should matter is a parent's demonstration of *agape*—self-sacrificing love—for the child. This, in essence, is what Lynda and Natasha wanted the law to focus on. They asked the court to recognize Lynda as a parent not because of the women's relationship with each other but because of the substance of the relationship between Lynda and Elaan.

Though Lynda valued the symbolism of being recognized as Elaan's mom, she was more concerned with the legal and financial consequences if the court refused to deem her his parent. Elaan would be denied access to her health insurance and pension. Were something to happen to Natasha, Lynda wouldn't be able to make medical decisions on Elaan's behalf; she would have no rights as a parent. Elaan would be disadvantaged because of his parents' relationship status. Unfavorable legal treatment like this falls under the banner of what the legal scholar Nancy Polikoff calls "the New Illegitimacy."

Lynda and Natasha had just left a parent-teacher meeting when Lynda got a call from Marta, their lawyer. Lynda was worried that something was wrong. Marta said, "I really just wanted to call you, Lynda, to let you know that you're a mama." The court had declared Lynda Elaan's parent, the first time platonic co-parents were recognized in Canadian history. Lynda fell to her knees. She sat down on the sidewalk until she could gather herself. Natasha pulled Lynda into a tight hug. They walked back into the school and shared the news. After some whooping and cheering, a pack of people—including teachers, educational assistants, physiotherapists, and the school principal—converged in a group hug, with the two mothers at the center.

———

For many people, a family helmed by a husband and wife is the gold standard because it's synonymous with the "traditional family." That's the thinking of people like James Dobson, the evangelical author and founder of the conservative Christian organization Focus on the

Family. In a 2006 column for *Time*, Dobson shared his disapproval of same-sex couples raising children, reasoning that "the traditional family, supported by more than 5,000 years of human experience, is still the foundation on which the well-being of future generations depends." Claims like this imply that older norms should be trusted more than newer ones. One chink in Dobson's logic is that the two-parent family gained prominence centuries, not millennia, ago. Before that, people raised children in extended families. In the overwhelming majority of preindustrial societies, polygamy was common, binding together adults and children in complex webs of support. If we really want to scroll back the timeline, we'd find cooperative child-rearing. Mothers—who gathered food, farmed, fished, made clothing, and did chores, among other labor—needed help raising their biological children, who are dependent for years. Parenting was often handled by people other than biological parents, known as *alloparents*. The anthropologist Sarah Hrdy writes, "Without alloparents, there never would have been a human species."

With the help of economic prosperity and government programs that encouraged a male-breadwinner/female-caregiver family, the nuclear family thrived in 1950s America. "The legendary white middle-class family of the 1950s," the historian Elaine Tyler May writes, "was not, as common wisdom tells us, the last gasp of 'traditional' family life with roots deep in the past. Rather, it was the first wholehearted effort to create a home that would fulfill virtually all its members' personal needs through an energized and expressive personal life." Despite being an anomaly, this period has become the source of so much contemporary nostalgia and the yardstick against which other families are now measured.

In reality, the *Leave It to Beaver* ideal was always inaccessible to large swaths of the American population, including enslaved Black

Americans and immigrants. Enslaved Black Americans couldn't establish nuclear families because states didn't legally recognize their marriages or parental relationships. The family units they informally built were constantly threatened because owners could separate them with impunity. Enslaved Black Americans adapted to having absent family members by creating what historian Herbert Gutman describes as "networks of mutual obligation" that enlisted support from people who weren't necessarily related by blood or marriage. Scholars use the term *fictive kin* to describe people who took on roles like these—they feel and function like family—and they remain a vital feature of many Black American families.

Immigrant households in the nineteenth and twentieth centuries rarely consisted of two parents and their children. Many immigrants couldn't keep their families in one place because the earner moved wherever was necessary for work. Split-household families—an arrangement where married workers are separated from their spouses for years—were common among Chinese Americans; laws passed in the late 1800s made it difficult for women to emigrate from China while bans on interracial marriages kept married couples, generally composed of white American men and Japanese women, from living in the United States together. Mexican Americans similarly had to cope with long separations from spouses and relied on caregiving networks among extended family.

Anti-immigrant sentiment at the end of the nineteenth century fueled some of the push for a "true American family"—that is, a nuclear family in which neither women nor children worked. The irony was that the very people who were maligned for not having a nuclear family made it possible for others to have theirs. Black Americans, immigrants, and working-class women labored outside the home and often couldn't live with their own kin. Meanwhile, same-sex couples couldn't marry or adopt children. Many queer and trans people were (and still are) pushed out of their families of origin, leading them to forge "chosen families" with people with whom they aren't related. Innovative family forms have thrived among people who've been excluded from the idealized nuclear model.

Despite claims from people like Dobson, the heterosexual nuclear family is neither the dominant family structure across history, nor does it seem to be clearly better for children. Susan Golombok, a professor of family research at the University of Cambridge, says that family forms that have recently become more common—such as single mothers by choice or families headed by same-sex couples—haven't harmed kids, as critics claimed they would. She's been studying family structure and child well-being for more than forty years, and in her longitudinal studies of children born into these types of families, she's found that kids fare well on outcomes ranging from psychological development to parent-child relationship quality. Far from being less capable than parents of conventional families, "those who have children against the odds become highly involved and committed parents," she writes. To the extent children suffer harm, it tends to come from outside their family: the stigma against them. That's a social failing, not one inherent to the family structure. "Children are most likely to flourish in warm, supportive, stable families, whatever their structure," she writes in her book *We Are Family*, "and are most likely to experience emotional and behavioral problems in hostile, unsupportive and unstable families, whatever their structures."

Four years before Lynda heard the words *You're a mama*, she thought, *I'm in deep*. She had already sold her three-bedroom house and, in

2012, moved into Natasha's building to cut down on her commute to visit Elaan. She bought the condo directly above Natasha's, and she and Natasha called themselves "vertical neighbors." Lynda established a routine. At 7:00 a.m. every day, she walked downstairs to see Natasha and Elaan and usually ended her day over dinner with them. She helped Natasha draft emails to Elaan's doctors and make medical decisions about their son.

Lynda could no more imagine life without Natasha and Elaan than without other defining parts of her life, like music or spirituality. But she became concerned about a factor outside of her control: What would happen if Natasha ended up in a romantic relationship and wanted to move? Lynda tried to make sure that she and her friend were on the same page. She told Natasha that if either one of them had a partner and considered relocating, she wanted to keep the family together. Natasha agreed.

Ultimately, Natasha was responsible for shaking up the family dynamic, but not in the way Lynda had predicted. Natasha connected Lynda to a friend of a friend, Justine, who was moving to Ottawa from France and needed a place to live. Natasha knew that Lynda sometimes felt lonely when she'd leave Natasha and Elaan each night, so she encouraged Lynda to consider having Justine as a roommate. Lynda decided to let Justine move in, the first time in twelve years that she wouldn't be living alone.

Natasha and Lynda tried to be welcoming to Justine while giving her space. But they found that Justine enjoyed spending time with them and with Elaan. She read books to him in French, translating the text along the way. She made an effort to understand how to care for him. Early on, Justine asked to learn how to feed Elaan and how to vent his gastric tube. She showed more than polite interest.

Lynda told Natasha about evenings in which she and Justine

watched TV and she rested her leg on Justine's legs as they sat next to each other. Natasha thought that was a bit more than standard room-mate friendliness. About a week later, Lynda shared that she and Justine had begun a romantic relationship. Natasha was delighted to see Lynda so happy. Still, she worried what would happen if it didn't work out. Lynda and Justine already lived together, and Justine and Elaan had bonded.

Lynda had her own concerns. When she was young, her mom dated a man, and on the weekends, they lived as a family. But three years in, the relationship ended, and so did his presence in Lynda's life. That ex-perience dangled in the back of her mind, even though she had ample evidence to suggest that Justine wouldn't abandon Elaan if the romantic relationship changed. Justine had a connection with Elaan that was independent of her romantic relationship with Lynda or friendship with Natasha.

Over the last several years, Lynda has watched Justine go through the same process that she did: realizing that she's central to Elaan's life but experiencing lag time before other people recognize it. Nurses and doctors ask questions about who Justine is. During a recent hos-pital stay, Natasha said she and Lynda were the moms and Justine the stepmom—not quite an accurate description, and it ran the risk of suggesting an acrimonious relationship between Justine and the others. But Natasha just wanted to get to the health care issues at hand with-out having to map out their unusual family tree.

Though people have generally been understanding, their three-parent family has run into administrative barriers. Doctors' offices typically don't allow more than two parents in the room. In 2021, the hospital called Natasha to say that because Elaan was at high risk for COVID, his parents were eligible for vaccines. When Natasha ex-plained they have a three-parent household, the hospital administrator said that the hospital could only give them two vaccines. Justine would have to wait.

Besides the challenges posed by people outside the family, Natasha notes that introducing a third adult does add a layer of complication. "I don't use the word *complication* in a necessarily negative way," she says. "But yeah, you have a third opinion suddenly about things." There are more schedules to coordinate on their family calendar, more needs to attend to. These parenting relationships haven't been systematically studied, so it's hard to know whether having several parents makes the family more or less likely to rupture than a two-parent one. You could make plausible arguments in either direction: that more parents produce more opportunities for disagreement or that more support reduces pressure on the parents and their relationship— in alignment with research I wrote about in chapter 2, that finds people are happier when they have multiple relationships to rely on.

Natasha and Lynda's accounts echo how Nick's girlfriend, Morgan, in chapter 4, described her family. They all acknowledge the added complexity of having more people in the mix but find the rewards to be far more salient. Justine has brought support and freedom to their family. If Lynda is too tired to lift Elaan, who's now a lanky teenager, Justine steps in. Having three adults means not only three bodies and three incomes but three skill sets and temperaments, three approaches to vexing challenges. For instance, Natasha and Lynda had long struggled to get Elaan to brush his teeth. Because he receives food through a gastric tube, he's not used to having objects in his mouth and gets upset by a trespassing toothbrush. But soon after meeting Elaan, Justine delivered the right joke that made Elaan willing to have his teeth brushed.

In 2022, Elaan had to undergo an eight-hour hip surgery in Toronto and stay in a rehabilitation hospital for two and a half months. Justine wanted to make Elaan's hospital room feel like his own and asked Lynda and Natasha for favorite photos of Elaan, which she would print. It was the last thing Natasha wanted to be thinking about when she had so many logistics to manage in advance of the surgery. Her living room had become clogged with open suitcases, which she packed with Elaan's specialized formulas, clothing, and supplies that he might need. Justine insisted that the photos were important.

"And of course it ended up being hugely important," Natasha says. Justine hung fifty large photos on the wall behind Elaan's hospital bed, creating a visual timeline for the family as well as the pediatrician and occupational therapist and surgeon and other health care workers who cycled through. They could see the full life Elaan had when he wasn't in the hospital: there were photos of him horseback riding, hanging out with his cousin, swimming with his grandfather.

The three women found the constant caregiving manageable because they shared the load. They rotated nights at the hospital to distribute the sleep deprivation—those off hospital duty slept at Lynda's parents' condo. They offset the emotionally challenging aspects of supporting Elaan with joyful moments. Whenever they spotted the pair of hospital-employed clowns who made Elaan laugh with their knock-knock jokes and music, one of the women would run out the door to grab them, saying, "Elaan is here! And he would love the clowns." ("But actually," Natasha says, "it was us who were like, 'Could we have this uplift, please?'") Having three parents allowed them to take breaks from the persistent demands of parenthood, and with that extra energy, more opportunity to experience its pleasures. Several health care workers at the hospital commented that they'd never seen a child who had so many people supporting him.

Debates about family structure rarely address the possibility of families like these. Instead, they tend to compare one-parent households to two-parent households, holding up the latter as the ideal. People who are worried about the rise of single-parent families argue that one parent can't provide as much economic security or emotional support as two parents (and sometimes oppose government support that would create more economic stability for these parents). The late sociologist Sara McLanahan, a leading expert on family structure, made that argument to the BBC: "Having two adults who co-operate to raise the child, who give time and money, means there are just more resources than one doing it." But by that reasoning, three or four parents should be even better. In a case in which several adults sought custody of a child, West Virginia's Supreme Court of Appeals remarked, "Oh that all of the children whose fates we must decide would be so fortunate as to be too loved."

————————

In 2016, a few months after Natasha and Lynda filed the paperwork to legally declare Lynda a parent, a new law passed in Ontario. The All Families Are Equal Act makes it possible for up to four people to be named as parents on a child's birth certificate. The law's purpose is to give parents who conceived their children through ART equal status to other parents; this change matters especially for same-sex couples, who may want their surrogate or egg or sperm donor to be a third or fourth parent. Though it seems like this law would have made Natasha and Lynda's case simpler, they're in fact relieved it wasn't on the books at the time. To be recognized as parents under this law, unmarried people who use ART need to make a formal agreement to co-parent before conception. Under this law, Lynda, who applied for parental rights years after Elaan was born, would not have been eligible to be on the birth certificate. (On the other side of the border, multiple US states allow a child to have more than two legal parents.)

Natasha and Lynda did not plan to be co-parents before Elaan was an embryo; the idea hadn't crossed their minds. This is true of other platonic parenting arrangements I've seen; there was already a kid in the picture when the friends slipped into the mode of co-parents, often because someone's life had jolted off the expected track. In one case, two women who are best friends had more childcare to handle once each of their husbands began traveling frequently for work. The friends merged households, bought a car that they share, and raised their collective six kids together; they referred to the friend's family as their "co-family." To avoid managing parenthood alone after having split with their partners, single mothers have created "Mommunes"—whether organically or by finding each other through the house-sharing platform CoAbode. Paula Archey, whom I wrote about in the introduction, started to feel like she had a family when she took on a larger caregiving role for her friend's kids during the COVID pandemic. She was watching after them frequently enough that the parents gave Paula a pair of car seats. Paula doesn't consider herself a parent; maybe, like Lynda, it would take years of acting as a parent for Paula to see herself as one.

Friends who have the foresight to draw up parenting agreements before conception tend to do so because they had no choice but to get creative. Some are same-sex couples and need a third person's sperm or egg to conceive. Others had banked on raising kids with a romantic partner but didn't end up in that kind of relationship. Tens of thousands of people have turned to sites like Modamily and CoParents that match them with other people who want to have a child with someone else but not necessarily be in a romantic relationship with them.

It's easy to view these arrangements as a tolerable plan B for people whose lives take a turn or who don't have typical options available to them. But these families, constructed around deep friendships, appear to have advantages over the gold-standard "traditional family."

Many platonic partners say their relationship is stabler than a romantic relationship because they aren't visited by the storms that accompany romance or sex—much the way Wilcox describes his ideal of a family-first marriage model. In difficult times—say a job loss or a pandemic—their larger household allows them to keep steady. Natasha says she doesn't think she and Lynda would have survived the pandemic if Justine weren't around. Same-sex friends like Natasha and Lynda appreciate that their relationship with their co-parent isn't predetermined by gender roles; they say the division of labor is more equal than they imagine it would have been with a man. As friends, Natasha and Lynda also had the liberty to arrange their lives in a way that made sense to them rather than conform to the pressure of what a marriage is supposed to look like. Lynda says she and Natasha aren't cut out to live together, because she's messy and chaotic while Natasha is "the tidiest person I've ever met." They've separated the question of whether they're suitable roommates from whether they're capable co-parents, a possibility that romantic partners rarely consider (though maybe they could if romantic partners were freed from the "relationship escalator"—the specific course romantic partners are expected to follow, which includes becoming exclusive, living together, and marrying.)

Even though this three-parent family has proved sturdy—and another set of parents remarked that they want to steal Justine for themselves—Lynda is quick to note that the structure of her family isn't superior to others. She's not trading the moralizing push for a traditional family for a different one-size-fits-all family form. Whether families work well, she says, comes down to the chemistry of the individual people involved. But as of now, most people only test that chemistry with potential romantic partners; many will never consider whether they and a friend—or friends—are suited to be co-parents.

Perhaps they would if the idea was put in front of them. In a 2017 survey of hundreds of women, just over half responded that there should be ways of raising children without a spouse or a romantic partner. Of the unmarried mothers who were surveyed, 58 percent reported that they would consider raising children with someone other than a spouse or romantic partner. Nicole Sussner Rodgers, the executive director of Family Story, the think tank that ran the survey, told that me that our limited cultural imagination curbs the options that we, as individuals, contemplate for our lives. "You need to see somebody doing the thing that you might want to do and doing it successfully," she says.

The thing you might see, if you visited Ottawa, is Lynda, on the fly, making up a cheer and repeating it with gusto to elicit an ear-to-ear smile from Elaan. Natasha might be harmonizing with Lynda or speaking to Elaan in his third language, Urdu. You might see Justine doing one of her spot-on imitations of Lynda or Natasha, which Elaan finds hilarious, or maybe she'd be sitting with Elaan to help him write a letter to his grandfather by using his eye gaze to select words on a screen—with a letter template that she created herself. Natasha's parents, who moved into the same condo building in 2022, might be over, schmoozing just as easily with Lynda and Justine as with their daughter and grandson. (Natasha's father often says that no one can make Elaan laugh the way Lynda can.) You'd hear the women speak in glowing terms about one another. Lynda would be reflecting on how remarkably compatible she and Natasha are as co-parents and how she thinks it must be destined that she and Natasha were brought together.

THE LONG HAUL

Aging and adaptation

The great thing, if one can, is to stop regarding all the unpleasant things as interruptions of one's "own," or "real" life. The truth is of course that what one calls the interruptions are precisely one's real life.

—C. S. LEWIS

When she was thirty-one, Inez Conrad took a trip to Washington, D.C., that gave her the first glimpse of a new life. Her marriage, the backbone of her current life, had felt fractured for a while. Though Inez had a way of seeing the best in people, even she knew that her husband had little to offer her. He had withdrawn from their suburban family life. His preference, it seemed, would have been to have a spate of women and no children around. When he wasn't absent, he was cold to their two sons, so much so that Inez found herself trying to explain to them why their father didn't act like the other fathers they knew—even by the standards then, in the 1960s, he was completely disengaged. She chalked up their dad's behavior to a "hard beginning," but her younger son, Scott, didn't buy it. Everyone has a hard beginning, Scott said. When Inez proposed a family vacation to D.C., her husband responded in character: *Take the kids yourself.*

As a step toward independence, she'd started an administrative job with Family and Children's Service of Greater St. Louis and one bright spot in her life was a new friend she'd made there. Like Inez, Barb Buettner was in a state of transition, having temporarily moved back to the St. Louis area to stabilize her parents' dire finances. At twenty-nine, she was living in the house where she'd grown up, sleeping in the same bedroom she'd had as a child to save money and maximize how much of her paycheck she could siphon to her parents. Her hopes of having children of her own had been dashed two years earlier when, after an emergency surgery, she was told she wouldn't be able to have biological children. Because she was an adopted only child, she'd never met anyone who looked like her and dreamed of bearing her own kids. But once that was off the table, her interest in marriage waned.

In each other, Barb and Inez found a mirror. They shared a sunny stoicism—they didn't dwell on hardships and instead drew attention to all the ways they'd been blessed. (Even when Inez is talking about a hard moment in her life, she will shoehorn in a story of a person who's "marvelous" or whom she "just loved.") They liked to laugh with others, never at them. They were quick to lend a hand to anyone in need as if it were as obvious and undemanding as holding a door open for someone. "I grew up thinking that . . . if somebody has a need, you fill that need," Inez says. "There's never a question, 'Should I do this?'"

One day at work, Inez mentioned the upcoming vacation with her kids to Barb, who'd never been to D.C., and Barb essentially invited herself for the two-week road trip. Without hesitation, Inez welcomed Barb's suggestion to join, and off to the nation's capital they went, Inez at the wheel of her husband's Oldsmobile with the boys in the back. While they were camping in Shenandoah National Park, they woke up to find a skunk on the table next to their tent, taking a single bite out of each doughnut they had bought the day before. Mostly, they stayed in hotels, sharing one room. The boys slept in a double bed, and Inez and Barb each took a twin.

They discovered they were compatible travelers. The boys were relaxed around Barb and didn't complain when she set boundaries. If she was intrigued by an exhibit display, they would drift over and ask what she found interesting. When they toured sites, Rick, three years older than his brother, walked alongside Barb and Inez while Scott jumped ahead to scope out the setting. Then, he'd return to let them know what lay ahead. Rick was shy—"a gentle soul," Inez would say. Not like her gregarious Scotty, who might chat up a stranger at a museum.

In Washington, they couldn't find the White House: Inez steered the Oldsmobile in circles around downtown as they looked for it, but they kept arriving at the river instead. Each time, Scott announced they were at the Potomac, which he pronounced "Pot-oh-mack." Inez and Barb would correct him, swing around again, and repeat the bit. At one point, Barb said, "If I go to that river one more time, I'm going to commit hara-kiri with my sandwich." Then, suddenly, it dawned on them that they had seen the White House several times, from behind, and at last, they figured out how to get to the front.

The comfort they felt around one another, the shared jokes and memories, and the respect the boys had for Barb—it all contributed to what Barb would remember as a "family atmosphere." Inez felt like they were two sisters with their kids. There was an ease she'd never really experienced with her husband. While neither of them could have anticipated, back then, the depth and longevity of their continued friendship, that trip to Washington laid the foundation for a life together.

When I first interviewed Barb and Inez, in 2019, at the home they now share, they requested that we wrap up our conversation before the start of *Jeopardy!*, which they watch together every day. Since 1998, they've lived in Kirkwood, Missouri, a suburb of St. Louis, in a one-story brick house they call "the Hermitage," to mean a place of refuge. The décor of the dining room, where we sat and talked, matched the wholesome and unassuming air of the women themselves. Prints of flowers and animals hung above the dark wood table, a rocking chair with a tapestry pillow sat in the corner, and long windows in their living room looked onto rustic woods. They told me about their lives: volunteering together at the local library, cooking and cleaning together, going to doctors' appointments together. Once, Barb went alone to the grocery store and ran into a friend there, and the friend's wife later called Inez to check in on her—since the two women seemed to do everything together, she'd wondered whether Inez wasn't feeling well.

When it comes to recounting their lives, the two friends tend toward understatement: both narrate their challenges matter-of-factly and quickly move on to what action they took. They'd rather talk about the novels they're reading or remark on some generous gesture someone did for them than dramatize their own past difficulties. But the twists and turns they've steered through with each other reflect the reality that whatever we might envision for ourselves at age twenty-five or fifty-five, life can take us by surprise. Relying on a close friend is one way to adapt.

More than fifty years ago, Inez and Barb met each other after veering away from marriage, and their friendship has in turn helped them avoid some of that standard path's pitfalls. Although one selling point of the long-term, romantic relationship is its promise of caregiving and companionship in old age—*How to Not Die Alone* is the title of one recent dating advice book—there are, of course, no guarantees. In fact, a growing proportion of Americans won't have children or a spouse to take care of them; marriage and birth rates have declined with each new generation, and divorce rates among older Americans have risen.

Older women are particularly affected. Above age sixty-five, women are far less likely than men to be married: 47 percent of women are married versus 69 percent of men in the same age group. (Many of the unmarried women at this point in life are widows—in 2017, there were more than three times the number of widows as widowers.) Women who survive their spouses often live alone and need social and practical support. Many older women also struggle financially, the premise of the Netflix show *Grace and Frankie*, about an unlikely pair of women who become friends and share a home together, as well as the iconic sitcom *The Golden Girls*: four women (three widowed, one divorced) share a house in Miami to save money and eventually become family to one another. Though *The Golden Girls* debuted decades ago, the financial gap between older men and women hasn't changed much. The median income for older women remains far lower than that of older men, the poverty rate higher. Break the numbers down by race, and the differences are starker. Reflecting a lifetime of pay gaps and other forms of discrimination, poverty rates for older Black women are two and a half times that of older white men.

Financial constraints are one reason Inez and Barb live together; they couldn't afford to maintain two homes. But they are much more to each other than roommates who share silverware and rotate chores. Their decades of history as friends make their relationship a true partnership, in which they each have an interlocutor, confidante, companion, and caregiver.

Life's later years are a time when the rewards of platonic partnership can be most potent and effortless. "It seems like when we're younger, we're searching," Inez says. "We're searching for ourselves and what our inner core is and what's important to us. I think then as you get older, you've established those things." Once you know yourself and what you need to be content, Inez thinks, it may be easier to share a home. And, Barb says, people are less judgmental as they age because "we've all seen enough, done enough, been privy to enough things in our lives . . . Judging everything and being rigid about a lot of things is not a good way to go, because you're not going to have a very comfortable old age if you do that." At a certain point in life, you're not only freed of others' judgment but of your own.

During my visit, Barb and Inez pulled a half dozen boxes from a shelf in the guest room and set them on the dining table. The envelopes from the photo developer lined the boxes, and within the envelopes, images that document their years of shared experiences: a photo of Barb with Rick's grandson. Photos of Inez, her sons, and Barb around the Christmas tree. While romantic relationships are often characterized by their intensity, Barb and Inez's photos are a record of another kind of partnership—quieter and less heralded but no less meaningful. In another envelope, they found a photo of a smiling Scott, who sports a tuxedo that's very 1970s, burgundy with black lapels. He's about to head off to his high school prom, while Barb stands by his side, looking every bit the proud parent.

It was in large part because Inez was a mom that Barb was drawn to her, back at Family and Children's Service of Greater St. Louis. Barb gravitated toward all the mothers at the office, noticing the warmth in their voices when they talked about their families and the interest they showed in each other's children. She had always loved kids—indeed, her job centered on them—but in her work she was helping kids manage challenges. She didn't have many opportunities to spend time with them casually. And she hit it off with Scott and Rick, then eight and eleven. In them, the traits that drew her to Inez were multiplied. She saw Inez's kindness: the boys were never rude and wouldn't dare to hurt someone's feelings. Like Inez, they each had a sense of humor, sophisticated for their age. Whereas Barb was used to bending conversation to fit what kids care about, Rick and Scott were happy to discuss the many interests they shared with Barb and Inez: museums, history, reading, travel. Each boy had a sweet side; Scott was particularly affectionate. Barb grew accustomed to getting a hug from Scott when he greeted her and when he said goodbye, a habit he didn't abandon in his teenage years as many boys do. "He never outgrew that desire to let you know how much he cared about you," Barb says.

But Barb had moved from Phoenix to St. Louis only to help her parents get their finances in order. Once she'd done that, she started chafing to get back to Phoenix, which felt like her true adult home. In 1971, a psychologist she knew there told her he had the perfect job for her, and not long after that, Barb drove down with her mom to look for a house.

After Barb left, Inez made a move of her own, at last. When she announced that she was separating from her husband of more than a decade, even her devout Christian Scientist parents asked, "What took you so long?" She and the boys moved in with them as she tried to figure out what a permanent situation would look like. Meanwhile, Barb sent letters describing Phoenix as a great place to raise kids, highlighting features she thought would be of special interest to Inez's sons, such as the city's zoo, library, and art museum, along with well-regarded Catholic schools. On a long-distance phone call, Barb said if Inez and the kids moved to Phoenix, she would do whatever she could to help. She had a three-bedroom house, with plenty of space for Inez and the boys to stay while they looked for a place of their own.

Rick and Scott were game, and so once their school year ended, they loaded up their belongings and headed west. The boys rode in the back, while the family dachshund, Gus, sat shotgun. As they drove toward Phoenix, the boys were enchanted by their first encounter with the American West. One morning, eating breakfast as they looked out over the hills of Santa Fe, Scott asked whether they could return to New Mexico if they didn't like Arizona.

In Phoenix, they moved into Barb's house, a concrete box with a light green façade and surrounded by eight grapefruit trees. For months, Barb's house was Inez's home base as she assembled her family's new life. When the job lead she'd been counting on fell through, she took a temp position at the sheriff's department. A few months later, she waited in the lobby of an American Red Cross office, which, with its shabby folding chairs and antiquated switchboard, looked run-down. But the office décor proved less important to her than the staff. "I fell in love with everybody I met," Inez recalls.

Inez tends to frame an unexpected event as "an adventure," whether it's moving to a new city or working at the sheriff's office while the department was the subject of a national controversy. And her sons adjusted quickly to Phoenix, making friends and finding work-study jobs at school that helped pay for their tuition. Adapting with grace to new circumstances, Inez thought, was their inheritance. From early on, she says, she'd considered her family of origin to be one that "lands on their feet. You kind of grow where you're planted." When Inez was a kid, her parents taught her that when there's an obstacle, you can either bang your head against it or walk around it and make new life. Her takeaway: "The better thing is to walk around it and make a new life."

As they had on the D.C. trip, the four of them comfortably shared space. At night, they gathered for dinner, and the boys told Barb and

Inez about their new schools, sports teams, and friends. After staying with Barb for about six months, Inez and her kids moved into a house around the corner. It was a yellow house with a big backyard, and she christened it "the Mustard Seed."

Even in separate homes, they continued to treat one another like family. While Barb recovered from a surgery, Inez brought her meals for several weeks. Barb would host the boys and shuttle them around the city when Inez had work trips. One spring, Barb came down with the stomach flu and was out of commission for weeks. Scott walked into her room, and Barb told him to call his mom because she was going to be sick. Instead, thirteen-year-old Scott found a dishpan in the bathroom and ran back to hold it by Barb's bedside as she vomited. Then he wiped off Barb's face with a washcloth. "People have to really love you when they do that, especially a young boy," Barb told me.

Their bonds grew stronger. The four of them dined together, celebrated holidays, and established traditions. Rick referred to Barb as his "angel mom," and Barb was named Scott's godmother when he was an adolescent. Inez added canned pineapple to a favorite recipe, and the experiment bombed; this recipe became a family joke. When Barb's parents visited her in Phoenix for monthlong winter sojourns, Barb's dad taught Scott about construction, and they worked together to build a porch. "We were doing so many things that maybe a family would do if there had been a father in the picture," Barb says. "Whether it was totally conscious or even unconscious, we began functioning as a unit—we would back each other up."

From the start, Inez says, Barb gave her a sense of comfort that she associates with relatives. The border between friend and family had always been porous for both of them. When Inez was growing up, one of her aunts or uncles was often living in her house, and she learned "by osmosis" that you should take care of the people around you, whether or not they were officially kin. Barb's dad converted their two-car garage into an apartment, and the long-term renters, a mother and daughter who were both widows, became part of their family. Barb says she grew up understanding that "anybody can be family given the right circumstances."

Barb and Inez's shared family history would eventually encompass a terrible loss. When Barb first told me about how Scott had held the dishpan for her after the surgery, her voice broke. Inez stepped in to explain that Scott had died. Barb grabbed a tissue. Losing "our Scotty," Inez said, "was very hard for us."

On the night he died, but before she found out what had happened, Inez dreamed of a black stallion, an animal she associated with her father. While he was growing up in Ridgway, Illinois, he would sometimes race his horse through town so fast that his mother fielded repeated complaints from the sheriff. In her dream, Inez looked up from her computer and noticed a black stallion walking toward her house, coming through the oleander bush in the backyard. He was angry, so furious he was shaking his head and foaming at the mouth. When he got to the window, he stared at Inez for a long time until his expression turned peaceful. He walked off. Halfway up the mountain, he turned back to look at Inez. Then he continued walking and disappeared.

At this point, Inez heard the back door open in her house—her real house. It was about three o'clock in the morning. She heard Barb's voice say, "It's me. It's only me. Don't be frightened." Barb came down the hall, sat on Inez's bed, and took her hand. "I have to tell you that Scotty is gone," she said.

Scott, then stationed in Pearl Harbor, had suffered a heart attack while out on a run. He was just thirty-seven years old. Scott had requested that if anything ever happened to him in the navy, the commanding officer should call Barb first. Sharing the news with Inez, Barb says, was "probably the hardest thing I've ever done."

Inez made a pot of tea, and they sat in the living room, exchanging stories about Scott's childhood. Inez figured she'd had the dream about the stallion just as Scott was dying. Through the dream, Scott had been telling her goodbye. After sunrise, Scott's commanding officer called Inez, and Barb called Inez's friends to tell them what had happened.

Though Inez was no longer in contact with her ex-husband—he'd disappeared after the divorce—she relayed the news to one of his relatives. Later, Inez got a call from her ex, who said, "Well, Inez, I don't know what to say."

"You know, that probably was the whole crux of the problem with our whole relationship. You never knew what to say," Inez replied. He was distant at all the wrong times. He told her, "Have a good day," and hung up.

Though Inez's ex-husband didn't exactly grieve alongside her, Inez didn't feel like she was coping with Scott's loss alone. Rick and his wife made a trip to Phoenix, and after, Barb, in mourning herself, would go to Inez's house in the morning, then leave for work while Inez, who was retired, was home. Barb always returned for dinner.

Inez was the one to explain most of this to me because Barb still finds it hard to talk about Scott—a place where her sunny stoicism falls away. The memories of Scott, Inez says, "are beautiful, marvelous things, but they can also just pierce your heart." Some parts of the year are harder than others. May is especially tough, Barb told me. Both of her parents died in May, and Scott's birthday is one day after her father's death.

Inez knows that Barb misses Scotty's hugs and misses singing with him while trimming the Christmas tree. The two of them still associate a specific Christmas ornament with him: a little mouse wearing a striped sweater and holding a football, which he'd picked out at a souvenir shop on the D.C. trip. Every Christmas, the last thing that Inez and Barb hang on their tree is Scotty's mouse.

————————

As Barb approached retirement, she was haunted by the question of how she would live in her later years. She had moved her parents into a nursing home in Phoenix so that she could help care for them in the final stretch of their lives. But in that sprawling city of seemingly endless thoroughfares, she spent hours languishing in traffic just to get them to their doctors' appointments, and she became convinced that Phoenix was not a good place to grow old—"I don't care what the chamber of commerce says," she tells me. Her life had been an endless loop: from home to work to the nursing home, maybe with a pit stop for fast food since she didn't have time for a proper meal. Her dad had been lonely: Parkinson's had worn down his body, but his mind was still sharp. His wife had Alzheimer's, and he had few peers at the nursing home who could offer stimulating company. At least he had a daughter to care for him. Barb wondered, *What's going to happen to me?*

The question Barb asked herself is increasingly pressing for many Americans, who now live longer and frequently suffer from chronic illnesses that require years of caregiving. The US Census projects that by 2060, life expectancy will increase by about six years, from 79.7 in 2017 to 85.6. But because of that rising life expectancy, cancer and dementia cases are predicted to increase substantially.

Unlike Barb's parents, who were married and had a child who devoted years to caring for them, older people today are less likely to have family members to turn to. In the United States and other Western countries, more and more people reach retirement age unmarried. Though only about 6 percent of Americans sixty-five and older have never married, that number has been growing in younger cohorts. Marriage isn't even a guarantee of companionship at the end of life. Many of those who have been married will reach old age without their spouse, whether because they outlived their spouse—as is the case for about a quarter of adults sixty-five and over—or the marriage dissolved. Divorce between spouses aged fifty and older has been on the rise; between 1990 and 2015, the divorce rate for this group nearly doubled. The Population Reference Bureau projects that the number of seventy-five-year-olds without a living spouse will more than double from 875,000 in 2010 to 1.8 million in 2030.

But it's more than an absence of spouses that complicates caregiving and companionship later in life. People are having fewer children, if they have children at all. This, in combination with marriage trends, has increased the number of older adults with no close family ties—a group of people whom sociologists call "elder orphans," "solo agers," or "kinless." Researchers estimate that one in five older adults is an "elder orphan" or at risk of becoming one, a figure that is likely to grow in coming years. Like marriage, having children isn't a surefire insurance policy for caregiving. Adult children might not live close to their parents, or their kids might not have the capacity to help. Daughters, historically the country's default caregivers of aging parents, can't be taken for granted as a source of uncompensated caregiving these days. Far more women are in the paid labor force and would jeopardize their economic security or their family's if they quit their jobs to take care of their parents. (Nevertheless, on average, daughters spend far more time caring for their aging parents than sons do.) Because Americans are having kids later in life, it's common for children with aging parents to be raising children of their own at the same time; these are members of the so-called sandwich generation. Unable to manage both forms of care, these adults may focus on their kids and outsource care for their parents.

Because Barb doesn't have children, a spouse, or siblings, she fits squarely into the sociologists' kinless category. In Phoenix, she was close to Inez and some other friends, but she was wary of burdening them. She also didn't think she and Inez could be each other's primary caregivers because they were close in age; they would likely have health issues around the same time. Barb had younger cousins and other relatives in the St. Louis area, and she figured she'd be better off leaning on them collectively. Inez, though she had a living son, was not in so different of a position; Rick lived far away.

One night at Inez's house, after eating a dinner that Inez had cooked for the two of them—a weekly habit of theirs—they settled onto the couch to watch TV. During the commercial break, Barb broke the news: "I'm absolutely pretty sure that I'm going back to Kirkwood," she said. Inez, who had expected to live in Phoenix for the rest of her life, was astounded.

"Well then," Inez said, "I don't know if I want to stay here by myself." Besides, Rick lived in Chicago; if she followed Barb to Missouri, she'd be closer to her son.

Initially, they thought to replicate the arrangement they had in Phoenix: each would buy a house in the same neighborhood. Home prices in Kirkwood, Missouri, were too high, though, so Barb and Inez had to come up with a plan B. In the past, they'd visited two different sets of friends who lived in houses that seemed designed for harmonious co-living, with bedroom suites on either side of a common area. Unable to find such a house in Kirkwood, Barb and Inez moved on to plan C: they'd buy a two-story house that had separate units. Again, they were thwarted by high prices. That left the option of being conventional roommates—buying a house together that they'd share.

"We thought, well, we never killed each other on a trip," Barb says. "Maybe this could work out."

Barb searched for a place while Inez stayed back in Phoenix to manage the sales of her house and Barb's. Inez, without giving Barb a heads-up, fired Barb's real estate agent—a real estate agent "from hell," Inez tells me before chuckling. One day, Barb called Inez to describe what she'd found: a ranch-style house that met Inez's simple criteria: a lot of windows and a fireplace. But the house's interior suffered from decorative malpractice. With disapproval in her voice, Barb describes the house to me: "It had metallic wallpaper all over the living room. It was so 1950s, you can't believe!" Inez reminds her of the metal window frames—another design offense to tally. Its interior untouched for decades, the house wasn't selling. The owners had lowered the price repeatedly. It was a good deal. Inez told Barb to make an offer—even though she hadn't seen the place. "Talk about trust!" Barb says as if still incredulous a quarter century later. Their bid was accepted.

Sharing a house would allow them to live in the setting they preferred, which is hardly a given for older adults. A 2021 AARP survey found that the vast majority of older Americans want to stay in their home and community, though a considerably smaller proportion believes they'll actually be able to do so. A nearby caregiver, such as a child or partner, could attend to an older person's everyday needs; without such a person, it may be too difficult or unsafe for an older person to stay in their home—especially those who live alone and now comprise 27 percent of Americans age sixty-five and older. Barb and Inez's demographic characteristics—both unmarried, one without children—would suggest they'd have trouble living at home as they age. In their case, demographics has not been destiny.

Older Americans have become increasingly open to the idea of sharing a home. According to an earlier AARP survey, the number of adults age fifty and older who share their homes grew from 2 percent in 2014 to 16 percent in 2018. Among the people I've interviewed, affordability—along with a desire for companionship—drove older friends to live together. Pooling resources saves money; this is the idea behind a home-matching website for older adults, Silvernest, which launched in 2015. Wendi Burkhardt, one of the company's cofounders, told *USA Today*, "Many baby boomers want to stay in their homes, but the harsh truth is many of them can't afford it." Though financial concerns have motivated the vast majority of people who have placed an ad on Silvernest, its users stress the social benefits of sharing a home. About a year into living with a roommate she found through Silvernest, Becky Miller enthused both about the cost-saving and company she now enjoys: "It's companionship. I know I don't have to eat supper alone." A few years later, another company, Nesterly, teamed up with the City of Boston to run an intergenerational roommate matching service, connecting older adults who have extra space in their homes with younger people who need affordable rent. As with Silvernest and similar nonprofit home-sharing organizations, Nesterly sought to lessen both financial difficulties and social isolation. The program in Boston was popular, and Nesterly expanded to several other regions.

Long before Inez and Barb decided to live together, the women in their mystery book club got into a conversation about wanting to mimic the living situation depicted in one of the books they read. The story followed five women who bought a big house together after their husbands died. A lot of people share this dream to live with friends as they age. In 2011, a group of eight friends had an architect design a compound of tiny homes for them to retire in together, balancing their desire for both privacy and shared space. They called this community on the Llano River in Texas the "Llano exit strategy"; the press dubbed it "Bestie Row." After the compound's viral coverage, the architect received more than five hundred calls and emails from people asking to create something similar for their group of friends. Stories like these from around the world seem fated to go viral because they tap into an idea friends may fantasize about but not realize is possible to pursue. In a video viewed nearly four million times, a group of Chinese friends show off the mansion they renovated to live in once they retire. The camera pans across the lush landscape that's visible through the floor-to-ceiling glass windows, and it lingers on the house's minimalist tearoom. Not long before that, the internet took to the story of three Australian couples in their sixties who had a house built for them and called themselves "the Shedders." One of the Shedders wrote in *The Guardian*, "We've made a long-term commitment to each other . . . Even though we are not biologically related, we have each other's backs in the way a functional family does." They gather most evenings over a shared meal, clean the house together most Friday mornings, sit down together every New Year's Eve to reflect on the year, and take a weeklong vacation each January to an arts camp for adults.

Deborah Carr, a sociology professor at Boston University, says that living arrangements like Inez and Barb's could be the "wave of the future" for two reasons: many older adults will need a form of support other than a nuclear family, and there is a persistent paid-caregiver shortage in the United States. (Low pay and difficult working conditions for nursing assistants and home health aides contribute to the high turnover in those fields.) She also points out that caregiving between friends has the appeal of being egalitarian, unlike a parent-child relationship, where the older person may feel like a burden.

Barb and Inez alluded to a fear of imposing on others when they talked about who would take care of them as they aged. Barb listed off people she and Inez considered getting support from. Inez's son Rick was an obvious caregiver, but he lived in a different state, and they didn't want to expect Rick to do everything. Their cousins lived far away and were preoccupied with caring for their own families. Besides, Barb says, stumbling as she tries to couch what she's about to say, "I don't want to sound like I'm bragging or anything," but she and Inez have "always tended to be more on the caregiver side in our relationships with people," and she wouldn't describe these relatives in those terms. As Barb knocked one option after the other off this list, she said, "There you go again, back to poor Rick." The implication was that Barb and Inez would weigh down family, but they wouldn't feel like burdens if they took care of each other.

It was 1998 when Barb and Inez moved back to Kirkwood, and they knew their arrangement would be unusual. Some people might assume they were gay. Before they left Phoenix, Barb and Inez talked about what they would do if people made snide remarks or excluded them from events. Rick asked about it, too: Did they worry about how they'd be perceived? People were going to think what they were going to think, he went on to say. All that mattered was that if something happened in the middle of the night, they wouldn't be alone.

Moving day brought double the usual madness, as the movers had to pick up belongings from their two houses in Phoenix—two toasters, two blenders, two everything. They sorted out the mundane logistics, obtaining a debit card for shared household expenses, and dividing up the bills. Inez warned her cat against eating "blue food" (i.e., Barb's blue parakeet, Tweety Sylvester). Inez gardened and kept the bird feeder topped up. Barb mowed the lawn and used matchsticks to say the Rosary. It wasn't hard to determine who would take on the cooking. When Inez read aloud recipes she was excited to try, Barb would respond, "What I'm hearing is 'blah, blah, blah.'" But Barb enjoyed her routine of cleaning the dishes at night while observing the birds out the window.

Sharing a home called for some adjustments. Barb woke up considerably later than Inez, so Inez couldn't water the plants in the morning because the squeak of the hose would rouse Barb. They'd notice that the other forgot to turn out the light or close the garage door, and they'd gently point it out. This was the extent of their friction; Inez says they're "peaceful souls" who are adaptable.

Though they had originally wanted to live in different homes, they recalibrated to having almost no private space, even virtually. The house had a single computer; Barb had never owned one. After they moved in, the kid next door set up internet access and created an email address that refers to the Hermitage, under Inez's name, that they went on to use jointly. Even though Barb sometimes has to correct people when they reply to her emails with "Hi Inez" (a mistake I made early in our correspondence), it didn't seem worth the trouble for Barb to create her own account.

A few years after their move, Inez had to go to the hospital for emergency surgery for a broken wrist, and after she came home, in the middle of the night, she called out for Barb in pain. Even though Inez left her door open when she slept and their bedrooms shared a wall, Barb didn't hear her. The next day, they agreed that Inez would put a bell by her bed—the same bell her mom used to summon the family to dinner. Though Barb had once thought they were too close in age to be each other's caregivers and needed someone younger to be in that position, sharing a house "changed it mentally in both our minds," Barb says. "Our determination then was that we would take care of each other as long as we could." Living together had opened up new possibilities for interdependency.

As it turned out, they never encountered prejudice or prying questions because of their living situation. Barb guesses that this is because older adults aren't expected to center romantic relationships in the way that younger people are. Had she and Inez wanted to move in together in their thirties or forties, Barb says, "I think there might've been a whole lot more negativity from friends or questions about 'why are you doing this?'" She thinks people might have asked them, "Don't you want to get married?" Stacey, from chapter 3, has faced exactly that question, at a time in life when others assume sex and romantic partnership are paramount. But by retirement age, societal expectations swing in the other direction. Older people are stereotyped as asexual.

Both stereotypes harm people: Stacey feels pressured by a culture that makes sexual attraction compulsory for younger people, while older people who care about sex are jeered at or given labels like "MILF" or "cougar"—exceptions that reinforce the implied rule that most older people aren't sexually desirable. But this latter stereotype comes with a silver lining for friends like Inez and Barb. People may not jump to the conclusion that older friends are in a sexual relationship or scrutinize them for deprioritizing romance. Barb says most people she knows around her age are looking for companionship or emotional intimacy, and a physical relationship is less important.

When I ask Barb whether she might compare her friendship with Inez to a spousal relationship, she's flummoxed. The thought had never occurred to her. She rattles off the differences: They keep their money separate (other than the joint debit card). Though they were welcoming of each other's families, they felt they could choose how much time they spent with the other's parents. They don't take each other for granted. "This has always been, I'm sharing a house with my best friend," Barb says. She wonders whether she never entertained the comparison because she's never had a spouse.

Inez sees that the friendship has similarities not so much to her former marriage but to a relationship with a man she met later in life—"We weren't in the lusty teens," she says. (He died unexpectedly, so their relationship was brief.) "What I felt with him was the same that I felt with Barb. I always felt that we had an honesty in our relationship. And a kindness." Theirs was a "peaceful relationship," like her friendship with Barb.

That peacefulness arises from their willingness to accommodate each other. Barb and Inez deliberately go to the same primary care doctor, someone who can make sure that the friends are aware of each other's needs. At one point, Inez was having trouble walking because she was often dizzy. Their doctor asked Barb how she and Inez walked when they were out and about: Were they side by side, or was one ahead of the other? Barb responded that she tended to walk faster. The doctor told Barb she should walk at the same pace as Inez, to help keep her safe.

They're neither annoyed nor bored by the familiarity they have for each other. When I sat at their dining room table with them, the sound of wind chimes pealing outside, Barb started laughing at a story Inez told even before she got to the punch line. "Obviously, we know each other's stories," Barb said. She looked at Inez: "I know where you're going."

———————

Inez and Barb have seen what can happen when someone doesn't have a clear candidate as their caregiver. A friend invited them to an English tea at the local library and, Inez says, "a new part of our life started." They made friends and started volunteering at the library. They ran the gift shop, buying items to sell there and creating displays.

One day, Barb and Inez stopped by the shop to make sure everything was set up because they were about to leave for a three-week trip to England. Another volunteer, Ann, who was working a shift, asked them to bring back postcards for her and mentioned she had a sore throat. A doctor in the neighborhood told her not to worry; it was just a swollen gland. Barb recognized the doctor's name because he'd treated her cousins when they were all children. Now he was retired and in his nineties. Barb thought this doctor is "probably way too old to be telling you anything." Barb encouraged Ann to consult another doctor—that is, a practicing doctor, in a medical office.

A few weeks later, Ann told Barb and Inez that she'd gone to a throat specialist, who had ordered a biopsy. Ann was too afraid to hear the results on her own. Her closest friend was a teacher, and she didn't want to ask her to miss work for the appointment. Barb and Inez said they would go with her.

When Barb and Inez arrived at Ann's house on the day of the appointment, she didn't answer the door. Eventually, Barb tried the knob and discovered it was unlocked. Ann was on the carpeted floor of her living room, curled in a fetal position and crying. Ann said she knew the doctor was going to tell her she had cancer. Barb and Inez were able to coax Ann into sitting up. Ann said she had no family whatsoever. No siblings or kids. She was divorced. Her parents weren't alive, and they were both only children, so she didn't have extended family. Barb and Inez hadn't known any of this; before that day, they had only had a couple of lunch dates together. They promised Ann they wouldn't let her go through treatment alone.

They sat in the waiting room during Ann's appointment. The nurse came to get Barb and Inez because Ann wanted to see them. Ann shared what the doctor had told her: she had cancer. Barb and Inez again assured her that they wouldn't let her go through this by herself.

Not long afterward, they made the commitment official; Ann had her lawyer put down Barb and Inez on her medical power of attorney documents. Ann's teacher friend and another woman had legal power of attorney rights, and the four women became Ann's family. For the next three years, they fielded phone calls from Ann's doctors, took her to her surgeries, and saw her through radiation treatment. They made sure she had the best quality of life possible.

Ann entered hospice, where she stayed in a room she loved: it looked out onto landscaped grounds and was a couple of doors down from a common space that housed brightly colored finches in a large aviary cage. When an administrator announced that Ann would have to move to a smaller room, she protested, telling Inez and Barb in her elegant handwriting on a yellow pad—the form of communication she used at this point in her illness—that her insurance covered the current room. Inez pushed, and the administrator checked on the insurance policy. She came back and said Ann could stay in the room as long as she wanted to. It was in this room that a half dozen friends gathered in April 2004 to reminisce with Ann. Around 9:00 p.m., Barb and Inez headed home, and two hours later, they got a call: Ann had quietly slipped away. Her fear that she would end life alone hadn't come to pass.

———

Friendship plays a significant role in the mental and physical well-being of older adults, and several studies suggest that friendship plays a *more* significant role than marriage. A study from 1987 found that different types of relationships affect health differently depending on people's ages. People under sixty were at greater risk of dying earlier if they weren't married. But that wasn't the case for people over sixty; close relationships with friends and relatives had more sway than marriage. A study published thirty years later, based on a survey of hundreds of thousands of people, similarly found that friendships become more predictive of mortality as people age and marriage relatively less so. People who valued friendship were healthier and happier across their lives, and those effects were particularly strong for older adults. By reducing loneliness, friendships ward off the host of negative physical and mental health effects that cascade from loneliness.

Friendships also buoy older people as they manage difficult life transitions like divorce, death of a spouse, or disease. By caring for Ann, Inez and Barb softened the edges of their friend's illness and her upsetting confrontation with mortality. Barb and Inez's willingness to care for each other and their friends initially struck me as exceptionally generous, but I discovered it is not that exceptional.

Friends make up a considerable portion of caregivers. A 2020 AARP survey found that 10 percent of caregivers for adults were providing care to a friend or neighbor. Caregiving between friends is especially common in LGBT circles. According to a study from 2010, LGBT baby boomers were more likely than the general population sample of baby boomers to have cared for a friend in the last six months, were twice as likely to have involved friends in discussions about their end-of-life preferences, were more likely to live with friends, and were four times as likely to have a friend as a caregiver. The social scientists Anna Muraco and Karen Fredriksen-Goldsen interviewed lesbian, gay, and bisexual caregivers, who reported that they often viewed providing care as a natural extension of their friendship, not as an extraordinary act. There are several explanations for the disproportionate caregiving among queer friends: queer friends have long become chosen family—often because they've been rejected by their families of origin. This sense of kinship was particularly evident during the AIDS epidemic. LGBTQ older adults also may not have the types of relatives who commonly step up as caregivers: compared to other adults, they're less likely to have kids or be partnered. Getting help from paid caregivers may not feel viable, either. Many worry they'll be refused care or mistreated in an institutional setting because of their identity.

Even older adults who have close relatives rely on friends for caregiving. One study found that one-third of chronically ill people being cared for by a friend had children who did not provide help. Those with kin can find themselves without care while people like Barb, who are technically "kinless," swim in support.

————

Though Inez always looks forward to mystery book club at the library, she enjoys the dinner after even more, at a beloved pub where their drinks are waiting for them when they walk in—a glass of wine for Inez, iced tea for Barb. One morning before book club, Inez wasn't feeling well, but she mustered some energy, and she and Barb drove to the library. As Barb stopped by the reference desk to talk to a friend, Inez walked to the elevator, and a friend of Inez's came up to her. "Oh, Cookie, I've got a book for you" was the last thing Inez said before her vision went black. She collapsed, hitting her head on the fire extinguisher attached to the elevator wall.

During her hospital stay, Inez was diagnosed with critical heart failure. The doctor told her, "You were just steps from death." Inez and Barb left the hospital with a prescription for heart medication and newfound motivation to grapple with end-of-life questions. Though they had plenty of experience making medical decisions for Ann and their parents, it took this brush with death to deal with the power of attorney paperwork by which each appointed the other to make decisions on their behalf.

Barb and Inez feel sure that Rick would step in if either friend dies before the other. But neither of them wanted to place caregiving entirely at his feet, consigning him to spend the prime of his life taking care of them.

Barb and Inez looked into assisted-living options. At a Q&A session for one facility, they were pleasantly surprised to hear someone else ask about whether it would be okay for two unrelated people to share a unit; apparently, they weren't the only ones with this sort of friendship. (The facility was fine with it.) Barb and Inez considered adding their names to the wait list, but once the COVID pandemic shut residents into their rooms, Barb and Inez were even more grateful than usual to be sharing a house with each other, to have someone to play Scrabble with or discuss their worries about everything that was happening in the world.

Over the years, friends of Inez and Barb's, especially single women, have said that they would have liked to have a similar arrangement; one friend expressed regret that she didn't have a friend she trusted enough to live with. After COVID began, these notes of envy became a chorus. Widowed and divorced friends confined to compact assisted-living apartments told Barb and Inez that they longed for companionship. Married friends stuck at home with their spouse longed for a different kind of company. Inez realized, "Just because you have someone with you doesn't mean that your life is going to go well."

COVID has been a black light, revealing the latent dissatisfaction of other people in Barb and Inez's lives. Their friends who had middling marriages found those relationships were tolerable as long as the spouses could keep some distance. In lockdown, too much familiarity bred discontent. The undercurrents of loneliness among

Barb and Inez's friends who lived in assisted-living homes rose to the surface once COVID restrictions kept them from seeing other residents. In the first several months of the pandemic, researchers found that nearly half of the older adults surveyed felt more isolated than they had before the pandemic, and about a third reported feeling less companionship than before.

Over time, Barb and Inez's preferences have evolved together. In the last few years, they've both been content to adjust to a quieter life with fewer cultural activities and social engagements. They've come to appreciate how aligned their outlook on caregiving is. After Inez was given her heart diagnosis, she says she and Barb "realized how important it is to share a home with someone who will take care of you and doesn't find that a burden." They can talk openly about how they're feeling. They each know that the other will gladly deliver a heating pad and hot tea to her bedside.

While living with friends can help older adults economize and find companionship, it doesn't resolve the deeper structural problems they face toward the end of their lives: the exorbitant costs of long-term care, the fact that many older adults live in poverty. And as much as Inez and Barb have constructed their lives outside the bounds of marriage, they confront some of the same risks as married people do. Like spouses, Inez and Barb would be left on their own were the relationship to end—though they have a robust social circle. They recognize that as content as they are with their shared life, they're likely to end up in a situation in which at least one of them needs care that the other can't provide.

Barb and Inez are growing increasingly dependent on each other. The once-fixed household division of labor has become more flexible. Inez had always taken out the trash. Now Barb will check whether she's okay doing it herself or wants help. Barb, whose instinctive reaction to recipes is "blah blah blah," now cooks alongside Inez; her chopping job, Inez raves, is better than what a Cuisinart can do. Barb reminds Inez to turn off the hose if she forgets, and Inez reminds Barb to take her medication. Barb has told Inez, "Help me with this, but don't help me too much, because what if the day comes, you're not here, and I need to be responsible for myself, too." Until that day comes, they plan to continue enjoying a life, together, in their hermitage.

GIVE THEM GRIEF

Platonic love lost

A single person is missing for you, and the whole world
is empty.

—PHILIPPE ARIÈS

When M moved to the UK in 2018 to begin a master's program, I
imagined her carrying out her routines I knew well, just in a parallel
English universe. Instead of journaling over a glass of wine at the Lao-
tian restaurant in D.C. that she frequented, she would be in a pub,
writing in an unlined Leuchtturm notebook because she couldn't find
her beloved Moleskine brand in the UK. Instead of spending her Sunday mornings singing in an Episcopal church, she would be sweeping
into a centuries-old chapel in a white cassock and surplice to sing even-
song around dusk. Because I had lived in the UK a few years earlier,
my picture of M felt familiar, yet far removed from my current life.

During the second year of her program, I wrote in my journal
about how I felt lonely even though I was sitting in the same room as
Marco and had seen two close friends that day. I longed to be pulled
into M's embrace, to have my forehead pecked with her exaggerated

kisses. I wrote, "How did I manage when I was single or Marco and I were long distance? My desire for touch feels insatiable. Maybe I didn't know what I was missing—in the same way that my sex drive was abstract until I had actually experienced sex—but now I know how good it feels." Forced to live without M's copious physical affection, I understood that our friendship had brought me a form of fullness I'd never had before. I also understood that, with us living so far apart, I was unlikely to feel that fullness anytime soon.

Our friendship lived as much in our bodies as in our minds—how we wrapped ourselves into each other and filled our friends' stomachs with budget-friendly stews when we gathered them for dinner. I felt the loss of that dimension of our friendship now that the Atlantic Ocean separated us. By her second year of grad school, I found it tougher to cope with the physical distance between us because we had grown apart in other ways, too. M, eager to immerse in life in the UK, was trying to reduce her dependence on her phone. This meant that the digital threads I'd been relying on to keep us close were, one by one, beginning to snap. Gone were the days of being bcc-ed on M's important emails and ping-ponging voice memos with her. We were giving each other summaries days later, often interspersed with phrases like, "I can't remember if I told you this," reminders that we were no longer walking together through the thickets of each other's lives. I scaled back the frequency of my contact to match hers because I didn't want to bother her.

Even the thought that I might be bothering her unnerved me. It was such a departure from the period in our friendship when it was clear that we completely fascinated each other. That was one of the things I most appreciated about being so close to M: the knowledge that someone who I thought the world of always wanted to be with me or talk to me—and never feeling like I was asking for more than she wanted to give. Now, her schedule was maxed out with classes, musical ensembles, a solidifying group of friends, and a new, serious romantic relationship.

When we were talking from afar, it didn't feel possible to share my disappointment. During a break from school, M briefly visited D.C. and came over to my apartment. I was eager to experience the bliss of being together in person, but I also knew that I'd have to give up that warm glow if I wanted to finally share what had been on my mind. That night, she and I lay horizontal on my couch, our bodies layered like pancakes. I told her that I didn't feel as close to her as I used to; I missed what our friendship had been. Our faces just inches apart, she stroked my tear-dampened cheeks and comforted me. But her words were not what I had wanted to hear: she said the time in our friendship that I missed was in fact beautiful, but we now had to figure out what this new phase would look like. I felt she was saying we had no power to resist our friendship weakening, as if that outcome was inevitable.

I had wanted her to assure me that we could make decisions to return to that earlier way of life. I thought we could prioritize each other by living close by or scheduling regular time to be together. If we didn't do so, it felt like we were admitting that we weren't all that important to each other. In friendship, where exchanging rings and holding public ceremonies aren't standard, it's decisions like these that convey what we mean to each other.

That spring, in 2020, M moved back to D.C. and sublet an apartment a twenty-minute walk from me. I nursed hope that living in the same place would recapture the closeness we shared before we lived continents apart. The changes in our friendship, to me, felt circumstantial, and now the circumstances were shifting in our favor.

Though M moved, her return felt transitory—the furniture and kitchen supplies and novels belonged to the apartment's owner; M could pack up and leave without having to take much more than clothing with her. Despite living close to each other, concerns about pandemic safety meant we saw each other sporadically, often outdoors, parting with a hands-free goodbye routine that ended with a pair of hip bumps, like the twins in *The Parent Trap*. That summer, M and her partner began to rove around the country, staying with their families. M talked about D.C. like it was home, where her people were, but I wasn't sure if or when she'd move back. I was coming to terms with the possibility that we weren't going to have the sort of lives where we made impromptu visits to each other's houses, where I knew her thoughts so intimately that she was a shadow mind, handing me ideas even when she wasn't in the room.

It would take time for me to grasp exactly what I had lost. I might have understood it sooner had we been in a different kind of relationship. I think most people realize that romantic breakups are devastating because you lose at least two things at the same time: an existing intimate relationship and a joint future you had imagined. When our friendship changed from its earlier form, I felt a relationship that anchored me and a kind of future I had wanted had drifted away.

As our friendship began to feel less like a partnership, I wasn't sure how to articulate what I was missing. M and I hadn't had a falling-out. She hadn't vanished from my life. We had merely stepped down from being exceptionally close to being best friends—though there was a period when I felt uneasy even using that label for us. The change in our friendship was in degree, not kind.

It's not surprising that I had trouble describing what I was feeling.

Our collective vocabulary offers little in the way of language about friendship challenges. Ann Friedman and Aminatou Sow, who hosted a podcast about friendship for years, coined popular terms like *Shine Theory* to describe positive friend dynamics. "But it has been much harder for us to find a language for the difficult parts," they write in their book, *Big Friendship*.

Besides lacking language, the kind of loss I was experiencing—one that had no definitive end—is, as a rule, difficult to manage. Pauline Boss, professor emerita at the University of Minnesota, coined a term for this: "ambiguous loss." Ambiguity, rather than alleviating the sense of loss, can make the coping process more complicated. Without a well-defined conclusion like death or divorce, loved ones may not realize they should step in to help. The loss may not even be clear to the person who's experienced it; a mourner needs to know there's something to grieve before she can start the grieving process. Ambiguous loss can lead to "frozen grief"—Boss's term for being ensnared in sadness.

Working on this book sharpened my understanding of the loss. As I interviewed friends who remained committed to each other for years or decades, who regularly went on vacations together and scheduled "date nights," I knew that my current friendship with M didn't belong to the same genre as theirs. I instead found some commonalities with people whose friendships had declined in a slow fade or flatlined.

Often it was a romantic relationship that spelled change for those friends, eclipsing their once-devoted friendship. It's common for romantic relationships to transform established platonic connections. According to the evolutionary psychologist Robin Dunbar, the inner ring of our social circles usually contains five "shoulder-to-cry-on friendships," but a romantic relationship takes up "two rations," so they typically knock out two friends once they begin. The journalist Rebecca Traister writes about how she and her friend Sara "pushed each other to become hardier versions of ourselves, more able (and, I suspected, more likely) to form healthy, happy alliances with partners," which was a win-win situation until Sara moved hundreds of miles away to live with her boyfriend. It was one of the hardest losses of Traister's adult life. "Through one particularly self-pitying lens," Traister writes, "I saw [the friendship] as the rocket that propelled a shuttle into orbit . . . and then, inevitably, fell away."

I had heard again and again in my reporting that romantic relationships and close friendships don't have to compete like this. There's Andrew, the physicist in the introduction, who has both a romantic and platonic partner, and Nick Galluccio, the youth pastor from chapter 4, who thinks his relationships with his girlfriend, Morgan, and best friend, Art, enrich each other. In the first couple of years of our friendship, M and I had talked about how a future romantic partner of hers would fit into our lives. Those decadent moments when M and Marco each held one of my hands showed me how effortless that integration could be.

But when M and I became friends, Marco and I were years into our relationship, past my stage of walking around town with a steady high because I was falling in love with a charming, bookworm Dutchman. M and her partner were in a different place. From the start, they were more enmeshed than Marco and I were. They were infatuated, and from what I could tell, the pandemic ushered them into enveloping domesticity. I wanted to spend more time with M, but I didn't want to introduce a dynamic I had experienced in a different relationship, in which someone's attempts to pull me in tightly felt stifling and sapped me of motivation to become closer. After a year and a half of living far apart, the constraints of a pandemic, coupled with M's relatively fresh, impassioned romantic relationship, chipped away at my closeness with her.

Talking to Boss, the loss expert, I was struck by a simple question she told me she asks her clients. After 9/11, she moved to New York to work with the relatives of people who had died in the attack. It was a far more diverse crop of clients than those she'd worked with for decades in Minnesota. She soon realized she couldn't make assumptions about the significance of a loss based solely on the relationship between the patient and the deceased. Boss started to ask, "What does this loss mean to you?"

Had I been asked or asked myself that question, I might have cited a scene from the novel *How Should a Person Be?*, when two characters who are best friends are repairing their relationship. In the book, Margaux tells Sheila, "Well, it's like in life—you have the variables and you have the invariables, and you want to use them all, but you work around the invariables. I thought *you* were an invariable—and then you left without saying a word." Sheila thinks, "Very deep inside, something began to vibrate. I was an invariable. An *invariable*. No word had ever sounded to me more like love." I had lost the feeling that I was an invariable for M.

Experiencing an ambiguous loss was only part of what made the change in our friendship hard to talk about with other people. The larger obstacle was something that could better be described as *unrelatable loss*. I didn't know if I could explain the sense of bodily loss I felt; most people I knew didn't physically intertwine themselves with their friends as M and I had. I didn't expect others to understand what there was to mourn because I didn't know many other people who had a friendship that had reached the closeness M and I shared. It would be like complaining that the amenities at the Ritz went downhill to people who'd never stayed in a swanky hotel.

The forms of closeness that I found hard to describe were exactly what I missed. Together, M and I had built a frame that marked the perimeter of our specific relationship, in an unconventional shape no one had told us we could make. We delighted in that discovery. When our friendship changed, I felt like I had lost the frame we had constructed and the person it contained. For a short while, I considered whether those losses were inextricable or if I could separate them. It was M I wanted: her incisive questions, her gentle voice singing jazz standards as she padded through the house. But I also wanted the permission to be effusive, the feeling of being chosen, the access to someone with a dazzling mind. What I felt wasn't so different from what my brother described in the aftermath of a yearslong romantic relationship. He missed his partner in particular, but he also missed everyday pleasures like waking up next to someone—the infrastructure of a romantic relationship. My friendship with M had shown me a new form of intimacy and altered my expectations for what constitutes a full life. Those expectations weren't elastic that could be stretched and then contract back to their original shape.

I shied away from talking to other friends about what I was feeling. I thought it was embarrassing to admit, even if implicitly, that M was more important to me than I was to her. I also feared others would think this ebb in a friendship was the natural course of things. My reputation as a friendship enthusiast didn't help; I had made it my mission, personal and professional, to help people realize how meaningful and devoted a friendship like ours can be. Our friendship was undermining my argument.

As hard as I found it to keep my feelings unspoken, I was spared the deeper shame felt by people who've had a decisive falling-out rather than a leveling down of their friendship. Yesel Yoon, a psychologist based in New York, wondered if there was something wrong with her after two intense friendships ended. As I saw it, Yesel was a woman who frequently assumed the role of helper and enjoyed being wanted—until it became clear that the friend in question wasn't going to reciprocate. It hardly seemed like a character blemish. Self-flogging is par for the course after a romantic relationship ends, too, but when a platonic relationship folds, a particular breed of shame can set in. The editors of an anthology called *The Friend Who Got Away* write that compared to romantic relationships, "friendship is supposed to be made of sturdier stuff, a less complicated, more enduring relationship. Because of this, the story of a breakup with a friend often feels far more revealing than that of a failed romance, as if it exposes our worst failings and weaknesses." You can part ways with a monogamous romantic partner believing they're a wonderful person, but you simply weren't compatible enough to wake up next to each other for the rest of your lives; it's more disheartening when someone drops you as one of their many friends, as if you'd failed to pass a much less demanding test.

The writer Patti Miller describes friend breakups as "shameful; it is certainly not something to talk about with other friends. I've been found unworthy by one friend—why would I advertise the fact to another? Somewhere in all the neural pathways of memory, or perhaps further back in the DNA of our survival, there is the dark sliver of fear of being cast out of the tribe. I must not talk about the rupture in case it spreads." That isn't an outlandish concern. One woman told me that when she says she "used to be friends" with someone, people are aghast. "*Used to?*" they ask with disapproval, as if she must have done something wrong—a judgment they probably wouldn't have leaped to if she had referred to an ex-boyfriend. Stigma feeds on shame and silence, and friend breakups are nothing if not shrouded with shame and silence.

The odd part about the shame is that friendship endings aren't unusual. A study from the Netherlands found that most of the adults surveyed replaced half their friends by the time of the follow-up survey seven years later (though many maintained some contact with these former friends), and only 30 percent of friends who were close were still close. In the United States, a 2021 survey found that Americans report considerably fewer close friends than they did in 1990, suggesting that many Americans have suffered the loss of a good friend.

———————

Joy Loughry doesn't feel judged that her closest friendship ended—there's no way to view her as culpable. But she has felt judged for the way she's grieved the loss—one that took years to unfold.

While playing darts at a bar after work, Joy's best friend, Hannah Friedrich, told her that she was trying to get doctors to figure out what was wrong with her body. For years, doctors at the women's clinic she went to wrote off her symptoms as fibroids. While pregnant with her second child, she felt an unfamiliar form of pain, which made a reprise several times after the birth, so she went to a series of doctors' appointments. But she got no new explanation for her persistent bloating and pain.

Her answer arrived on April 6, 2011, a few days after her bar hangout with Joy. Hannah had forced her way into the clinic, and she was immediately given a CT scan. A fresh-faced resident called Hannah while she was at work to share the results and said, "Oh my god, it's cancer, and it's everywhere."

Thirty-four-year-old Hannah couldn't help but notice the parallels to her dad's experience. For years, he told doctors that he knew something was wrong. By the time they discovered his rare form of cancer, it had metastasized to his lung, the cause of his eventual death. About five years after he died, Hannah was learning she had stage 4 stomach cancer, and it had spread to her liver and lungs.

Hannah sounded petrified when she called Joy to explain what the resident told her. Hearing Hannah, Joy says, "My world just stopped." Hannah was the axis around which her adult life turned. As geology majors at the University of Minnesota Morris in the late 1990s, they quickly became "bonded besties." They spent a summer driving around small-town Minnesota in a university-owned maroon Buick to map a glacial river and its terraces. They dismissed the guys at a party who asked them to make out, insinuating that Hannah and Joy were a couple. Even after Joy relocated to Milwaukee to get a master's and Hannah moved to Utah to work as a ranger at Zion National Park and set up a side business baking wedding cakes, they made time to see each other. Once Hannah was back in Minnesota, Joy would drive ten hours round trip just to catch her for dinner. In 2004, Hannah and Joy downed frozen vodka shots before Hannah walked down the aisle for her wedding, and Joy signed the marriage certificate as her witness. That night, Hannah set off fireworks—her favorite way to celebrate any occasion—leaving her wedding dress with a blue streak across the side and butt. No, the dry cleaners said, they couldn't get the mark out. To Joy, Hannah made everything feel like an adventure.

The same year, Hannah was the witness for Joy's wedding. When Joy later expressed ambivalence about her marriage, Hannah nudged Joy to consider that it wasn't enough to be loved; she deserved to be in a marriage in which she felt *in* love. Joy and her husband went on to divorce. At the memorial service for Hannah's father, Hannah had entrusted Joy—not her brother or another family member—to read aloud a letter she had written to him. The funeral felt like a big to-do; Hannah's father was an esteemed psychologist at the Mayo Clinic, and the imposing, cavernous chapel was packed with his colleagues, friends, and relatives. Holding Hannah's handwritten letter, Joy kept her eyes fixed on Hannah's face, terrified she'd mess up the delivery. Joy says, "I just felt like it was a really big responsibility to be her voice."

In her online journal, Hannah titled an entry she wrote in 2011, "Resident needs an anatomy lesson." The resident was wrong about where the tumors were, and Hannah's cancer hadn't spread to her liver. But the prognosis still wasn't good. She'd ultimately be diagnosed with stage 3c ovarian cancer.

Step one in treatment was abdominal surgery that pilfered one organ after another: her ovaries, fallopian tubes, uterus, cervix, appendix, the layer of tissue over her intestines, and whatever else the doctors deemed necessary. She wasn't allowed to lift anything for weeks, a problem for managing her intrepid daughter. "I am literally defenseless against this 19 month old," Hannah wrote. She signed up for a clinical trial and took notes on how to correctly say the chemical name of the experimental drug: "BEV-a-SIHZ-a-MAB"—she wanted to get on the good side of the clinical trial nurse, who told her she should learn how to pronounce it.

Once Hannah's treatment began, Joy's calendar swelled with activities and errands related to her friend. With Hannah's husband and mom spending so much time at the hospital, Joy would pick up the kids from day care and spend evenings making crafts with them. Joy ordered teal silicone bracelets printed with HANNAH ROCKS—as geologists, they said "You rock!" as a compliment. She organized a team for a fundraising walk/run by the Minnesota Ovarian Cancer Alliance. Hannah was determined to have the biggest team—she wanted the banner that would be awarded to the largest group. With seventy-five friends and family members in matching HANNAH ROCKS T-shirts and teal face paint, Hannah won and got to hold the vertical, person-size banner. At the agency where she and Hannah both worked, the Minnesota Department of Natural Resources, Joy kept her colleagues in check. They were showing up at Hannah's house uninvited while Hannah was in treatment. Later, as if she were a pregnant woman whose belly is treated like public property, they asked to touch Hannah's hair, which had grown back fuzzy after chemotherapy. Joy felt protective of her friend.

Not long after Hannah's diagnosis, Joy was baking a cake for a nephew's birthday and told her sisters about her frustration with her intrusive coworkers. Joy's oldest sister said she needed to settle down. Joy felt like her sister didn't grasp how devastating this news was. It would be bad enough to know that your friend's body was being cut into and pumped with chemicals to stop a grisly disease. But Hannah was not an ordinary friend. She was Joy's person.

About five months later, in September 2011, Hannah's CT scan was clear—no sign of ovarian cancer. On the day of her last infusion of chemotherapy, she posed in the hospital with her fist held up in a sign of victory. She wrote, "A suffocating blanket of fear has smothered me since my diagnosis. Hardly a minute goes by without me thinking about something related to my illness. What an energy sucker, I have so much else I want to do and don't have any more time for this damn cancer."

For Valentine's Day in 2013—about a year and a half after she became cancer-free—Hannah's son gave her a handmade card that read, "I love you mom, I am so glad you are back to normal."

"Yeah, it about broke my heart," Hannah wrote. "I so so so wish I was back to normal." She'd just learned that her cancer had returned. Denial, anger, and sadness blurred together. Her oncologist wouldn't perform another surgery, so Hannah parted ways with her and searched for another doctor. She switched to the Mayo Clinic and got a second surgery and more chemotherapy. About five months later, her oncologist told her the term she'd been waiting to hear: "NED!!!! No Evidence of Disease!!!!! I'm beyond relieved," Hannah wrote. But the cancer returned for a third time. Her oncologist at the Mayo Clinic worked with her until he, too, told her there were no other options. Hannah thought, *Yes, there are.* She found a doctor in the Bronx known for delivering specialized chemotherapy and bringing ovarian cancer patients back from the brink.

In 2015, Hannah and Joy flew to New York and laughed as the taxi driver sped and swerved his way to the Bronx, not knowing how else to react to his recklessness. The oncologist they saw the next morning was optimistic about what his treatment could do for Hannah and arranged for a doctor in Manhattan to put stents into her liver. In Manhattan, Joy ushered a jaundiced Hannah into the emergency room—if she was admitted to the ER, insurance would pay for her treatment. Hannah got several stents, and she and Joy called it "the stent tent," one of the many nicknames they came up with for treatments and doctors.

Hannah was flying out to New York every other week because a foundation helped pay for her treatment in the Bronx. In her journal posts, Hannah repeatedly thanked her coworkers for donating vacation hours so that she could keep her job and, with it, her health insurance. Hannah's friends, including Joy, organized a spaghetti lunch fundraiser to pay for Hannah's medical bills. When it came to Hannah, money was no object; Joy spent what she could to support Hannah's treatment.

Joy joined Hannah for many of her New York trips. The hospital room didn't have a recliner or pullout bed, so Joy slept on a chair with metal arms that cut off her circulation. She told the hospital staff that she was Hannah's wife because she feared she would get kicked out; she wasn't related to Hannah by blood or marriage—only one example of how official classifications of which types of relationships matter would leave out their friendship.

By this point, Hannah's self-deprecating humor ("I could be related to the Simpsons. I am so yellow!") and strings of exclamation marks had become rarer in her journal posts. What remained was medical jargon and a log of her latest test numbers, as if she were in the doctor's rounds, reducing her own life to a medical chart. Hannah scared Joy by signing up for whatever promising drug trial she could find, regardless of where it was taking place in the country. One trial, as Joy understands it, amounted to cooking Hannah's blood at a high temperature to kill the cancer. Hannah turned out not to be healthy enough to join that trial.

The cumulative effects of chemotherapy were wearing on her: "My fingers and toes are getting numb, my brain feels pickled, I have the teeth and gums of an 80 year old, my skin is fragile and dry," and when she listened to people, "it is as if I am wearing earmuffs." Still, she sang with abandon in the seventh row of a Red Hot Chili Peppers concert, her favorite band. Joy had bought them tickets to celebrate Hannah's fortieth birthday, just as she'd done for Hannah's thirtieth birthday. Every few songs, Hannah had to leave to go to the bathroom or get water but told Joy not to accompany her because she'd miss the show. In Hannah's absence, Joy was too busy worrying whether Hannah was okay to fully tune in to the music.

The next month, Joy took them on a trip to Miami. They came across a boat rental, and when the guy at the rental stand asked if they needed to pay for a driver, Hannah declared, "We are from *Minnesota* and are on boats *all* the time! We will be fine!" Except neither of them had ever been on a boat like this one. They faked it, Hannah at the wheel with her skirt blowing in the wind, and made it out into the ocean.

In March 2017, they flew back to New York. Joy wheeled Hannah into the same ER for another stent tent. Over the next few days, they did a tourists' romp through New York City because Hannah wanted to make sure Joy had a good time. The wheelchair they'd gotten from their Manhattan hotel didn't have a place for Hannah to rest her feet, so Joy ran across traffic to snag caution tape and tied it to the bottom of the wheelchair as a footrest. They spent their time in the hotel room watching cooking shows while lying on their double beds. One of Joy's favorite chefs, Rick Bayless, prepared a Mexican chocolate pepper cake, and intrigued by the recipe, Hannah said they had to make it someday.

Joy's life was playing out in split screen, divided between the fun she and Hannah had together despite Hannah's health and the calm that shattered when Hannah wasn't present. During the first trip to New York, Joy stayed up two nights in a row and tracked the rise and fall of Hannah's chest because she worried Hannah could die while away from her mother and children. On this latest trip, Joy set off on her own to get a prescription for Hannah at a corner pharmacy in the Bronx and argued with the pharmacist, who was giving her trouble as an out-of-state resident. Joy, who gives off the impression of a reserved nerd, got in the pharmacist's face. She explained what was going on with Hannah and told him to call whoever was necessary to get the medication or tell Joy where she could get it. During the hour it took to get the prescription in her hands, she sat on a metal chair, in the smallest pharmacy she had ever been in, and cried. The inescapability of Hannah's mortality, all the drugs and liver numbers and side effects—it had taken its toll. She couldn't keep it together anymore.

Though Joy could see the end, Hannah never admitted that she was dying, never broached the topic of death with Joy, never signed a do-not-resuscitate order. Hannah had just bought an annual pass to the arboretum, thinking she'd get good use out of it. Joy would later see that Hannah's reaction wasn't so unusual; Joy's father also never accepted that he was dying. Still, Joy was horrified by Hannah's unwillingness to prepare for the end; she didn't have a will and hadn't talked to her kids about dying. Joy thought, *My God, when she was in remission, why wasn't I more forceful about these things?*—as if she, not Hannah or even Hannah's husband, bore some responsibility for Hannah's decisions.

During all the weeks Joy took off work to be in the hospital with Hannah, she wasn't entitled for leave through the Family and Medical Leave Act because she and Hannah weren't related by blood, marriage, or adoption. Instead, Joy used her vacation days; because her employer offered generous vacation time, she counted herself lucky.

Joy never stopped feeling torn between the desire to honor Hannah's wish for autonomy and the urge to stare into reality's menacing glare. Six years after Hannah was diagnosed with ovarian cancer, she entered hospice. She agreed to go because she wanted a hospital bed that was adjustable and would make her comfortable enough to sleep; insurance would only pay for that through hospice care. Even in hospice, an institution focused on improving the quality of life during the time a patient has left, Hannah asked staff to give her new treatments.

For the previous month, Hannah had been living at her mom's apartment, which had turned into a maze of medical supplies. A hospice nurse gathered Joy, Hannah, and her mom around the small dining room table. The nurse insisted that Hannah understand that this was "the end"; Hannah couldn't get the feeding tube she requested because she was too far gone, and besides, hospice doesn't provide treatment. Sitting next to Hannah, Joy asked the nurse to promise that she would look into getting a feeding tube. Joy wished she'd had a few minutes to talk to the nurse before this meeting to give some context: she knew Hannah was on the cusp of death, but Hannah was trying hard to stay alive for her children. Hannah was still searching for the next treatment because that's what she had done for more than six years. Not knowing all of this, the nurse seemed to think Joy was in denial.

After the meeting, the nurse took Hannah's mother and Joy into the hallway outside the apartment and said, "You do understand that Hannah is so sick she has maybe a few days left?" Yes, they said.

"I felt like I was betraying Hannah because all I ever did was support her in every treatment option," Joy says. "I didn't want her to know that I believed she was close to death with zero realistic options to stop it." Joy didn't think it was her place to convince Hannah that she was dying.

Two days later, Hannah couldn't keep down liquid morphine without getting sick and throwing up. Hannah's mom didn't know what to do and called Joy. They decided to dial 911 to get Hannah to the hospital. After the ambulance reached Hannah, shutting down the block with howling sirens, Joy drove to her parents' house because it was Father's Day. Sitting at the picnic table in their yard, she cried. No one tried to lift Joy out of her somber mood as they had back when Hannah had gotten her diagnosis.

The next day, June 19, 2017, Hannah's mom called Joy and told her to come to hospice. Hannah's husband was going to sign the do-not-resuscitate order. Joy left work and joined Hannah's mom, husband, kids, brother, and a few close friends. They all held Hannah at the end. It was the same day as Hannah's son's eleventh birthday. Joy and a childhood friend of Hannah's had bought gifts for Hannah's son, and they tried to celebrate despite the cruel convergence of occasions. That night, Joy drank herself to sleep.

A memorial service was scheduled to happen a few weeks later at the arboretum, and Joy helped plan it. When she stopped by Hannah's mother's house to do some errands for the memorial, Hannah's mom gave her two blocks of chocolate Hannah had ordered from Mexico so that she and Joy could make the chocolate pepper cake together, the one they'd seen prepared on a cooking show that they'd watched from their New York hotel.

Joy couldn't bring herself to give a speech at the memorial because she didn't think she could deliver one without crying. She communicated instead through her selection of the Red Hot Chili Peppers song "Otherside," about crossing over to another realm after death; Joy and Hannah listened to it on heavy rotation when the single was released, and now it was playing at the memorial.

Joy returned to work three days after Hannah died because she wasn't entitled to bereavement leave; again, Hannah didn't fit the official criteria of being Joy's relative. Joy thinks it's unfair that she could have taken time off to attend the funeral of her dad's brother, whom she'd never met, but not to mourn Hannah's death.

From family leave to bereavement leave to hospital rules about who can be in the room with a patient, the policies Joy ran into reflect and reinforce a hierarchy of grief. In the penthouse is enfranchised grief; most people understand that losing a spouse, parent, or child can raze even a flourishing life. In the basement is what bereavement expert Kenneth Doka has termed *disenfranchised grief*—grief that isn't or can't be openly acknowledged or mourned or supported by others. He arrived at the idea while teaching a class in the 1980s about grief. One student who had been through a bitter divorce told the class, "If you think it's tough to have your spouse die, you ought to see what it's like when your ex-spouse dies." People didn't rally around her as they would have if she and her ex-husband were still together, yet she experienced his death as a loss. There are multiple pathways that can lead to disenfranchised grief; one is a relationship that's unrecognized—say, if your employer and government don't treat the lost relationship as deserving of caregiving or bereavement accommodations. Another cause of disenfranchised grief is ambiguous loss.

When grief is avowed, those around the mourner know what to do: send flowers, sit shiva, drop off meals. There is no playbook for someone who wants to help a loved one who has lost a friend. "Try to find a card for 'I'm sorry your friend died,'" Doka says. Friedman and Sow, the authors of *Big Friendship*, propose a similar challenge: "Try calling your boss to announce you've experienced a devastating friend breakup and need to take a day off to grieve." When mourners don't have support, they can suffer even more. Disenfranchised grief is a risk factor for complicated grief—a form of grieving that's so long-lasting and severe that it's debilitating.

Joy once heard that grieving is like a ball that rolls in a box. At the beginning, the ball is enormous and strikes the sides with force. As time passes, the ball gets smaller and doesn't jostle the sides as frequently. But it still hurts when it hits. Although this analogy has been validating for Joy, as it normalizes the grief she's felt for Hannah, people around her don't seem to expect that ball to bump well after her friend's death and for the pain to be as wretched when it does. Joy says she doesn't think her grief "is out of bound, but I get the feeling from people that they're just like, 'Oh, geez, you're still on this. You're still talking about this.'" Comments from friends and family had the pretense of looking out for Joy, but she felt like the message was to let go of her grief. They wouldn't say those words directly but instead would tell Joy that Hannah wouldn't want her to feel so bad. Or they'd compare their own grieving of Hannah to Joy's; they'd tell her that they focused on the happy feelings and asked Joy why she was so sad.

"I'm sad because my human's gone," Joy says, her face reddened. "The person who chose to love me unconditionally isn't here anymore. And I don't think I'll ever have that again for the rest of my life." She brushes a tissue underneath each lens of her teal glasses. "I can't believe the world still spins when she's not here," she says.

It's taken Hannah's absence for Joy to understand what the friendship gave to her. Since Hannah died, Joy has come to understand how rare a friendship like theirs is. "When I was living it, I knew it was special," she says, "but I didn't know how special it was until she passed away."

This is the dark irony of disenfranchised grief: the depth of Joy's mourning should be the strongest evidence that her friendship was significant; it's that classic Joni Mitchell line that you don't know what you've got 'til it's gone. But her grief didn't secure her recognition, whether in the form of workplace or government policies or from the people in her immediate vicinity.

Even when people try to offer support after the loss of a friendship like Joy's, they may cause more pain with their misunderstanding. Nicole Sonderman, a woman whose best friend died by suicide, felt alienated because people around her didn't grasp how important her friend (whom she called "wife") was to her. They'd bring up someone they'd known from high school who died, as if her loss was the equivalent of dealing with the death of an acquaintance.

Some part of the reaction Joy received reflects a more general Western impatience with grief, regardless of who has passed away. Psychologists describe the typical grieving process just as Joy has experienced it: grief strikes in oscillations that are spaced farther apart over time but still can pummel when they arrive. These psychologists also say that healthy reactions to loss are often treated as pathological. Terms like *closure* and *over it* send an inaccurate message that grief will have a punctuation mark. The philosopher Judith Butler compares the way people talk about grieving to a misguided use of the Protestant work ethic. She says you can't solve grieving by thinking, "I'll apply myself to the task, and I'll endeavor to achieve the resolution of grief that is before me." Grief is something we live with, not something we complete.

Other people may want Joy to think about something else, but she doesn't. She says, "I feel like I can't let it go because if I do, I'm letting her go. I want to think about her every single day. I want to remember her every day and celebrate her every day." When we talk, Joy is wearing a T-shirt from the Minnesota Ovarian Cancer Alliance walk that reads HANNAH ROCKS and a HANNAH ROCKS silicone bracelet. If "Dark Necessities" by the Red Hot Chili Peppers comes on, Joy says, "I'll just close my eyes, and I'm right there in row seven with her right there, cheering and smiling and having a blast."

For a while, Joy didn't have the opportunity to remember or grieve. A few weeks after the memorial service for Hannah, Joy found cancer in her breast. Her treatment consumed the next six months of her life. Even so, Joy says, "I felt like I won the cancer lottery" because she only needed surgery and radiation, not chemotherapy. She knew that Hannah hated how much money was raised for breast cancer whereas more deadly diseases like ovarian cancer received scant attention by comparison. Joy was racked with survivor's guilt.

During Joy's treatment, a college friend who was also close with Hannah sent Joy soap to ease her radiation burns and a card that read, "I know the person you want most to be here, especially through tough times, isn't." With that comment, Joy at least felt that someone understood the gravity of what she had lost.

On the first anniversary of Hannah's death, done with her own cancer treatment, Joy was finally able to mourn. She took the chocolate that Hannah had bought from Mexico and made the Mexican chocolate pepper cake that Hannah herself never got to try. She turned this into a ritual: she'd bake this cake on the anniversary of Hannah's death every year.

The specificity of this ritual is part of what makes it meaningful. But had Joy wanted an off-the-shelf ritual for the friendship—intelligible to others and supported communally—she would have had trouble finding it. The central rituals meant to process grief that exist in major religions don't carve out space for friends. Doka, the grieving expert, is also a Lutheran minister, and he couldn't think of a Christian grieving ritual for friends. Jews follow the ritual of kaddish traditionally to mark the death of a child, parent, spouse, or sibling. In Hinduism, male descendants perform the rite of shraddha for specific blood relatives. Joy's loss was hers to manage, the rituals of recovery hers to create.

———————

I know I wasn't completely clear-eyed when I was longing for an earlier era of my friendship with M. I didn't appreciate that during the pandemic there were alarms going off in M's life that were more urgent to respond to than our friendship. She was struggling at work, she was in a job that wasn't well suited to do remotely. A lover of routines, she moved to a different state every few months. She worried about her immunocompromised family member. Between living far apart and deliberately curbing my contact with M, I missed opportunities to fully appreciate that she was trying to keep the clapboard house of her pandemic life together. Whatever

I thought about the space her romantic relationship had in her life versus friendships, her then-partner gave her pleasure and steadiness in a destabilizing time.

I only got a better picture of what was happening in M's inner life after M reacted to a draft of this book. It was then that I realized I'd missed something fundamental about who M is, which shaped how the transition in our friendship unfolded. I had been under the impression that M was a direct communicator and fearless about doing what she wants—qualities I admired in her.

More than once, M remarked early in our friendship that we should practice handling conflict together so that we'd be prepared when we eventually, inevitably had some sort of disagreement. I hadn't realized that comments like that and her willingness to buck social conventions were exceptions to M's discomfort with conflict. M is exquisitely sensitive to how other people feel—both the root of M's empathy and her struggle to share what she wants when it might hurt someone else. Take, for example, how, while she sometimes missed our closeness, our shift from platonic partners to friends created room for her to develop other meaningful relationships. Realizing how much had gone over my head about this person I thought I knew so well, to put it lightly, was humbling.

Even before M clarified what had been happening during grad school and the pandemic, I tried to make peace with the idea that we've changed the roles we play in each other's lives, and not all of those shifts were downward moves. We've become more vital to each other in providing professional counsel as our careers have increasingly overlapped. When I was navigating some major life changes that M had experienced firsthand, we returned to a steady cadence of exchanging voice memos, an indicator that our friendship can alter in intensity depending on what's happening in our lives. We were inadvertently following Meg-John Barker's proposal to move away from a breakup model of relationships. If we stop expecting relationships to come to a decisive end, Barker explains in *Rewriting the Rules: An Anti Self-Help Guide to Love, Sex and Relationships*, "it becomes possible to change one of these aspects [housemate, sexual intimacy, supporters in times of crisis] without necessarily changing all of the others. Which ones aren't working anymore? Which ones still are?" Unlike many romantic relationships that operate with an on-off switch—you're either each other's number one or absent from each other's lives—our friendship is more like a dimmer that can easily be adjusted.

Or maybe it's like a collage with components that can be added or shuffled around. M and I both became friends with a woman named Helen, and over time, we've formed a close three-way friendship. With three of us, there was more laughter to fill the room when I bought silver string decorations to celebrate Helen's pregnancy and inadvertently hung them in the shape of drooping breasts. We took a photo in front of those decorations: in jest, Helen hoists her breasts over her seven-month-pregnant belly as M and I hug her from either side. It's now the background image on my phone. A few weeks later, when M's mood was a weight too heavy to lift alone, Helen drove us an hour and a half north to where M lives and reused those decorations. The string of silver circles framed the exposed brick wall in her living room, on which we'd taped photos forming a record of our friendship. Like my initial friendship with M, so different from anything I'd experienced, this three-way friendship was not something I had known to want before.

As I became less attached to the early years of our friendship, I found that my relationship with M has acted as a lighthouse, illuminating which friends I should try to become closer to. That light beamed on Sigal, whose wacky nerdiness sends me into fits of laughter, like the time she and her partner sang the song they'd written about lichen. It beamed on Kim, who, once, when we were in a car and she was sitting a row in front of me, reached back to grab my hand—for no reason other than to show affection—and whose exuberance was infectious.

Though I would readily return to seeing M most days of the week if it were possible, I've come to view the first couple of years of our friendship as a point in history to appreciate rather than long to revive, like treasuring a memory from a vacation without expecting to return to the spot years later and find everything intact. I would never use the term *ex* to describe M, but I nevertheless recognized my own experience in Barker's idea to think of exes "as the people we've reached the height of intimacy with . . . Perhaps we can view these people as the most valuable and precious relationships in our lives, instead of hating them or relegating them to the past." Valuable and precious is exactly how I think of my friendship with M. Just in the first couple of years of knowing her, she reshaped my understanding of platonic relationships and expanded my sense of who I could be.

Being with M reacquaints me with the version of myself that I like best: unabashed about my enchantment with a song from a musical; animated as I move through the room as if there are springs beneath me. The last time I stayed over at M's apartment, she told me about a time a loved one withheld information from her, which spun into a conversation about the ethics of withholding information—when does it constitute harm, and when is it an act of care? I paused the conversation to go to the bathroom. When I returned, M was scrolling through a PDF of a political theory paper, searching for a relevant thought experiment she wanted to share with me. As we sat at her dining room table, I told her how much I love that she enjoys toggling between the interpersonal and the theoretical—a combination that makes every conversation with her captivating. She told me that's something she loves about me, too.

When I spend time with M, I can still feel a current of bittersweet feelings, like a draft invading a heated room. One night, I walked M home, and with our arms wrapped around the waists of each other's puffy coats, we were back in that familiar mode of building a tower of ideas together with interludes of humor. I felt a blend of nostalgia for our early friendship, annoyance with myself for still pining for the past, and disappointment for what the future won't hold. While working on the book, I learned there was a clinical term for this pain about a lost future: *intrapsychic grief*, which the hospital chaplain and writer J.S. Park describes as "grieving what could have been and will never be." Like reading about romantic friendships and sworn brotherhoods from earlier centuries, seeing this term assured me that my reactions weren't over-the-top. I've felt this form of grief, though with less intensity, when I've grown apart from childhood friends or friends who moved away.

While I expect my friendship with M to remain close as it evolves over the coming decades, Joy doesn't have the option to fantasize about moving forward with Hannah. Joy tells me about a hairdresser appointment before Hannah's chemotherapy started. Hannah and Joy both chopped off their waist-length hair and ended up with what Joy describes as "little old lady helmet hair." Over lunch afterward, Joy joked about the two of them having drinks together fifty years later, with blue wash in their hair. "I miss that future," Joy says. "Of having her and having those experiences and the time and camaraderie—the hopes and dreams I had of being just part of her life and her being a part of my life."

Joy no longer takes for granted that she's been chosen, a fundamental feeling so many of us seek in partnerships of any kind. "I just feel so much less special now," Joy says. "I don't have this human being who every day wanted to talk to me and smiled when they saw me."

Losing someone you love always means losing a particular person who can't be traded for another. But at least with a romantic relationship, you might have some sense of how to fill in that space eventually. With these unusual friendships, built with their custom frames, it's harder to imagine someone else occupying that space or how you'd even find such a person for the role. Whether friend or romantic partner, Joy has never felt connected to anyone the way she felt connected to Hannah. A widow could download a dating app to search for a new spouse or ask to be set up. But Joy says, "I can't just put out an ad that I'm interviewing for a new soulmate."

FRIENDS, WITH BENEFITS

The costs of the marriage monopoly

"Marriage" is the name that society gives to the relationship that matters most between two adults.

—*PERRY V. BROWN*

In comic books, invisibility is a superpower. In the law, it can be a liability. Amelie Zurn-Galinsky has long viewed the invisibility of lesbian women as an injustice and has spent her adult life trying to change it. In 1990, just a few years out of college, she was named the first director of lesbian services at the Whitman-Walker Clinic, a health center in Washington, D.C., that has the mission of serving gay and lesbian residents in the area. Each month, Amelie weaved through the prewar brick building in her standard ensemble of a clinic T-shirt and short hair combed to the side, to run a day of workshops. One or two hundred women would assemble in conference rooms, sit down in one of the folding chairs that Amelie or the scores of volunteers had dragged in, and learn about health issues ranging from safe sex to mammograms. One workshop helped participants write living wills, asking the women, *In a crisis or at the end of life, who do you want around you?*—"Because the state's going to say: it's going to be your parents, or your brother you're estranged from, or your kiddo who you don't talk to," Amelie tells me. The lack of legal recognition for same-sex relationships meant that lesbians' partners were legal strangers, as were the friends they considered chosen family. If women who came to the clinic got their papers in order, Amelie hoped, any life-altering decisions that needed to be made for them would be handled by people they wanted in that position.

Amelie knew of plenty of instances when the law undermined queer people's autonomy, including the story of Sharon Kowalski, which made national news when Amelie moved to D.C. in the mid-1980s. Kowalski sustained severe brain injuries in a car crash, and her parents shut out her partner of four years, Karen Thompson. The women demonstrated the commitment characteristic of spouses—they'd exchanged rings and named each other as insurance beneficiaries—but because they were a same-sex couple, they didn't have the rights that legal marriage afforded. It took years of court battles for Thompson to be allowed to visit Kowalski and have the right to make decisions on her behalf. Then there were the cases Amelie saw up close. She knew gay men who became sick with AIDS and, as they were dying, were cut off from the people who mattered most to them. "Their family, who were their chosen family—their friends who were taking care of them—suddenly were ripped away from being with their beloveds," Amelie says, "because the biological families came in and said, *You don't have any place here. You're not really family.*"

After Amelie finished her four-year run overseeing lesbian services, she gained personal experience with the indignities, time drain, and financial cost of having a relationship that the law doesn't recognize. That all began when, in 1996, she introduced herself to a woman named Licia at a meeting for a lesbian health project where they were both volunteers. Even though Amelie's friends had told her that they'd like each other, Licia, striking with her salt-and-pepper hair and mustache, seemed busy and not particularly interested in Amelie. But when Amelie sent a note with her phone number, Licia responded, and they started dating. The following year, Amelie and Licia took in a twelve-year-old child of Licia's ex. Even though Amelie and Licia had legally notarized permission for Jessica to live with them, the school system wouldn't enroll her and required Amelie and Licia to get guardianship, a more involved legal process. They sought the help of the same lawyer who led the will-making sessions at Whitman-Walker and became the first pair of women in the state of Maryland to be the legal guardians of a minor.

Two years later, Licia gave birth to Tova, whose birth certificate named Licia as the mother and listed the father as "unidentified." The certificate didn't have a spot for a second mother. Amelie had to adopt Tova, which meant following the same process as adopting a stranger's child. Amelie and Licia had to get a home study with an adoption agency; a fire marshal inspection of their house; neighbors and people in the community were interviewed; they had to petition the court for the adoption and pay hefty legal fees. The couple repeated this process two years later, when Amelie gave birth to their second child, Milo. None of this legal rigmarole would have been necessary had Amelie and Licia been allowed to get married.

But marriage wasn't Amelie's end game in her LGBTQ activist work. She says, "As a political movement, I always saw the limitations of the institution and its sanctioning by the state." Although legalized same-sex marriage would have made co-parenting easier for her and Licia, she says, "I didn't necessarily think it was going to be the panacea that everyone thought it was going to be." People in nonmarital relationships still wouldn't have medical, legal, and financial rights to the most important people in their lives. Indeed, when Amelie eventually developed a category-defying friendship, marriage rights would turn out to be of no use.

————

In the mid-1980s, there were few enough gay and lesbian legal advocates that they could all fit around a table—and they did, assembling at a conference twice a year to talk about nationwide strategy and priorities. There was no shortage of issues to consider. Sodomy was illegal. Lesbian and gay parents were losing custody rights to their kids, and LGBTQ workers didn't have protection against employment discrimination. One of the lawyers at the table, Thomas Stoddard, saw the Sharon Kowalski case as evidence that same-sex couples needed marriage rights. He was the executive director of the Lambda Legal Defense and Education Fund, the leading gay legal advocacy organization at the time. In an essay published in 1989, he argued that it was politically strategic for the movement to make marriage equality its top priority. He wrote that it was an efficient way to gain rights and was "the issue most likely to lead ultimately to a world free from discrimination against lesbians and gay men." The right to marry, he thought, would be the train pulling the cargo of other types of equality behind it.

Support for this strategy generally fell along gender lines. Compared to the men, the women tended to be more critical of prioritizing marriage equality, influenced as they were by feminism, a movement with a long history of disenchantment with marriage and its patriarchal roots. Paula Ettelbrick, a colleague of Stoddard's at Lambda, was a skeptic, and an essay she wrote appeared alongside his in the gay and lesbian publication *OUT/LOOK*. The headline above the essays read "Gay Marriage: A Must or a Bust?" Ettelbrick warned that making same-sex marriage a priority "would set an agenda of gaining rights for a few, but would do nothing to correct the power imbalances between those who are married (whether gay or straight) and those who are not."

American law codifies an imbalance between married and unmarried Americans. Among the more than one thousand federal rights and benefits afforded to married couples are: getting access to each other's employer-provided health care; making a foreign-born spouse eligible for a green card; passing any amount of money or property on to each other tax-free; collecting unemployment upon leaving a job to join their spouse who's been relocated; filing a lawsuit for their spouse's wrongful death; and refusing to testify against their spouse in a criminal case. Serena Mayeri, a law professor at the University of Pennsylvania, calls the legal privileging of marriage and families formed by married couples "marital supremacy."

Instead of concentrating on marriage, Ettelbrick endorsed a different approach that she believed aligned with the central goals of the lesbian and gay rights movement. She advocated for a legal agenda that expanded options for more types of relationships, and in doing so, narrowed the rights gap between the married and unmarried. She saw domestic partnerships as an important legal tool to advance equality, one that gay and lesbian activists had successfully passed at the state and local levels. Because domestic partnerships weren't limited to sexual or romantic relationships, Ettelbrick said they were part of "the groundwork for revolutionizing society's views of family." But things did not play out as she'd hoped. Decades after Ettelbrick's proposal, marriage is still the only legal partnership available in most US states, leaving many committed relationships without protection under the law.

In 2004, Massachusetts became the first US state to allow same-sex marriage. After all the legal trouble they faced with their kids, Amelie and Licia wanted the protection of marriage. They drove from Maryland to Provincetown, where they'd just bought a home, and brought their toddlers to the courthouse to file for an expedited marriage certificate. After a justice of the peace married them on the beach, Amelie and Licia had a marriage license to their name, but they weren't equal to straight spouses. As long as the federal government didn't recognize same-sex marriage, many big-ticket benefits such as tax advantages weren't available to them. Maryland didn't grant them rights either, because the state didn't recognize same-sex marriage. Based on the political conversation happening in Maryland, they thought their home state would extend marriage rights to same-sex couples in only a year or two. It ended up taking nearly a decade.

Within that decade, Amelie and Licia's relationship had shifted. Once rooted in romance, it now centered on co-parenting. Amelie moved out, and Licia had a new partner, Tamara. But the law wouldn't let them divorce. Massachusetts required at least one spouse to reside in the state, but Amelie and Licia had kids enrolled in Maryland schools and jobs that bound them there. Maryland didn't acknowledge the marriage in the first place, so they couldn't file for divorce in their home state. Until they divorced, Licia couldn't marry Tamara. They were all in marriage purgatory. Or somehow trapped in the plot of a cruel screwball comedy.

In 2012, about six years after Amelie and Licia's relationship had transitioned into being a queer blended family, a ballot initiative was introduced in Maryland to legalize same-sex marriage. Amelie, along with her close friend Joan Biren, volunteered outside a polling station to answer people's questions and encourage them to vote yes. Voters approved the change, and three months after the law went into effect, Amelie walked into court for her divorce hearing. Though only one spouse was required to show up in court, if both spouses weren't there, a community witness needed to attest that repair between the couple was out of the question. The witness was Joan.

She and Amelie had met about twenty-five years earlier, on the steps of Whitman-Walker when Amelie was running events for Lesbian Health Day, and Joan, a freelance photographer, was there to take photos. Amelie remembers Joan as "a very handsome butch" who had camera equipment slung across her body. Joan was twenty years older than Amelie, but unlike some of the other seasoned activists Amelie had met, Joan seemed to have deep respect for Amelie as an equal. Over a long conversation about lesbian health issues and having lost so many people they loved to AIDS, Amelie sensed that Joan was as interested in her ideas as she was in Joan's. She was right. Joan was immediately impressed by Amelie's smarts and admired the work she was doing. Both women were drawn to knowing more about the other.

Since their first conversation on the Whitman-Walker steps, they saw a lot of each other through organizing. Amelie learned important lessons from Joan, including that it's best to pace yourself if you're playing the long game as an activist. They were part of a group that launched an organization to support lesbians with breast cancer—the same one Amelie and Licia met through. They also worked together on a CDC-funded project to make health care for lesbian and bisexual women more competent and hospitable. Women with these sexual identities weren't going to the doctor as often as other women because they felt excluded or ignored from the moment they read the intake form, which asked them to fill in the name of their husband and indicate whether they were pregnant. Spending nights in a conference room drafting text for brochures isn't most people's idea of fun, but Amelie, Joan, and a third friend who made up "the Dream Team," as they called themselves, felt energized about the work they were doing. During creative collaboration, Joan experiences a special kind of closeness, and she felt that bond with Amelie, who became a trusted sounding board for her. A video Joan made for the project encouraged doctors and nurses to think about how they could include the families of lesbian and bisexual patients in their care—however these patients defined family.

Soon enough, Amelie and Joan saw each other as chosen family. Joan already had known Amelie's partner, Licia, for years. In 2000, Licia found Joan a house to buy on the same block as them. Having two homes extended the space where their family could roam, but that wasn't the only way Joan expanded the family. Aunt Joan, as the kids called her, imparted her love of theater, the arts, and women's basketball by taking them to plays, concerts, and games. A portrait Tova painted of Frida Kahlo now hangs on Joan's living room wall—one of relatively few pieces of art displayed in Joan's uncluttered home.

Joan enriched the family's Jewish life. Amelie had less familiarity with Judaism because she grew up Episcopalian, whereas Joan had designed lesbian feminist Jewish rituals with a group she was part of for thirty years. Together, Amelie and Joan would figure out what to change up that year in their custom Haggadah—the text read during Passover—or decide whether the upcoming celebration for Purim, a holiday in which people wear costumes, should be drag themed. Celebrating Shabbat together every week gave them an opportunity to discuss both day-to-day and spiritual questions.

When the divorce proceedings came around, Joan was Amelie's obvious choice as the witness. Besides her long-standing role as a member of the family, Joan, Amelie says, had been a "huge source of support" throughout the seven years since Amelie's relationship with Licia began changing. Amelie moved out of her shared home with Licia in 2011, and she bought the bungalow next door to Joan's, which she painted mint green with the word *Hope* on the periwinkle front beam. Joan often cared for the kids so that Amelie could work or take part in organizing efforts. She watched after the large mutt named Sadie that Licia had adopted and which ended up under Amelie's care after the separation. When Amelie picked up Sadie from Joan's house, she would often kvetch about her relationship with Licia but asked that Joan not hold it against Licia. The couple may have been breaking up, but they would continue to raise their kids as a family and remain part of their close-knit lesbian community. Amelie felt Joan "held us so lovingly as we went through this hard thing."

On that March day, Amelie and Joan drove to the court together and sat next to each other in the courtroom. The only person on Licia's side was her lawyer, so Joan was called on to assume the duties of a witness.

The whole divorce process felt intrusive and antiquated to Amelie; the state didn't only have ideas about how a marriage should work, like the expectation embedded into tax law that one person would be the primary breadwinner, but also judgments about how a marriage should end. The judge asked Joan, "Is there no chance of reconciliation?" and Amelie silently balked because she took "reconciliation" to be a euphemism for resuming a sexual relationship—according to Maryland law, a separation is only valid if the spouses lived in separate homes without "sexual relations" for twelve months. The question felt paternalistic to her. "I get to have sex with my ex-partner if I want to," Amelie says. "I mean, honestly. Why does the judge of the state of Maryland have to ask that question?" Amelie says that if there's anyone who would understand how uncomfortable that question made her—but also who she could trust to answer it—it was Joan.

Joan told the judge no, Amelie and Licia were not together and that wouldn't change. The judge granted the divorce. Because it took so long for Maryland to extend marriage rights to same-sex couples, Amelie says her marriage was merely a piece of paper; the only thing she got from Maryland's passage of same-sex marriage is the right to get divorced.

———————

Joan was a nineteen-year-old student at Mount Holyoke College when she had her first female lover, and she recalls, "I was beside myself with joy to finally be able to have sexual expression that meant something to me." But pursuing unbridled sexual expression didn't jibe well with being a student at a women's college in the 1960s, a time of housemothers and nighttime fire drills that conveniently doubled as an excuse to confirm that students had been sleeping in their own beds. In her work-study job as a waitress at the dining hall, Joan's housemother would lift Joan's smock and yell at her when she found rolled-up jeans below; this was Joan's way of dealing with the waitress uniform of a skirt. She hated skirts. So fiercely did Joan despise this job that she once started a food fight by throwing the Jell-O fruit dessert they served. "I was breaking a lot of rules, all the time. I was getting caught on some of them," she says. "I just didn't want to get caught on all of them." So, after curfew most nights, Joan would leave her room and literally sneak around in the bushes to get to her lover's dorm, which was on the other side of the campus's lake.

Later, Joan felt she needed to hide her desire for women for a different reason. The child of civil servants and a native Washingtonian, Joan expected to run for Congress one day. A political career was a dream she shared with her first lover, whom she'd met in student government. Joan hadn't been able to picture being a lesbian with the life she wanted "because there were no lesbians living out lives for me to see," she says. After Joan and her lover broke up, Joan took her chance to erase the evidence of their relationship for good, hoping to preserve their shot at a life in politics.

Joan's ex was staying at the Plaza Hotel after graduation and let Joan, who also happened to be in New York, into the hotel room to visit. When her ex went out into the city, Joan was left alone. She had packed everything her ex had written to her, as well as all the "young puppy-love poetry" and letters she had written her ex that were in her possession. Joan tried flushing the papers down the toilet, but that was taking too long, so she switched to burning them. She hadn't considered that smoke would leave the bathroom and creep under the door of the hotel room, attracting the attention of security guards. The guards banged on the door, but Joan, watching the papers burn with tears in her eyes, didn't let them in. "I was very, very romantic and very, very dramatic at that point in my life," Joan says.

After college, she headed to England for graduate school with the twin aims of developing her political credentials and turning herself straight. But burning her lover's letters proved easier than obliterating her desires. In 1970, Joan moved to D.C. and shelved her unsuccessful yearslong attempt at heterosexuality, and with it, her imagined political career. Newly out of the closet, Joan searched for images of lesbians, especially of women kissing. She paged through books and visited the photo collection at the Library of Congress, but she couldn't find depictions of what she thought was genuine connection between women—there were pornographic images and photos taken by men, for men, of women who seemed to be pretending to be lesbians. She decided that if she needed to see images of lesbians, she would have to create them herself. The only camera to her name was a cheap Kodak model she'd gotten as a kid, so she borrowed a 35 mm camera from a friend. With her arm outstretched, Joan turned the camera around and captured her and her lover kissing. The photo tightly frames their faces, which are in profile, and their cheeks swell with contentment. It was a selfie before the term existed, rendered in black-and-white film.

Joan's career as a self-taught photographer of lesbians had begun. She took on the moniker JEB (short for Joan E. Biren) and funded her work through financial support from the lesbian community. "I was the original GoFundMe girl," she says—another way Joan was ahead of her time. In the late 1970s and early '80s, she toured the country presenting a two-and-a-half-hour slideshow more than eighty times. The slideshow featured hundreds of photographs, which, after analyzing them and reading between the lines of the women's biographies, she thought had been taken by lesbians. One reviewer wrote that Joan's slideshow, affectionately known as *The Dyke Show*, exposed her to "images I had never seen before, images I had seen and not perceived. Images on which to build a future."

———

Domestic partnerships, initially embraced by activists like Ettelbrick for being forward-thinking and egalitarian, by the early twenty-first century, were sidelined as a knockoff of marriage. The California State Legislature is one place where the lofty vision got whittled down. In the late 1990s, a domestic partnership bill was up for consideration, and the governor was skittish about the optics—would he be seen as undermining marriage by giving everyone, straight couples included, access to a competing alternative? To assuage the governor, a lawmaker reworked the bill to limit eligibility to same-sex couples and different-sex couples over sixty-two. (Older couples, this lawmaker argued, could lose Social Security and pension benefits from prior marriages if they were compelled to remarry. Besides, with procreation off the table at that age, it made little sense to strong-arm them down the aisle.) Some queer activists weren't fazed by eligibility restrictions like those in California because they thought it was strategic to position domestic partnerships as a stepping stone to same-sex marriage; with this incremental move toward recognition, same-sex couples could eventually get matrimony.

Courts came to regard domestic partnerships as separate and unequal to marriage. In the 2012 case *Perry v. Brown*, the Ninth Circuit ruled that California's ban on same-sex marriage, known as Prop 8, was unconstitutional and wrote, "We are excited to see someone ask, 'Will you marry me?', whether on bended knee in a restaurant or in text splashed across a stadium Jumbotron. Certainly it would not have the same effect to see, 'Will you enter into a registered domestic partnership with me?'" After the Supreme Court's landmark ruling in *Obergefell v. Hodges* in 2015, declaring that same-sex couples have a constitutional right to marry, many states eliminated domestic partnership and civil union laws that had been on the books. In some cases, they automatically converted domestic partnerships to marriages, overlooking the possibility that some couples might not want to be married. Now, only ten states plus Washington, D.C., allow residents to enter some type of nonmarital legal partnership. Domestic partnerships vary so widely across states and localities that many people aren't aware they exist or what benefits they provide. Most Americans, if they want to formalize a relationship, have marriage as a take-it-or-leave-it choice.

The *Obergefell* ruling undeniably broadened popular definitions of family and fostered greater acceptance of LGBTQ Americans. But the Court's opinion simultaneously entrenched the importance of marriage above all other relationships. Both the majority and dissenting justices, despite their divergent opinions on the case, agreed that marriage deserved a hallowed position in the law. Justice Anthony Kennedy, writing for the majority, hailed marriage in soaring language: "No union is more profound than marriage, for it embodies the highest ideals of love, fidelity, devotion, sacrifice, and family." Though his rhetoric was stirring and validating for many same-sex couples—so much so that wedding officiants would go on to quote Kennedy's words with the reverence usually reserved for scripture—it also implicitly belittled relationships that aren't codified as marriage. "Marriage responds to the universal fear that a lonely person might call out only to find no one there," Kennedy wrote. It's the same sentiment you would have heard a half century earlier in the 1964 pop song "Chapel of Love": "Today's the day we'll say 'I do' / And we'll never be lonely anymore," the lyrics go—as if all unmarried people are lonely, and no married people feel lonely.

The same year Amelie moved next door to Joan, Joan's primary care doctor found a lump in her breast. Amelie attended Joan's biopsy and the appointment to hear the biopsy's results. Joan's doctor told her she had stage 2 breast cancer. After the diagnosis, Amelie promised to be with Joan at every single appointment and treatment.

Amelie kept to her word, accompanying Joan for a year's worth of doctor's appointments, chemotherapy treatments, and surgeries. Joan, typically anxious when she met Amelie in the morning to drive to the hospital, came prepared with printouts of information she'd found on the internet and a list of questions for the doctor that she read aloud and discussed with Amelie. By the time they got to the hospital, Amelie says that, despite everything, Joan was cheerful.

When Amelie recalls this pattern, Joan interrupts to explain why her mood shifted. She says, "I was so cheerful because I dumped all my worries on you on the drive."

Joan and Amelie each had ways of making the best of a difficult situation. As if her car were a force field, Joan decided to contain negative energy inside it, and she wanted to make the health care workers' days brighter. On the Tuesday mornings of chemotherapy, Amelie greeted Joan with coffee and oatmeal and dressed "fabulously"; her outfit typically featured fishnets, stylish boots, and clothing in vibrant colors. During the four-hour chemotherapy infusions, she told Joan stories—of her foibles and dating life, keeping the conversation joyful. They'd end the afternoon at a nearby ice cream shop. Joan almost found herself looking forward to her chemo sessions. "It meant I had all those hours to be with Amelie," she says.

Because Joan had written guidelines for health care workers as part of the CDC-funded project, she knew the hospital should let her have the people she wanted around her and insisted that Amelie was going everywhere. When necessary, she challenged the doctors. Because of the women's age difference, hospital staff would ask if Amelie was Joan's daughter. Joan would say no, Amelie was her "sister-neighbor-comrade." The staff assumed she was Joan's sister, and Amelie didn't mind the mistake. First and foremost, she wanted the health care workers to respect her role as caretaker and to consult her about medical decisions. Amelie and Joan faced the trade-off that translators do when they must either select words that have the same literal definition across languages or words that convey the same feeling. Like other friends in this book, as long as Joan and Amelie's relationship didn't fit into a traditional category, they wouldn't have a term that was accurate in both the literal meaning and the connotation. *Sister*, in this setting, was good enough.

Joan says that Amelie's constancy during her cancer treatment was "kind of the huge precursor to our whole relationship, everything about our relationship now"—even more committed and intertwined than before. In 2017, Joan and Amelie traveled to New York to help Joan's friend prepare a museum exhibition of her photographs. The friend, whose work had inspired Joan to become a photographer, was now impoverished. Joan saw similarities to her own life—they both had careers that were deeply fulfilling and poorly paid. Joan says, "If you spent your life as a lesbian photographer—surprise!—you have no retirement fund." Because she made little money in formal employment, she had accrued virtually no Social Security. Joan would see "bag ladies" gathered in downtown D.C. and worry she'd end up alongside them one day.

Amelie was also concerned about Joan's lack of financial security and the psychological strain that came with it. She knew many queer elders were in poverty, whether because they devoted their careers to modestly paid social justice work, like Joan; because their families, disapproving of their sexuality, cut them off from support; or because they faced employment discrimination. Amelie had offered to create a retirement fund for Joan, believing she had more than enough resources to share with her friend. Joan resisted. She thought of self-sufficiency as a "high virtue" and took pride in being able to say she taught herself everything she knew, professionally and otherwise.

During this trip, Joan was starting to feel differently. Sitting on their hotel beds in midtown Manhattan, she told Amelie that she had originally refused her offer of a retirement fund because she was afraid the money would mess up their friendship. But now, she felt their friendship was so secure that the money wouldn't get in the way. Joan says the regular financial help makes an enormous difference to her life. When expenses crop up unexpectedly—like $400 to tow her car because of a flat tire—she's no longer preoccupied with what she needs to eliminate from her budget to make ends meet. After decades of struggling to accept help, Joan has embraced mutuality, which she sees as a healthy midpoint between self-reliance and codependency. And mutual their friendship has been since they met in the '80s, both of them giving and receiving.

In his *Obergefell* decision, Justice Kennedy wrote that marriage offers spouses "the hope of companionship and understanding and assurance that while both still live there will be someone to care for the other." He could have just as well been writing about Joan and Amelie's friendship.

———

As part of the same Prop 8 decision in which judges referred to Jumbotron marriage proposals, they observed, "The designation of 'marriage' . . . is the principal manner in which the State attaches respect and dignity to the highest form of a committed relationship and to the individuals who have entered into it.'" In search of this respect and dignity, some pairs of committed friends have turned to marriage. One woman became TikTok famous after posting videos, some of which have amassed hundreds of thousands of views, in which she explained her "platonic marriage" to her friend. She presented platonic marriage as a reimagining of what marriage can be and who has access to the institution. In 2017, press from across the world picked up the story of a pair of devoted older male friends who took advantage of Ireland's recent legalization of same-sex marriage; the older man owned a small house that the two of them lived in and didn't want his friend to incur a €50,000 inheritance tax to receive it. (The stories about these men, often written in a heartfelt tone, didn't question why marriage was the only way these friends could get access to key legal rights.)

These pairs of friends have repurposed an existing legal structure, a resourceful strategy to get the legitimacy and practical benefits afforded to married couples. But Nancy Polikoff, a law professor at American University—who was part of the biannual meetings of gay and lesbian lawyers dating back to the 1980s—sees platonic marriage as a symptom of our limited legal landscape: "That's what's going to happen if there's only one thing"—marriage—"that has the name that gets this full panoply of rights and recognition."

Friends who opt for wedlock, hoping to remake it in their image, take a gamble. A pair of friends who moved together from Toronto to Berlin, Chiderah Sunny and Deidre Olsen, got married to affirm the importance of their friendship and ran headlong into other people's expectations of marriage. Specifically, others assumed that they would move through the world in unison, be exclusive, and have interwoven identities. If one of them attended a gathering alone, the first question they got was "Where's your wife?" or "How's your wife?" A friend of Chiderah's told her it was inappropriate to post a photo on social media with a person she was dating when she had a wife. Though Chiderah and Deidre explicitly entered marriage for unconventional reasons, the clay had already dried on marriage's meaning; their individual friendship didn't have the power to reset it.

The friends Terry McKeon and Anne Quinn had no interest in the symbolism of marriage but in its practical advantages. Terry, who's a gay man, and Anne, who's a lesbian, used artificial insemination to conceive and had three kids—their firstborn in 1989 and twins a couple of years later. Anne did per diem work while caring for their three young children, so she didn't have health insurance. Anne and Terry considered ways to get her on Terry's health care, maybe by writing up a contract. But marriage was the only viable option—an option they were averse to pursuing after having fought against marital supremacy in their LGBTQ activism.

During their wedding ceremony in a municipal building, Terry hoped the judge wouldn't instruct him to kiss the bride. Anne thought the ceremony was "ridiculous." People say "marriage is this sacred, sacred thing, and yet you can get married in ten minutes," she tells me. "It was like, you paid your money, you got a marriage license."

News of their marriage, which they'd tried to keep quiet, leaked quickly, and their families seemed to stop believing that Anne and Terry were queer. One day, Anne's ninety-nine-year-old grandmother slipped Terry a fifty-dollar bill and said, "I'm glad you took care of that business." Anne ended up in a romantic relationship, and after her partner moved into the house she shared with Terry, Terry and Anne's family finally acknowledged that the two of them weren't a straight couple. Anne and her partner wanted to get married, which meant she and Terry needed to divorce. As Terry sat in divorce court, the judge chastising one cheating or lying husband after another in the large courtroom, Terry was nervous he'd have to reveal that he and Anne had never been romantic partners. He worried the judge would tell him he'd broken the law. The ease of getting married, in contrast to the expense and intrusiveness of getting divorced, convinced Anne that "marriage is really about property." It was also not the ideal legal structure for their friendship.

Chiderah, Deidre, Terry, and Anne were living out an observation by the social critic Michael Warner: "It is always tempting to believe that marrying is simply something that two people do. Marriage, however, is never a private contract between two persons. It always involves the recognition of a third party—and not just a voluntary or neutral recognition, but an enforceable recognition."

Terry said that by forming a family with Anne, "absolutely everything I dreamed of I got" but wishes the state recognized devoted platonic relationships so that marriage wasn't the only avenue for access to important rights.

Other sets of friends never entertain marriage as an option, whether because they oppose the institution or because the connotation of a sexual relationship creates too large of a barrier to entry. When I asked Amelie and Joan if they'd ever considered marriage, Amelie said she was mystified by the question. After delivering a fervent critique of marriage, she said, "I had no interest in joining up an institution that would, again, select that I was the only person who could care for Joan, or Joan could only have access to me and not other people." Barb, from chapter 6, was flummoxed when I merely asked her to compare her half-century-long friendship to a marriage; she certainly never contemplated marrying her friend.

Barb's discomfort reflects the dual nature of legal marriage: it is both a status and a contract. While people might appreciate the benefits built into the contract, the status doesn't fit their relationship—as was the case for Anne and Terry. On the other hand, some people might want the status, but the practical consequences are a net negative for them. This is often true for older Americans. An older adult may not want to intermingle finances with a partner they met decades into their career or have their new spouse usurp their child's role as the designated decision-maker; marriage gives these rights to spouses by default. For some, marriage attaches too many rights to spouses with too little flexibility.

Others have relationships that are incompatible with legal definitions of marriage. Sure, friends could decide to enter a "platonic marriage." But siblings who function as life partners cannot get married and call it a "sibling marriage"; that would count as incest, which US states outlaw. Challenging the law would probably be quixotic, as it was for a pair of British sisters in their eighties who lived together their whole lives. They unsuccessfully petitioned UK and European courts to get the same inheritance tax rights as a married couple. (We are far removed from Bloxham and Whytton's time, when the figurative language of "wedded brotherhood" made sense to people.) Marriage also doesn't help Americans who have a constellation of important people in their lives but not a single partnership. Many types of committed relationships simply don't fit the mold of marriage.

What, then, justifies the bounty of benefits attached to marriage? History offers some explanations. Kerry Abrams, the dean of Duke Law School, explains that through the twentieth century, the public had both an economic and a moral interest in marriage. Essentially, marriage was a microcosmic welfare state, a unit where men and women exchanged not only wedding bands but caregiving and financial support. And as the sole acceptable venue for sex and procreation, both culturally and legally, marriage made sense for the state to encourage; otherwise, society might overflow with adulterers, "fornicators" (the term for people who engaged in the then illegal act of premarital sex), and "illegitimate" children.

In the mid-twentieth century, marital status determined eligibility for a growing slate of public benefits. The assumption was that husbands and wives were interdependent, and the state stepped in to encourage their mutual support or replace it once that support was gone. For instance, by offering widows Social Security benefits, the state effectively filled in for a lost breadwinner. In a society where matrimony was ubiquitous, marital status was an easy way to decide who got public assistance.

But the landscape has drastically changed. Marriage rates have plummeted, particularly among less advantaged socioeconomic classes. Mayeri, the UPenn law professor, writes, "The stakes of marital supremacy are higher than ever as marriage becomes the province of the privileged." That's because the benefits heaped on married couples exacerbate the inequality between people who are married and those who are not.

For some people, inequality between married and unmarried people is a feature, not a bug, of marriage. Rather than adapt the law to reflect the reality of marriage's waning relevance, they'd rather incentivize it.

At a panel I attended in 2023 at the American Enterprise Institute, a conservative think tank, researchers put forward a mix of moral and practical reasons for promoting marriage. The sociologist W. Bradford Wilcox led with an ominously titled presentation, "The Closing of the American Heart"—his term for the steep decline in marriage rates over the last several decades. He said these trends of moving away from marriage were "dark news because . . . we thrive most when we have deep and abiding ties to other human beings, and for most of us, no such ties are as important as those found in hearth and home." Describing marriage as "this most fundamental social institution," Wilcox suggested that marriage's benefits go beyond the individual and radiate outward.

Our laws echo this sentiment. The 1996 act now known as "welfare reform" begins with these words: "The Congress makes the following findings: (1) Marriage is the foundation of a successful society." The law also makes an economic case for boosting marriage, explaining that a key reason for overhauling welfare policy is to "end the dependence of needy parents on government benefits by promoting job preparation, work, and marriage." More marriages mean fewer people on government rolls.

These claims should give us pause. The idea that marriage will solve poverty has historically been fraught with racism; the infamous unmarried "welfare queen" invoked in politics and media was invariably a Black or Latina mother. The implication was that if only these women married—creating a private welfare state of two—they wouldn't be poor, effectively absolving the government from assisting Americans who are economically disadvantaged or of color.

Perhaps above all, advocates of marriage's special status believe marriage is the best environment in which to raise children. Much of the discussion on that AEI panel focused on research that's found that children of married couples fare better in education and employment, and how young people who get married are less likely to end up in poverty.

We should take very seriously the effect marriage might have on children. But understanding how marriage influences kids is a vexing research question. People who marry tend to be better off in the first place than people who do not, and while you can use all manner of statistical methods to account for this discrepancy, we don't have the gold standard for determining causality: we can't randomize who gets married. This is part of the reason there's a fierce debate among researchers about the relative importance of poverty, family structure, and family stability on children's well-being.

Even if you agree with the researchers who conclude that marriage is the optimal setting for children, as Brookings senior fellow Richard V. Reeves has put it, "I just don't see how you put this genie back in the bottle." The government has tried squeezing the genie back in, spending hundreds of millions of dollars from the welfare budget on marriage promotion programs—and studies have found little discernible effect on marriage rates. Today, about 40 percent of children are born to unmarried parents. Melissa Kearney, an economist and author of *The Two-Parent Privilege: How Americans Stopped Getting Married and Started Falling Behind*, told me that she believes "marriage has proven to be a unique institution, in terms of delivering a multitude of benefits, to children especially." But she explained that it makes sense to consider robust legal alternatives to marriage "given how many people are not married, and how difficult it will be to restore the prominence of marriage." "To my mind," she added, "this is especially true where children are involved." An alternative legal structure could offer families some stability that the parents' unmarried status does not.

As important as it is to factor in children's well-being, not every partnership has procreation as its purpose. But legal marriage, and the arguments for its primacy, is built around the interests of families with children. In 1999, California's state legislators recognized that marriage doesn't suit the needs of at least one major portion of the population—older people—when it made domestic partnerships available to different-sex couples ages sixty-two years and above. Then there are people like Amelie and Joan who surely have a "deep and abiding tie" but whose relationship doesn't conform to marriage.

Instead of focusing on the form a relationship takes, many legal scholars suggest looking at the function it serves. Vivian Hamilton, a professor at William & Mary Law School, argues that the state has an interest in two core functions: caregiving and economic support. She asks, "Why should [the government] privilege one form of companionate relationship over others that may serve the same societal functions?" Hamilton says marriage is a "ham-handed" proxy for caregiving and economic dependence and calls on the state to support those functions directly. The courts that ruled in the parental rights cases outlined in chapter 5 used similar reasoning; they determined who a parent was not by the structure of the family but by the role the person played: Did the adult in question act as a parent? It's the legal equivalent of deciding not to judge a book by its cover but by its content.

————————

A half century after Joan took the kissing selfie, her work started to garner more interest than ever before. A photography book she self-published in 1979 was reissued in 2021 and immediately went into a second printing. A museum in Cincinnati presented *The Dyke Show*— the slideshow she'd shared decades earlier in garages and community centers. The Leslie-Lohman Museum in New York City commissioned an installation; enormous prints of Joan's photos filled the museum's eight-foot-tall windows that faced out onto the sidewalks of SoHo. To celebrate the opening of the exhibit, which was set to coincide with Pride weekend in the city, Joan decided to have a party at the museum. She invited more than one hundred friends and relatives from across the country—the kind of convening of loved ones that most adults only get to have at their wedding. During the run-up to the party, Joan and Amelie discussed what term they could use to describe their relationship in a way that others would understand. Joan was increasingly finding herself in situations where she felt it was important for others to grasp who Amelie was to her. A couple of years earlier, Joan was given an honorary doctorate from her alma mater, Mount Holyoke. Joan didn't know how to talk about Amelie to the university's president or the other esteemed guests she met during the ceremonial events. Now, in meetings to select photos and approve mock-ups for the Leslie-Lohman exhibit, museum staff asked who Amelie was.

Joan and Amelie agreed that the term they were using, "sister-neighbor-comrade," was a mouthful. Amelie, ever subversive, took some pleasure in that. "I kind of like how much it really mixes people up. Like they don't know what to make of us," Amelie told Joan. But Joan was tired of seeing confusion waft over people's faces. "I'm a communicator. That's what I do," Joan says. "I was not amused that I wasn't communicating how I felt—the person that Amelie was in my life." Joan had spent fifty years trying to make lesbian relationships visible, but now she had a new challenge: helping people understand another kind of relationship that shaped her life—one that didn't involve sex. She and Amelie decided on the term "non-romantic life partner." They hoped including the word *life* would give the label the gravitas that was missing from the other options they had considered, to have it measure closer to "spouse."

At the museum party, Joan stood on a square platform to give a speech, microphone in hand and a gold lei resting over her loose Hawaiian shirt. She gave a heads-up to the attendees, a mix of museum staff and loved ones: "I am the crying kind of butch lesbian, so if I get choked up, I don't care." One by one, Joan lavished praise on museum staff members who worked on the installation with her. Then she looked at Amelie in the audience, tilted her head, and said, "Come on, Amelie." People cheered as Amelie stepped onto the platform. Joan explained how much she appreciated Amelie, and Amelie held her hands behind her back, an unassuming posture that contrasted with her black patterned tights, undercut hairstyle, and tank top emblazoned with the face of the trans rights activist Sylvia Rivera. Joan described how Amelie "inspires me to live up to my convictions" and holds her hand or gives her great hugs "when I'm elated or dejected or freaked out—which, of course, never happens," she said, and the audience erupted in a collective knowing laugh. Joan announced, "We have a non-romantic life partnership." Some people in the crowd went, "Mmm," one person said, "Hear, hear," and then the group broke into applause. Amelie felt Joan's remarks were a "beautiful acknowledgment" of their relationship. After the speech, friends told Joan they thought "non-romantic life partners" was a good way to put it. Since then, they soured on the description "non-romantic" because it defines the relationship by what's absent, and, besides, like Stacey in chapter 3, they see elements of romance in their friendship. They've opted for the term "friendship love."

Apt language, but not labels the law recognizes.

Friends who don't want to or aren't entitled to marry have two options: live without legal rights or fashion a DIY solution. Joan chose the latter. She found a lawyer, Michele Zavos, who prides herself on devising creative legal solutions for people who can't get married or aren't married. For forty years, she's specialized in providing legal protection to LGBTQ and unmarried clients.

During the summer of 2021, deep into the COVID pandemic, a half dozen people convened on the porch of Michele's house for the occasion of signing Joan's will. Seventy-seven-year-old Joan, Michele, two witnesses, a notary public, and Amelie, who was set to become the executor of Joan's will, sat six feet apart from one another at foldable TV tables. With bins to designate dirty and clean pens and masks covering the lower half of their faces, they passed documents around and around. *Initial here. Sign here.* Joan says, "I thought it was some kind of slapstick movie because the documents just kept coming."

This relentless roundabout of paperwork was the culmination of months of discussion Joan had with Amelie and other loved ones in their community about end-of-life questions: When Joan says she would rather have the plug pulled on her than become a "vegetable," what does that mean for the purposes of her advance directive? How much memory loss did she need to have for it to count as dementia? These detailed conversations that foregrounded Joan's mortality weren't easy, but Joan felt relief afterward, as did Amelie. Joan had articulated exactly what she wanted and feared; decisions for her wouldn't be made by default or without her consent, as Amelie had seen happen when she'd been with many AIDS and cancer patients as they died. Joan's discussions resulted in more than a dozen pages' worth of legal documents and cost thousands of dollars.

Though their friendship is grounded in mutual support, their legal paperwork isn't reciprocal. Amelie's will doesn't name Joan. Because she's twenty years younger than her friend, Amelie expects to outlive Joan; Amelie's brother is currently tasked with making decisions related to her health and money—though if anything were to go wrong for Amelie while Joan was alive, Joan would work with Amelie's brother to make decisions. Amelie says that it would seem natural for them to both include each other in their wills "to validate the relationship, but it doesn't make practical sense."

Bespoke contracts provide rights on paper but, without the status to go with them, are unlikely to affect other people's perception of a relationship; you don't typically introduce someone at a party as "the executor of my estate" or "the person who holds my legal power of attorney." Barb and Inez, who have lived together in the Hermitage for more than two decades and been friends for more than fifty years, discovered the consequences of this disconnect between formal rights and social meaning. In 2020, Inez had a hernia and as the EMTs loaded her into the ambulance, the driver warned Barb that she might not be allowed to see Inez in the hospital. Barb followed the ambulance anyway. Outside the hospital, a nurse asked if she was a relative. Barb said, "No, a friend," and the nurse told her to come back in thirty minutes. While Barb sat in her frigid car on that February day, she watched a man and a woman who appeared to be spouses get screened by the same staff and enter the hospital together. When Barb returned after a half hour, the hospital staff member asked if Inez had designated someone with medical power of attorney rights. Barb said she had those rights and was brought inside. In the end, the legal rights the friends had lined up protected them.

But there's a less sanguine interpretation of what happened. Yes, the law ensured that Barb was ultimately able to be with Inez—at least for some part of the hospital visit—but it didn't spare her the indignity of being literally left out in the cold, treated as inessential to Inez's life, and isolated from her ailing friend when she could have been by her bedside. Kaipo Matsumura, a professor at Loyola Law School, told me what Barb faced is "the burden of always traveling with a piece of paper that identifies your status" lest your rights not be believed. It's a burden that married people don't face.

Friends can explicitly ask for recognition, as Joan did from her community during the museum party, but there's no guarantee people will grant it. Apart from declaring Amelie her "non-romantic life partner," Joan specifically requested that any invitation to her also be extended to Amelie, a gesture that touched Amelie. Nevertheless, Joan had to keep reminding people to include Amelie as her plus-one when they sent invitations for backyard barbecues and birthdays. Since same-sex marriage became legal and same-sex spouses have become assumed plus-ones, Joan says "it's a little worse" that her friendship with Amelie is overlooked. "Now that the state approves of [same-sex marriage]— and I hope it will continue to do so—then it becomes harder for the people who don't have the government stamp of approval to assert what their relationship is," Joan says. She had tried to convey the weight of their friendship in her speech, but "that doesn't mean it lands forever in a way that [it does] if you have a huge party and wedding celebration." Joan says, after a wedding, "people don't tend to forget to invite your spouse."

There are two main approaches for reducing the current inequities between marital and nonmarital relationships: create a legal alternative to marriage and strip marriage down to its essentials.

Polikoff, the law professor and advocate, suggests a simple way to provide legal protection to nonmarital relationships: create a registry to designate a default decision-maker, much like an emergency contact form. When people get a license or register to vote, they could mark down their designated person.

A more elaborate but flexible solution could involve using a little-known Colorado law as a template for states across the country. In the late 2000s, Colorado state senator Pat Steadman wanted to design a legal structure that was more customizable than marriage and which extended rights to any two adults, regardless of the kind of relationship they had. Steadman said, "We didn't want the designated beneficiary law to make the same discriminatory choices as the marriage code." Beginning in 2009, Coloradans have been able to register for a designated beneficiary agreement by filling out a two-page form that lists rights in sixteen categories, mostly related to health and finances. Unlike marriage, the designated beneficiary agreement uses an à la carte model; the two people can choose to grant or withhold each of the rights, and rights don't have to be assigned reciprocally. If a father and son were to register, the father could make his son his health care proxy, but the son doesn't have to designate the father. It's simple and inexpensive, covering many of the core rights that are part of a costly estate-planning process. (In contrast, the remaining domestic partnership laws in the

United States tend to offer few rights; Joan's lawyer couldn't recall ever recommending Maryland's domestic partnership law to clients because she believed it offered too little to be worth it). There are advantages to getting a lawyer's expertise to draw up legal documents and, with it, a prompt to have hard conversations with loved ones, as Joan did. But Colorado legislators knew that many people don't or can't afford to do so and, as a result, may end up with someone they wouldn't have chosen making serious medical or end-of-life decisions on their behalf. Amelie and Joan know this, too—they emphasized to me that they have financial and educational privilege that allows them to access solutions that most people can't. The designated beneficiary agreement at least encourages people to think through each of the sixteen rights rather than sign up for the Costco-size rights bundle that comes with marriage. The law strikes a balance between intentionality and accessibility.*

Several legal scholars suggest allowing more than two people to enter into this agreement. A few city-level domestic partnership ordinances already have this feature, and this structure could serve people like Andrew and Toly, the physicist friends, who have both a platonic partner and a romantic partner. Joan has talked to people who would, for instance, prefer that their best friend rather than their spouse make certain health decisions on their behalf. In marriages, Joan says, "the two partners are not always the best to do all the things that they're expected to do and forced to do legally." For administrative ease, the

---

* There are compelling cases for the abolition of state marriage, for instance, as the philosopher Clare Chambers argues in her book *Against Marriage*. However, Chambers admits that she doesn't address the political viability of the changes she suggests; it's an argument built on logic and ethics. I instead propose reforms that scholars I've spoken to see as a vast improvement on the status quo and in the realm of possibility.

state would probably need to set some limit on the number of people given rights, but it's not clear that one person needs to be the maximum. Already, those with the know-how and means can spread rights across multiple people in a will, as Joan did. (Joan doesn't believe you should ask one person to fulfill all your needs while you're alive, so, she asks, "Why should you have one person who's supposed to fill all the needs when you die?") A simple agreement like a designated beneficiary agreement that enables people to register more than one person would just make it more accessible to do so.

A legal alternative to marriage that carried important rights would likely tap into a significant, unmet need, including for couples in romantic relationships. California offers a preview because of what happened when it lifted restrictions on who could enter domestic partnerships—first, in 2002, opening up domestic partnerships to different-sex couples in which only one partner was over sixty-two, and then in 2020, allowing different-sex couples of any age. After each change, the number of people who filed for domestic partnerships spiked. Straight couples were among them. Capital Public Radio interviewed couples, including Kristy Snyder and Michael Halverson, who opted for a domestic partnership because they didn't like the roles they'd slipped into as husband and wife in their previous marriages. "Now I had this expectation, I'm a wife and it's supposed to be this certain way and I'm supposed to do a certain thing," Snyder said. "And I spoke to a lot of women that felt like they lost their identity when they got married." A legal partnership unburdened with marriage's calcified cultural meaning worked for them. Couples' use of prenuptial agreements—often entered into by those who have family fortunes to safeguard, and which can cost thousands of dollars to draw up—also shows that the off-the-rack version of marriage doesn't work for everyone. A legal structure like the designated beneficiary agreement could make it easy and cheap for people to pick and choose which parts make sense to them.

France's registered partnership, PACS, is nearly as popular as marriage. In 2019, about 196,000 PACS were registered, compared to 225,000 marriages. This marriage alternative appeals to people who want official recognition as partners, but who don't feel ready for marriage, object to marriage in principle, don't want to be financially intertwined, or don't want to risk a lengthy divorce process. Having been introduced nationally, PACS is a well-known option in France, unlike American domestic partnership laws that operate on the state or local level. If something like the Colorado-style designated beneficiary agreement were to exist, a national campaign that used the same template across states could ensure that Americans know it's available.

Along with creating a legal alternative to marriage, the institution could get the Marie Kondo treatment, retaining only what's necessary. Marital status determines whether Americans are eligible for an enormous range of benefits, and Polikoff suggests running an inventory. She says, "Ideally, I would take every single law that makes marriage the dividing line between who's in and who's out of the law, ask the question: Why does this law exist? What is its purpose? What is it trying to accomplish?" Then she would adjust the law so it achieves its purpose without using marriage as the deciding factor. "And you can do that for every single law," she says.

Polikoff rattled off a long list of relevant areas of the law, including zoning, rent control, taxes, house deeds, decisions about medical care and burial, and inheritance. Take workers' compensation survivor benefits, in which a state provides payment to a surviving spouse of someone who died on the job. Polikoff identifies the underlying purpose of the law: to compensate someone who was financially dependent on or interdependent with the wage earner. It therefore makes sense to base eligibility not on marriage but on dependency, which is exactly what some states, like California, have done. This more precise filter does a better job of satisfying the purpose of the law than marital status does. Paring down the benefits attached to marriage could temper the current extreme: spouses who are flush with benefits on the one hand and, on the other, unmarried people who enjoy neither societal standing nor legal protection.

By giving rights to nonmarital relationships, the state could bolster their stability and offer people greater freedom in their private lives. In his *Obergefell* decision, Justice Kennedy links marriage to autonomy and liberty, but Matsumura, the law professor, says, "If we accept that autonomy and self-definition is an important part of what the law's protecting through marriage, then giving [marriage] as the only option to people who don't see their relationships that way is denying them that valuable aspect of the law." More options would enable people to explore a wider set of possibilities for their lives. Nancy Cott, a history professor at Harvard University, writes in her book *Public Vows: A History of Marriage and the Nation* that the legal institution of marriage defines "the realm of cognitive possibility for individuals." Extending legal rights beyond a monogamous, conjugal relationship could make it easier for people to imagine finding companionship in other types of relationships. This expansion of possibilities could especially benefit Americans who aren't married or living with a romantic partner and who constitute nearly 40 percent of Americans ages twenty-five to fifty-four.

American law is an outdated map of the real-life landscape of relationships. We live in a time when sex doesn't have to lead to procreation, procreation can happen without sex, and marriage is far less pervasive and permanent than it used to be. Amid all this change, the solutions still have decades-old dust on them, waiting to be cleared off. They are part of the same approach Ettelbrick wrote about in 1989, and which Amelie, Joan, and countless others advocated for. If the law broadened its attention beyond marriage, it would, at last, validate the range of relationships that are the cornerstones of Americans' lives.

EPILOGUE

It's a narrative trope to conclude with a wedding. In movies, when newlyweds drive off in their car, we glimpse them from behind as they speed toward the horizon with their "Just Married" sign slung across the rear, signaling their passage into a world full of promise.

This book instead began with weddings and questioned what they do for us: how, as long as they remain the singular happy ending, they can just as easily close off our worlds as open them up. The expectations of modern romance risk narrowing the scope of our imaginations, making us believe that romantic relationships are our sole legitimate option, that we must find everything we need in one person, leaving little room to picture others as potential significant others.

But romantic relationships are not the only unions that can shape our lives. Much like spouses, the friends featured in this book act as a unit. They share money, homes, and a private language of shorthand.

They take care of each other without hesitation, relish each other's brightest moments, and commemorate their friendship. They transform each other: Kami gained the confidence to expect more of a romantic partner and her life; Nick learned to parse his feelings and what mattered to him; Joan realized it was okay to depend on other people. These friends are each other's invariables.

To a question posed in the novel *A Little Life*—"But how was one to be an adult? Was couplehood truly the only appropriate option?"—these friendships offer an emphatic answer: absolutely not. They point toward a society that doesn't encourage a monoculture of monogamous romantic partnerships but instead recognizes a variety of profound connections. In this society, where people could lean on many types of relationships, a romantic partner and nuclear family wouldn't have to be the sole reprieves from American individualism.

Like most one-size-fits-all items, the single model of romantic coupledom does not accommodate large numbers of people, who can't find or don't want a one-stop-shopping romantic relationship. And as long as we have only one option, we aren't freely choosing romantic coupling. Even if everyone coupled up, marriage would not be the cure-all for America's loneliness epidemic. We need other forms of close connection, too.

To get past the idea that a long-term romantic relationship is the fulcrum of a full life, it helps to recognize a larger truth. As Kieran Setiya, a philosophy professor at MIT, writes in his book *Life Is Hard*, "When something has value, that doesn't mean we should or must engage with it." He adds that a well-lived life is inherently limited: "It has good things in it, but the many it must omit don't necessarily make it worse." We cannot simultaneously spend our days scuba diving in Costa Rica, live next door to our nieces and nephews in Tennessee, become a performer of Beyoncé-level acclaim, and be a groundbreaking mathematician. All are worthwhile pursuits, but the absence of any of them doesn't lessen life's richness. While we can acknowledge that, for plenty of people, romantic partnership is meaningful, it doesn't follow that a life without this type of relationship is, by definition, deficient. There is an abundance of ways to live well.

People who have fulfilling romantic partnerships would still benefit from more models of deep relationships. That's because our adult lives are not one continuous scene; they're extended stories with unpredictable turning points. You can be like Inez, married and raising two kids in the suburbs by age twenty-five, and eventually decide that you need to make a new life for the sake of yourself and your children. You can discover your sexuality as an adult and realize that conventional relationships are stifling or incompatible with your desires. You can become a parent and be overjoyed for extra support, or you can find yourself so smitten with your friend's newborn that you'll wake up at dawn just to get the chance to gaze into the baby's eyes. Maybe you'll be mesmerized by someone standing across the room at a bar and, soon enough, learn that there are more forms of love than you'd been told about. One model of a fulfilling adulthood is not enough to accommodate the scene and character changes in the long drama of our lives.

———

There is freedom in the unfamiliar, when the kind of relationship you have exists outside of well-worn categories. Most of the friends I talked to reveled in how unclassifiable their relationship was, speaking of their connection in terms that were practically spiritual. Joy, from chapter 7, doesn't believe in soulmates when it comes to romantic relationships but believes Hannah was a soulmate of a different kind. Oprah Winfrey said about her best friend, Gayle King, "Something about this relationship feels otherworldly to me, like it was designed by a power and a hand greater than my own." A woman who'd read my article about platonic partnerships, Valentina Espana, surrenders to the mystery of her friendship, which she and her friend refer to as "THE FRIEND-SHIP." She wrote, "Understanding this relationship is like reading a recipe and expecting to taste the food. Not even we understand how or why it works how it does."

Because friendships don't have a prewritten script to follow, friends must decide everything for themselves. Despite the time and work involved, Stacey, from chapter 3, values this aspect of their friendship. They feel more confident in the future of their partnership with Grace because, they say, "we've been our own narrators" of it. Stacey and Grace's commitment spurs conversation; it doesn't suggest everything can go unsaid and unasked for—a contrast to romantic partners who can conveniently glide up the "relationship escalator." The escalator's predictable path—from dating to becoming exclusive to moving in together—can make partners feel securer as they navigate their relationship. But it can also encourage partners to take each other's beliefs for granted—sometimes to tragic effect. A couple's therapist recounted to me how a monogamous couple discovered during their therapy session that they had different definitions of monogamy. To the woman, going to a strip club or watching pornography constituted cheating. Her partner revealed that he had done both of those things, unwittingly crossing her line. The woman broke up with him on the spot. The preset template of an exclusive romantic relationship meant they had never discussed their boundaries explicitly, giving them the illusion that they were on the same page.

Platonic partnerships and conventional romantic relationships diverge in another key way: platonic partners tend to be deliberate about keeping their friendship from becoming too encompassing. Art, the former youth pastor from chapter 4, warned viewers of his webinar, "If we're not careful, we do to friendship what other people do to romance: we idolize it, and we expect it to fill all our needs." I often interviewed a pair of friends only to learn that there's a third friend who is just as important or that the pair is embedded in a group of friends. Amelie emphasized her community because she didn't want me to imply that she and Joan were all that mattered in each other's lives, replacing one kind of privileged dyad with another. The fact that Amelie's kids aren't the only ones who consider Joan an auntie or grandma "diffuses the dyad stuff," Amelie says, but "it's not diffusing how important Joan is to me. That Joan has other kiddos that are beloved, as well as my kiddos, just feels like it's all value-added, and we're all creating this intentional quilt of connection."

Just because people put deep thought into these friendships doesn't mean they escape all friction and harmful dynamics. When a friend who's a clinical psychologist read a draft of a chapter of this book, she commented that a set of friends I wrote about seemed to have an avoidant-anxious attachment pairing, which she'd been taught to detect in couples. Just like personal and professional relationships of all kinds, these friendships can have power imbalances, uneven commitment, and unhealthy enmeshment.

One difference is, when things aren't going well in platonic partnerships, there's not much help to be had. People who need guidance for a friendship don't have the wealth of books and resources that are available for romantic relationships. Good luck finding someone who specializes in friend therapy. (A few years ago, my colleagues at NPR's *Invisibilia* doggedly searched for such a therapist, to no avail.) A friend in mourning will have to console himself with songs about romantic love, as the *New Yorker* music critic Hua Hsu did after his close friend was murdered; music about friendship was scarce and didn't speak to the magnitude of his grief. It can feel like a blessing to land in the supportive embrace of a platonic partnership. But the costs include being exiled from the realm of popular comprehension and being forced to come up with your own solutions to challenges. Not to mention, if you want to stay in the hospital to care for your friend or have legal rights to a child you're raising as your own, recognition and protection are absent when they matter most.

To honor these friendships and other life-defining relationships, compulsory coupledom would need to fade—including in the law. We could get there by reforming the law from two directions: breaking up marriage's monopoly on legally recognized relationships and unbundling the many rights attached to marriage. A legal alternative to marriage would give important protections to people whose relationships don't fit into the confines of wedlock.

Laws that focus on the function rather than the form of a relationship could equalize the rights of married and unmarried people. Elected officials could repeal zoning laws that create obstacles to unrelated people living together. Legal recognition of more than two parents and bans against discrimination on the basis of family structure could protect a wider range of loving families whereas now, people in unconventional relationships live in danger of losing child custody, their jobs, and more. Workplace and government policies could expand eligibility for family and bereavement leave so that people like Joy could take the necessary time to mourn.

There's precedent for these reforms. Legal alternatives to marriage are scattered across US states and municipalities; statutes in several US states already allow a child to have more than two legal parents; and courts have recognized multiparent households, in a quieter way, for decades. In 2023, Somerville, Massachusetts, passed the first non-discrimination ordinance that explicitly protects nonnuclear families. Outside the United States, national-level changes have already been underway. In 2022, Sweden's Supreme Court ruled that a pair of friends who lived together on a farm counted as a couple for the purposes of the Cohabitation Act, making the friend eligible to receive a $30,000 insurance policy following her friend's death. (The parents of the woman who died had unsuccessfully argued that the two women shouldn't be considered a couple because they didn't have a sexual relationship.) The legal status of an "Adult Interdependent Relationship" in the Canadian province of Alberta allows two people, including relatives and friends, who function as an "economic and domestic unit" to have rights that are similar to marriage. At the time that I turned in the manuscript, Germany's Federal Ministry of Justice was working on a family law reform that could afford friends similar rights to married couples.

Legal changes could drive cultural shifts—perhaps, to prevent the kind of situation Barb faced, in which she had paperwork with official protections but was kept out by the hospital staff because her friendship with Inez was unintelligible to them. Right now, a feedback loop between the law and culture keeps friendships down: the invisibility of friendship in the law perpetuates the idea that friendships are less valuable than romantic relationships, which then justifies the absence of legal protection for friendships. Laws that acknowledge the potential for friendship to be devoted could interrupt this cycle.

But the law won't change cultural norms on its own. We'd need movies and TV shows and books that are driven by a platonic—not romantic—plot, like on *Insecure* and *Broad City* and *Booksmart*, whose protagonists are inseparable friends. We'd need music that celebrates and aches about platonic love. It also wouldn't hurt if our culture encouraged us to build skills to discern and communicate to others what we want—a change that could benefit relationships of all kinds.

Cultural representations of devoted friendships have the power to alter people's conception of platonic love. A professor who researched a romantic friendship between two women in the nineteenth century told me that, having been married for twenty years, she's missed the spark of new connection with people. The only kind of relationship available to a married person that had previously occurred to her was an affair. She has no interest in that kind of spark. Having learned that friendship once stretched far beyond our contemporary definition, this professor now knows that platonic relationships can offer the flash of excitement and depth of connection she craves. It energizes her to think about the people she will meet and what those friendships can become.

Many of the people I interviewed decided to go on the record about their intimate lives for a simple reason: "I'm interested in making sure that other people feel like there are other models and other ways to live their lives," Amelie told me. "Something other people can create for themselves." Joan said that living in a different way "has to be seen for other people to know about it, to want it, to fight for it with us, to change the way it is." As she said this, I thought of the title of her 2019 photography installation in New York: *Being Seen Makes a Movement Possible.* Joan says she and Amelie are trying to show "a vision for a different future." These friends are emissaries from the world as it could be.

The expectations we have for different kinds of relationships can affect our behavior, which, in turn, affects the shape that those relationships take. We know it's possible for someone to vault, in a matter of months, from being a stranger who sends us flirtatious emojis on a dating app to the first person we want to hold us when our eyes are swollen from crying. Though it may sound too dramatic to admit to, on a first date, many of us are tacitly evaluating whether we could fall in love with the person sitting across from us or imagine building a life with them.

But when we're getting to know a new friend, we're not taught to extrapolate to a shared future. We're also not taught to expose as much of ourselves as we do in romantic relationships. Art has found that people don't let friends see them in their less neat states. Suburban middle-class people, he says, "we love a manicured lawn—emotionally and otherwise. The house is a mess, but the lawn is really manicured, and no one's going to come over until the house is cleaned up . . . And that's fine until we realize that what that means is that no one can ever just show up and just live life with us because we have to clean before anyone comes over." He thinks that, by hiding the messier parts of our lives from friends, we limit our ability to develop intimacy with them. Whereas it's considered normal to have conversations with a romantic partner about how the relationship is going and what each person wants from it, in friendships, many of us operate according to the same principle that Nick heard as a kid: "If you're talking about your friendship, you're trying too hard." We don't always notice this cause and effect, though—how our behavior feeds an intimacy gap between romantic and platonic relationships. If we feel emotional distance in friendships, we may attribute those feelings to the limitations of friendship rather than ask whether our expectations got in the way.

We can create the conditions for intimacy by allowing friendships to take up more room in our lives. Platonic partnerships show that there's little a friend cannot do. These friendships can also help us to spot which relationships have potential to grow. Like the professor whose encounter with centuries-old romantic friendships made her realize she could invest more in friendships, Art's friendship with Nick made him reflect on the other platonic relationships in his life. Before he met Nick, he didn't feel like he had the freedom to ask what he wanted from friendships. Having touched friendship's edge with Nick, Art says he's learned to look at the people in his life and "to imagine, what is the fullest version of this friendship?"

The fullest version doesn't necessarily mean a friendship as intense as his and Nick's. Not every set of people has the compatibility or space for such an involved relationship; Nick adds that "trying to copy and paste" what he and Art have onto their other friendships is unlikely to work well. But there are still opportunities for deeper connection, as Art found when he suggested to a couple he's friends with that they co-work. Their weekly co-working sessions have made Art more productive and strengthened their friendship. He's around these friends enough to witness them argue or be handed their baby while they resolve an issue in another room. "We end up sharing a lot of life side by side," Art says, messiness and all.

When M and I lived a five-minute walk from each other, our friendship accelerated and intensified because it was so easy to live life side by side. We could spend an evening on opposite ends of M's couch, legs stretched toward each other and noses buried in our own books, and it wouldn't feel like we had wasted each other's company. The casual time we spent together acquainted me with M's everyday behaviors that, once known, added up to intimacy: how she heats water for sixty to ninety seconds (the duration depends on the microwave) to get it to her preferred temperature. How M moves each hand in the opposite direction—one hand clockwise, one hand counterclockwise—when she rubs shea butter into her hair. How, when we spot a rat skittering by us during a nighttime walk in D.C., she'll trill, *Rat-tat-tat-tat-tat-tat!* As neighbors, we quickly devoured what psychology professor Lisa Diamond calls the three "magic ingredients" of attachment: time, togetherness, and touch. We hadn't planned on becoming so close—I would have had trouble even imagining a friendship like ours—but because we lived in such proximity, we had license to ignore whatever norms usually limit friendship. Like Art, my friendship with M made me wonder about what my other friendships could become.

———————

The first bullet point in the email from two friends, whom I'll call Naomi and Daniel, read that living with my husband and me "would be quite the dream." The subsequent bullet points listed reasons they thought we wouldn't want to live with them: they observe Shabbat, keep kosher, have a baby, and will hopefully have more in the coming years. Inconveniences for us, surely, as a child-free and secular couple. The idea of sharing a home had come up earlier that week, when Marco and I had dinner with Naomi and Daniel over Zoom. As we caught them up on what had been going on in our lives over the last few months, Marco and I mentioned that we'd talked to two friends about the possibility of buying a house together. We were drawn to the vibrancy of being surrounded by friends, and when we eventually had a kid, we wanted a home setup that prevented family life from feeling hermetic.

After Marco described the conversation we had with the other couple, I added that we'd of course love that sort of arrangement with Naomi and Daniel if they were ever interested. But I didn't expect them to seriously consider the idea. It would be an unusual way for a religiously observant young family to live. And even though we were close enough to Naomi that she officiated our wedding, she and Daniel weren't our closest friends. Marco and I had joked that they were out of our league as friends, beloved by too many for the two of us to be the chosen ones in their lives.

Apparently, they didn't think so. They daydreamed with us on the Zoom call about how we could create a mini urban kibbutz—the Hebrew term for a communal settlement. Marco was unfazed by the list of downsides Naomi and Daniel itemized in the follow-up email they sent us, subject line: "Kibbutz D.C." Marco replied, "Shabbat with many babies, MY DREAM! \:D/" (If the all-caps didn't adequately convey his enthusiasm, Marco's signature grinning emoticon was sure to.) By living with Naomi and Daniel, we thought we'd get more than friends as housemates; we'd get a different way of life—a life with the door open to guests and a clock that forced us to pause our work- and technology-oriented lives for Jewish holidays.

Because Naomi and Daniel were going to move from Massachusetts to D.C. in just a few months, we realized we wouldn't have enough time to make the arrangements that were necessary to buy a home, especially because our situation would be complicated. We didn't expect real estate agents or banks to have much experience evaluating a mortgage application for two couples, and we'd need to write up a contract to ensure we had a plan to sell or exit the shared home. We turned to the idea of renting. On a hike, Marco and I talked about this option, and I explained that as excited as I was to live with our friends, I had financial concerns. The one-bedroom apartment Marco and I lived in was a bargain. If we moved into a larger space with Naomi and Daniel, our rent would increase, and we'd fall behind on our goal of saving for a down payment. Marco didn't contest those facts but instead questioned the importance of them. He asked me how much we cared about buying a home soon. Was it just a default next step? He pointed out how special an opportunity this was, to live with these particular friends at this stage of their child's life.

That Marco had to say all this made me shrink. I had spent years thinking about the significance of friendship and interviewing people who built their lives around friends. I may have gotten past compulsory coupledom (I would later brush off my mom's remark about the co-living setup: "Is Marco not enough?"). But I hadn't escaped all societal programming; my instinct was to prioritize financial gain over friendship. I had absorbed the idea that it's worth making sacrifices to pursue a career and nurture certain relationships—romantic partners, parents, children—but I'd left friends off that list. And this wasn't a particularly big sacrifice because Marco and I didn't have a strong desire to own a home.

As Marco and I roamed through the woods, we decided that what mattered most to us was community. Naming that value clarified my decision. It's easy to see the downsides of an unconventional choice like this—from the financial costs of delaying homeownership to the extra work of strategizing in a Google doc about how to fit four people's furniture into a house. It can be harder to notice the drawbacks of going down a standard route, like the relative isolation Marco and I would have felt if we continued living without anyone else or how much work it would have taken for just two people to manage an entire home. Whatever might come in our shared house, I understood the drawbacks as one side of a trade-off that I had entered into deliberately. Kibbutz D.C. was a go.

Together, the four of us rode the waves of anticipation and disappointment of D.C.'s tight housing market. One owner declined to even show us his apartment because he didn't think it was suitable for "two families." Through her compulsive Craigslist refreshing, Naomi found an ideally located row house that was out of our price range, but she persuaded the owner to decrease the rent by more than 10 percent. When we moved into the house months later, in the summer of 2021, I discovered Naomi was the Tasmanian Devil in reverse—instead of tearing a path of destruction, she whipped through the house solving problems. Within two weeks, she'd had all the art hung on the walls, completed the babyproofing, and gotten the landlord to resolve the many malfunctions in our century-old house.

Over Shabbat lunch one Saturday, we discussed answers to a set of questions Marco had sent us, modeled off premarital counseling he and I had done with a rabbi. He included a "premortem" question— the opposite of a postmortem; we'd try to imagine a scenario in which we'd decided to disband the house after a year and then predict what the likely causes were. That way, we might be able to avoid those risks. Hearing all of us utter our concerns and acknowledge that our living arrangement was potentially fragile, instead of making it feel doomed, brought me closer to Naomi and Daniel.

Living with Naomi, Daniel, and their one-year-old son, who I'll call Yonah, immediately varied the tune of what would have otherwise been a one-note pandemic life. Empty cardboard boxes became vehicles to speed through the living room, with Yonah as the giggling passenger. I came to associate Saturday nights with the smell of cinnamon and blaze of a braided candle to mark the end of Shabbat, followed by the ritual we quickly established of snaking through the house in a conga line while singing the song "Shavua Tov." When Yonah learned to talk, our names (adjusted for toddler-speaking capabilities) were among the first words he learned: "Coco" for my husband and "Nana" for me. During our mothers' respective visits, he called them "Coco-mama" and "Mamanana," and I felt our household stretch.

Before living with Naomi and Daniel, I had held them up on a pedestal—a position of admiration but also, by definition, a distancing one. I stood somewhat in awe of Naomi's wise and nearly regal presence, only enhanced by her blended German/British/American accent and expertise in philosophy. Daniel's knowledge, from bird cognition to Mormon history, is encyclopedic and his intellectual judgment exacting; he'll ditch a book within ten pages if he's not impressed. (I've joked that my goal is to get him to read past the first ten pages of my book.)

Since we became housemates, my admiration for Naomi and Daniel, if anything, has grown. From our living room, I've watched Daniel hinge his torso like a rag doll and look between his legs at Yonah, whose dimples then burst from his cheeks. I've seen how Naomi's eyes glow with intrigue when a conversation touches on death, the subject of the legal project she's devoted herself to for months. They've floored me with their thoughtfulness; they gave a gift to Marco and me as a thank-you for caring for Yonah while they were in the hospital for the birth of their second child. (Our loot included coconut-printed socks for Marco, a.k.a. Coco, and a shirt for me that read #NANALIFE.) When did they find time to assemble this gift? Scouring the internet for presents, Naomi said, turned out to be "the perfect activity for early contractions."

And yet the space between my housemates and me has narrowed because I've witnessed their marriage in the mundane but intimate ways that we're rarely privy to for relationships other than our own. I learned that their term of endearment for each other, "gorge," is a shortened version of "gorgeous" (not the geologic feature, as I'd thought when I first heard it). I sensed tension in a disagreement between them over the seemingly trivial decision about whether to use expired, off-brand antibacterial cream on my cut finger. I had observed their relationship well enough to guess that the cream was a proxy for longer-standing differences in opinion about vigilance over health and frugality. My lesser angels and eccentricities, too, have been on full display for Naomi and Daniel: how I can snipe at my family, how I took over Marco's desk because mine had become a nest of papers and books, how I'll save, as Daniel once put it, "one-fiftieth of a banana." A few years ago, Naomi and Daniel had been sketches to me, and I to them. Now, we have detailed portraits.

———

On one of the last nights he'd spend in his D.C. apartment, my friend Adam invited Marco and me over for dinner. This is the same person who'd asked me what the difference was between my connections with M and Marco. With a spread of soul food takeout in the center of the table, the three of us ended up in a conversation about relationships, and Adam clarified that while he's had polyamorous relationships, he wasn't stalwart about polyamory. The serious romantic relationship he was in—and which was the reason he was about to move across the country—was monogamous. So he's not against monogamy. What he's against is adherence to defaults—he spitballed a term: "defaultamy." Hearing Adam say this, I realized this is why I've felt such a strong urge for people to learn about platonic partnerships: they are a case study in resisting defaults. Whether you're in one or you simply take time to understand them, these friendships take us off autopilot.

That's what happened to Andrew's mom, Lisa. After talking to her son about his friendship with Toly, she reflected on the degree of intentionality she brought to the decisions in her life. She grew up with parents who were Holocaust survivors and who pushed her toward security: a job that made money, a husband. Lisa was always asking herself, "What's the next step?" This wasn't like a rock-climbing wall where she could choose where to step next but a ladder set by society. The profession she picked, teaching, was a practical one. Marriage "wasn't even necessarily discussed," she told me. "It was just what we kind of knew was the path we were going to take." Seeing her son follow an unmarked trail in his friendship with Toly, Lisa wonders what would have happened if she had done something similar. She says, "Maybe it would have been more fun, rewarding, but I was too afraid to try."

Experiencing a friendship like Andrew and Toly's or witnessing one can sharpen our vision, allowing us to notice the trellis—as Art and Nick put it—that had been directing our path all along. An encounter with just one of these friendships can dislodge fixed ideas about who (and how many people) we can spend the rest of our lives with. The trellis may be ideally suited to some of us, its use by so many others a source of meaning and its preset structure reassuring. But for those who have doubts or are curious, these friendships can give us the nerve to detach from the trellis and grow toward the light.

ACKNOWLEDGMENTS

For clarity's sake, writers deliberately limit the number of characters who feature in their stories. It's simply hard for a reader to keep track of a lot of people. In the real world, though, there's an ensemble of people who shape us, and shape a project as big as a book. That's certainly true of this book.

My fiercely supportive agent Gail Ross understood my vision for this book from our first conversation and has been in my corner ever since. Dara Kaye's sharp, discerning edits helped me see that the book had larger things to say about society than I'd realized.

My editor Hannah Phillips was a champion for this book even before I had a proposal to send her and has never wavered in her enthusiasm or patience, despite my endless emails.

Gareth Cook and Karen Olsson raised the ambitions of the book and challenged me as a reporter and writer. This is a far better book, and I'm a far better journalist, because of them.

Emily Krieger, who assiduously fact-checked the manuscript, was an essential backstop—she caught errors that ranged from comical to subtle—and has been a cheerleader for the book.

Thank you to everyone at St. Martin's Press who's brought this book to life and gotten it into more people's hands, including Laura Clark, Amelia Beckerman, Laurie Henderson, Gail Friedman, Jen Edwards, Soleil Paz, Hannah Jones, and Jessica Zimmerman. I felt secure after Devereux Chatillon went through the manuscript with a fine-toothed comb. Courtney Wright compiled invaluable research and acted as an early sounding board. Molly Kovite had the brilliant idea for the title, *The Other Significant Others*. I'm indebted to Julie Beck for allowing me to write about these friendships at length for *The Atlantic*.

Shankar Vedantam, the first person in my professional orbit who I told about my book idea, didn't laugh off twenty-six-year-old me but instead gave me a sense of urgency to get a proposal out the door. Peter Slevin suggested I slow down and start by writing an article. Somehow both pieces of advice were right. Peter, it would be impossible to overstate the effect you've had on my education, career, and confidence. I wish everyone had a mentor as supportive as you.

Rebecca Traister, thank you for letting me be your fangirl when I was a college student, then your research assistant, and now, maybe almost your peer. Hanna Rosin, it meant the world that you supported this book idea from the start and that you've continued to be such an advocate for it. I'm grateful to these mentors and the other writers who demystified the publishing world, including Briallen Hopper, Linda Kinstler, Kayleen Schaefer, Matt Sheehan, and Logan Ury. Marisa Franco has been an exceptional guide through the publishing process. Thank you to the author support group for all the wise advice.

I've spent the better part of my adult life at NPR, and I've learned from too many colleagues to name individually, so I'll thank the teams of *Embedded, Hidden Brain, Invisibilia, Rough Translation, Planet Money, Louder Than a Riot*, and *The Sunday Story* for giving me master classes in storytelling. I've hit the jackpot with bosses, first with the inimitable Tara Boyle, then Nicole Beemsterboer, who ensured I could take time off to work on the book. (I bow to NPR's SAG-AFTRA union for getting sabbaticals into our contract!) My subsequent bosses, Liana Simstrom and Katie Simon, have been just as supportive. The grant I received from the National Endowment for the Humanities Public Scholars program made it feasible to take all those months away from my job and to give single-minded attention to the book.

Writing about people who have a societally invisible relationship is a tricky venture. I found several of the people who I profile because someone kindly acted as a bridge between me and their community. Thank you to Rachel Bergman, Katie Davidson, Julie Kliegman, Nancy Polikoff, and Eve Tushnet.

I spoke to many dozens of people who have this type of life-defining friendship, and I have deep gratitude that they were willing to let a nosy stranger into their personal lives. To each of you who I interviewed or who answered my survey: you meaningfully shaped the ideas in this book. I hope you see yourself in these pages.

The stereotype of writing as an isolating practice has only partially been true for me. Monson Arts and Jentel Arts each gave me picturesque, peaceful spaces to inhabit my own thoughts with little else to worry about. But I am just as appreciative for the company of extraordinary writers and artists who I met at these residencies. Kim Trowbridge, thank you for inviting me to sit in your studio as you painted and helped me restructure my chapter.

Angela Chen, Julia Craven, Natalia Emanuel, Betsy Feuerstein, Sarah Hurwitz, Ela Leshem, Jenny Schmidt, Roseanna Sommers, Emily Tamkin, Brandon Tensley, Luis Trelles, and Lia Weintraub are among the people who lent their time, subject-matter expertise, and editing prowess to give feedback on chapters of the book. Hannah Groch-Begley, I don't know what I did to deserve the history education you gave me.

Simo Stolzoff taught me to write crummy first drafts and then graciously edited many of those drafts. Simo, it's been such a pleasure to see you thrive as an author. Thank you to Smiley Poswolsky for being our friend yenta.

The mother of the writer Gustave Flaubert once complained, "Your mania for sentences has dried up your heart." During this project, I feared that I could be accused of the same. The irony did not escape me: to write a book about friendship, I needed to spend less time with my own friends. But my friends have been understanding and cheered me on. Thank you to Adam, Chigozie Akah, Alex Baron, Lisa Einstein, Becca Kagan, Sara Katz, Caroline Mehl, Katherine Nagasawa, Gabrielle Newell, Tanya Rey, Baleja Saïdi, Parth Shah, Leah Varjacques, and Anna Wherry. Thank you to the friends who make D.C. feel like home. My friends who served as accountability partners and organized writing retreats made work feel like a vacation.

I was raised in a family that valued asking questions and caring about the world around us. My dad, Herschel Cohen, gave me an immense sense of freedom by encouraging me to chart my own course. My mom, Tobey Wittlin, is an expert *kveller* and the original source of my feminist consciousness. Spending time with my brother, Jason Cohen, invariably makes me want to soak up knowledge the way he does. My sister-in-law, Ting Gong, embraced my family as her own. My uncle, Norman Wittlin, gave me an early model of an intentional, unconventional, and contented life. Cees and Leonie, thank you for raising the son you did (though I know it's not in your nature to take credit) and to both of you and Akkie for welcoming me into your family.

My housemates at Kibbutz Swann never seemed to tire when yet another Shabbat dinner veered into a conversation about platonic partners. Standing under the chuppah in 2019, I couldn't have imagined that the home I'd build with my husband would eventually include you and your kids. What a dream it's been. #Nanalife

Rachel Affleck, you were a supreme distraction but made up for it by showing me what it means to adore and be adored. Joan, you've given me the weekly joy of rave-and-runs, read the entire manuscript, and floored me repeatedly with your support. Sigal Samuel, thank you for staying up late at Swifflepoof Manor to talk about Wittgenstein and for toning my abs with your hilarity. Adrianna Smith Reig, you're an eternally generous reader and friend and have taught me the beauty of commitment, tradition, and poetry.

Helen Toner, what a remarkable person you are: wise, compassionate, always present with the people you love. I know I've written a book on friendship, but the truth is, I've learned so much about being a good friend from you.

Craig Pearson! I feel the need to shout because I want to make clear how pivotal you've been in the writing process. For years now, you've gotten me up in the morning to write, been my coach, and given feedback on so much of the manuscript when you had so little time of your own. This book has your fingerprints all over it.

There are two people without whom the idea for this book wouldn't exist. Coco, as I'm calling you here, writing a book only felt plausible, not laughably audacious, because of your insistence that I'd write a book. I know you didn't care about me turning out a book per se but wanted me to feel that I was capable of such a giant undertaking. That was a profound gift to give me. Working on this book made me reflect a lot on partnership, and I remain boundlessly grateful for the one we have—and that we're always ready to revise.

M, there would have been no rabbit hole to go down if not for our friendship. Thank you for letting me write about you, about us. Early on, you encouraged me to bring a sense of expansiveness to the book—to expand readers' sense of what's possible for their own lives. That's what you do: you encourage the people around you to open themselves up to new feelings, ideas, and experiences—however unfamiliar or uncomfortable. My world is immeasurably larger, richer, and more beautiful because of you.

NOTES

INTRODUCTION

compulsory coupledom: Eleanor Wilkinson, "Learning to Love Again: 'Broken Families,' Citizenship and the State Promotion of Coupledom," *Geoforum* 49 (2013): 206–13.

privileging of romantic relationships: The philosopher Elizabeth Brake coined the term *amatonormativity* to describe the societal expectation that everyone is or should be in a romantic relationship and that it's the best type of meaningful connection. Her term is inspired by the concept of *heteronormativity*, which is the assumption that everyone is heterosexual and that it's the only natural, normal way to be. Heteronormativity results in the societally imposed norm that being straight is mandatory (compulsory heterosexuality). As I see it, amatonormativity leads to compulsory coupledom—the norm that being in a couple is mandatory.

about half of adults: Richard Fry and Kim Parker, "Rising Share of U.S. Adults Are Living Without a Spouse or Partner," Pew Research Center, October 5, 2021, https://www.pewresearch.org/social-trends/2021/10/05/rising-share-of-u-s-adults-are-living-without-a-spouse-or-partner/.

wealthier Americans are more likely: Richard V. Reeves and Christopher Pulliam,

"Middle Class Marriage Is Declining, and Likely Deepening Inequality,"
Brookings Institution, March 9, 2022, https://www.brookings.edu/research
/middle-class-marriage-is-declining-and-likely-deepening-inequality.

neither married nor cohabiting: Fry and Parker, "Living Without a Spouse or
Partner."

politicians and policymakers: I write about this in chapter 8.

spent hundreds of millions: Philip N. Cohen, "Healthy Marriage and
Responsible Fatherhood: Time for Some Results," *Family Inequality* (blog),
November 11, 2014, https://familyinequality.wordpress.com/2011/11/14/hmi
-and-rf-results/.

"one-stop shopping": John Carroll is responsible for this clever term. I write
about him and his platonic partnership in my 2020 article in *The Atlantic*,
"What If Friendship—Not Marriage—Was at the Center of Life?," October
20, 2020, https://www.theatlantic.com/family/archive/2020/10/people-who
-prioritize-friendship-over-romance/616779/.

"When we channel all our": For more on this idea, see Esther Perel, *The State of
Affairs: Rethinking Fidelity* (New York: Harper, 2017), 41–45.

one-third of American women over sixty-five: Andrew W. Roberts et al., "The
Population 65 Years and Older in the United States: 2016," U.S. Census
Bureau, October 2018.

In 1960, the average marriage: Philip N. Cohen, "For Social Relationships
Outside Marriage," *Family Equality* (blog), February 10, 2018, https://
familyinequality.wordpress.com/2018/02/10/for-social-relationships-outside
-marriage/.

a "friendship recession": Daniel Cox, "American Men Suffer a Friendship
Recession," *National Review*, July 6, 2021, https://www.nationalreview.com
/2021/07/american-men-suffer-a-friendship-recession/.

surgeon general declared it an epidemic: Jena McGregor, "This Former Surgeon
General Says There's a 'Loneliness Epidemic' and Work Is Partly to Blame,"
Washington Post, October 4, 2017, https://www.washingtonpost.com/news/on
-leadership/wp/2017/10/04/this-former-surgeon-general-says-theres-a-loneliness
-epidemic-and-work-is-partly-to-blame/.

lack of social connection: Julianne Holt-Lunstad et al., "Social Relationships
and Mortality Risk: A Meta-Analytic Review," *PLOS Medicine* 7, no. 7 (2010),
https://doi.org/10.1371/journal.pmed.1000316. The longitudinal Harvard
Study of Adult Development likewise finds that social connection has the largest
bearing on people's health and happiness.

conservatives have been arguing: David Brooks, "The Nuclear Family Was a
Mistake," *The Atlantic*, February 10, 2020, https://www.theatlantic.com/magazine
/archive/2020/03/the-nuclear-family-was-a-mistake/605536/. On his website,

the Marginal Revolution, the influential libertarian economist Tyler Cowen
called the article "so far the best essay of the year."

falling church attendance: For declining worship attendance after the pandemic,
see Lindsey Witt-Swanson et al., "Faith After the Pandemic: How COVID-19
Changed American Religion," Survey Center on American Life, January 12,
2023, https://www.americansurveycenter.org/research/faith-after-the-pandemic
-how-covid-19-changed-american-religion; for declining religiosity over the
last few decades, see Jeffrey M. Jones, "How Religious Are Americans?," Gallup,
December 23, 2021, https://news.gallup.com/poll/358364/religious-americans
.aspx.

drop in the number of friends: Daniel A. Cox, "The State of American
Friendship: Change, Challenges, and Loss," Survey Center on American Life,
April 7, 2022, https://www.americansurveycenter.org/research/the-state-of
-american-friendship-change-challenges-and-loss.

depression and anxiety: Dan Witters,"U.S. Depression Rates Reach New Highs,"
Gallup, May 17, 2023, https://news.gallup.com/poll/505745/depression-rates
-reach-new-highs.aspx; Renee D. Goodwin et al., "Trends in Anxiety Among
Adults in the United States, 2008–2018: Rapid Increases Among Young
Adults," *Journal of Psychiatric Research* 130 (November 2020): 441–46, https://
doi.org/10.1016/j.jpsychires.2020.08.014.

CHAPTER 1: DEFINING THE RELATIONSHIP

shorn of sexual desire: I don't spend time in this book addressing the
possibility of having sex in the context of friendship; illustrating nonsexual
partner–like friendships already takes up a book's worth of space! If you're
interested in the role that sex can play within friendships, I explored that
question with my colleagues at *Invisibilia* in the 2021 episode "Friends with
Benefits."

"Mutually Assured Non Complacency": Kristen Berman, "The Family
Gathering: Aka Our 'Non-Wedding,'" Medium, July 18, 2018, https://bermster
.medium.com/the-family-gathering-aka-our-non-wedding-1201364b4cb7.

design mimicked those for husbands: Alan Bray, *The Friend* (Chicago: University
of Chicago Press, 2006), 80.

Their friendship spanned: Bray, 80.

Monks in the fourth to seventh centuries: Claudia Rapp, *Brother-Making in
Late Antiquity and Byzantium: Monks, Laymen, and Christian Ritual* (Oxford,
England: Oxford University Press, 2015), 4.

shared the same visions: Rapp, 160.

left the monastery they had joined: Rapp, 159.

the priest would say prayers: Rapp, 49.

seen as "brothers": Rapp, 6.

***wed brothers* or *blood brothers*:** P. J. Heather, "Sworn-Brotherhood," *Folklore* 63, no. 3 (September 1952): 158–72, https://doi.org/10.1080/0015587x.1952.9718120.

throughout Europe, Asia: In *Brother-Making*, Rapp writes about these relationships in Germany (page 178) and says there are reports of monastic pairs in late antiquity Egypt, Palestine, and Syria. The anthropologist David K. Jordan describes blood brotherhood in China. Across countries, there are different terms for this kind of relationship, for example, *affrèrement* in France and *pobratimstvo* in the Balkans.

deep fondness for one another: Rapp, *Brother-Making*, 229.

exist alongside marriage: Rapp's scholarship departs from John Boswell's interpretation of these rituals in his influential book *Same-Sex Unions in Premodern Europe*. Boswell sees these rituals as sanctioning same-sex romantic relationships.

buried with their sworn brothers: Bray, *The Friend*, 236.

"half of my soul": Craig A. Williams, *Reading Roman Friendship* (Cambridge, England: Cambridge University Press, 2020), 15.

***affrèrement*:** Allan A. Tulchin, "Same-Sex Couples Creating Households in Old Regime France: The Uses of the Affrèrement," *Journal of Modern History* 79, no. 3 (September 2007): 613–647, https://doi.org/10.1086/517983.

promised to live together: Allan Tulchin, "The 600 Year Tradition Behind Same-Sex Unions," History News Network, https://historynewsnetwork.org/article/42361.

Sworn brothers in China: David K. Jordan, "Sworn Brothers: A Study in Chinese Ritual Kinship," UC San Diego, March 1, 2001, https://pages.ucsd.edu/~dkjordan/scriptorium/jyebay.html#metaphor.

***wed* meant a pledge:** Bray, *The Friend*, 94.

medley of terms: Bray, 96.

"The confusion lies not": Bray, 104.

hair as gifts: For example, Sharon Marcus in *Between Women: Friendship, Desire, and Marriage in Victorian England* (Princeton, NJ: Princeton University Press, 2007) describes a woman sending her fiancé a hair brooch at the same time as she sent a loving letter to her friend (page 40).

"next to my Julie": Jean-Jacques Rousseau, *La Nouvelle Héloïse: Julie; Or, the New Eloise: Letters of Two Lovers, Inhabitants of a Small Town at the Foot of the Alps* (University Park, PA: Pennsylvania State University Press, 1968), 174.

"From our earliest years": Rousseau, 383.

join two creatures: Leila J. Rupp and Susan K. Freeman write in *Understanding* *and Teaching U.S. Lesbian, Gay, Bisexual and Transgender History* (Madison: University of Wisconsin Press, 2014), "Modern science, medicine, and culture since the eighteenth century established women and men as polar opposites: women defined by the heart, men by the head and hand. Heterosexual marriage was supposed to unite the two opposites into a whole" (page 144).

intensifying the difference: Marcus, *Between Women*, 39.

"In the circle of her private friends": Marcus, 39.

coed universities and some prestige professions: Lillian Faderman, *Surpassing the Love of Men: Romantic Friendship and Love Between Women, from the Renaissance to the Present* (New York: HarperCollins, 1998), 186–88; the University of Michigan and newly founded women's colleges such as Wellesley are mentioned in Nancy Sahli, "Smashing: Women's Relationships Before the Fall," *Chrysalis* no. 8 (Summer 1979): 17–27.

well-off or well educated: Faderman, *Surpassing the Love of Men,* 190.

"a union": Faderman, 190.

Queen Anne house: Helen T. Verongos, "Overlooked No More: Lucy Diggs Slowe, Scholar Who Persisted Against Racism and Sexism," *New York Times,* October 7, 2020, https://www.nytimes.com/2020/10/01/obituaries/lucy-diggs -slowe-overlooked.html.

helped found the first: Verongos; Carroll L.L. Miller and Anne S. Pruitt-Logan, *Faithful to the Task at Hand: The Life of Lucy Diggs Slowe* (Albany: State University of New York Press, 2012), 44.

Writers of the Harlem Renaissance: "Mary P. Burrill," DC Writers' Homes, November 29, 2020, https://dcwritershomes.wdchumanities.org/mary-p -burrill/.

letters to Slowe: Samantha Schmidt, "This Pioneering Howard Dean Lived with Another Woman in the 1930s. Were They Lovers?," *Washington Post,* March 26, 2019, https://www.washingtonpost.com/history/2019/03/26/this-pioneering -howard-dean-lived-with-another-woman-s-were-they-lovers/.

"to my good friend MPB": Karen Anderson, "Brickbats and Roses: Lucy Diggs Slowe," in *Lone Voyagers: Academic Women in Coeducational Universities, 1870– 1937,* ed. Geraldine Jonçich Clifford (New York: Feminist Press, 1989), 295.

a hub for students, educators: "Slowe-Burrill House," DC Historic Sites, https:// historicsites.dcpreservation.org/items/show/1085.

"My heart aches for you": Miller and Pruitt-Logan, *Faithful to the Task,* 232.

Slowe's papers sent to Morgan State: Miller and Pruitt-Logan, 233.

evidence of sexual relationships: For example, there's speculation of romantic or sexual involvement between Frances Willard and her secretary Anna Adams Gordon, as well as Walt Whitman and Peter Doyle. See Wendy

Rouse, "The Very Queer History of the Suffrage Movement," National Park Service, https://www.nps.gov/articles/000/the-very-queer-history-of-the -suffrage-movement.htm; Selbry Kiffer and Halina Loft, "Literally in Love: The Story of Walt Whitman and Peter Doyle," Sotheby's, June 20, 2019, https://www.sothebys.com/en/articles/literally-in-love-the-story-of-walt -whitman-and-peter-doyle.

decoded sexual references: Bray, *The Friend*, 271.

Americans during that period: Richard Godbeer, *The Overflowing of Friendship: Love Between Men and the Creation of the American Republic* (Baltimore: Johns Hopkins University Press, 2009), 3.

"smashed": Sahli, "Smashing," 21.

a "rave": Faderman, *Surpassing the Love of Men*, 246.

"When a Vassar girl": Sahli, "Smashing," 21.

"verged on romance": E. Anthony Rotundo, "Romantic Friendship: Male Intimacy and Middle-Class Youth in the Northern United States, 1800–1900," *Journal of Social History* 23, no. 1 (Autumn 1989): 1; Donald Yacovone, "Surpassing the Love of Women," in *A Shared Experience: Men, Women, and the History of Gender*, ed. Laura McCall and Donald Yacovone (New York: New York University Press, 1998), 207.

"this heart of mine": Godbeer, *Overflowing of Friendship*, 55.

Men shared beds: Godbeer, 36; Yacovone, "Surpassing the Love of Women," 20.

"obscure that wider frame": Bray, *The Friend*, 6.

idolize or caress their female dolls: Marcus, *Between Women*, 112–13.

"precisely because Victorians saw": Marcus, 113.

"The beauty of the girls": Marcus, 111.

Until lesbianism became a sexual identity: Marcus, 113.

"the mother I never had": Lindsay Powers, "Oprah Winfrey Cries to Barbara Walters: 'I Am Not a Lesbian,'" *Hollywood Reporter*, December 8, 2010, https:// www.hollywoodreporter.com/tv/tv-news/oprah-winfrey-cries-barbara-walters -57842/.

CHAPTER 2: OTHER SIGNIFICANT OTHERS

"True love in this differs": Percy Bysshe Shelley, *Epipsychidion: Verses Addressed to the Noble and Unfortunate Lady, Emilia V—Now Imprisoned in the Convent of—* (London: C. and J. Ollier, 1821), 13.

supposed to be the one-stop shop: Bella DePaulo, *Singled Out: How Singles Are Stereotyped, Stigmatized, and Ignored, and Still Live Happily Ever After* (New York: St. Martin's Press, 2007), 4.

singleness might not carry the same stigma: See Rebecca Traister, *All the Single*

NOTES 271

Ladies: Unmarried Women and the Rise of an Independent Nation (New York: Simon & Schuster, 2016).

Husbands could beat their wives: Reva B. Siegel, "'The Rule of Love': Wife Beating as Prerogative and Privacy," *The Yale Law Journal* 105, no. 8 (1996): 2117–2207, https://doi.org/10.2307/797286.

stronger emotional connections: Stephanie Coontz, *Marriage, a History: How Love Conquered Marriage* (New York: Penguin Books, 2005).

Some Enlightenment thinkers: Nancy Cott, *Public Vows: A History of Marriage and the Nation* (Cambridge, MA: Harvard University Press, 2000).

the *basis* for marriage: Cott, 150.

did not change in the same way: Deborah Valenze, *First Industrial Woman* (Oxford, England: Oxford University Press, 1995).

ideal of a "companionate marriage": Anya Jabour, "'The Language of Love': The Letters of Elizabeth and William Wirt, 1802–1834," in *A Shared Experience: Men, Women, and the History of Gender,* ed. Laura McCall and Donald Yacovone (New York: New York University Press, 1998), 120–1.

coverture: In a famous passage in his 1765 *Commentaries,* English jurist Sir William Blackstone writes that "the very being or legal existence of the woman is suspended during the marriage, or at least is incorporated and consolidated into that of the husband." Coverture spread from England and influenced laws in the United States. The Married Women's Property Acts in the late 1800s started to chip away at laws that were informed by coverture.

the legal picture had changed: Marital rape only became illegal in all fifty states in 1993. Raquel Kennedy Bergen, "Marital Rape: New Research and Directions," National Online Resource Center on Violence Against Women, 2006, https://vawnet.org/sites/default/files/materials/files/2016-09/AR _MaritalRapeRevised.pdf.

fulfillment of deep psychological needs: Eli Finkel's idea of eras draws on Coontz's historical work. Coontz writes in *Marriage, a History,* "Never before in history had societies thought that such a high set of expectations about marriage was either realistic or desirable."

Coontz interviewed women in the 1950s: Hope Reese, "Studying U.S. Families: 'Men Are Where Women Were 30 Years Ago,'" *The Atlantic,* March 27, 2014, https://www.theatlantic.com/education/archive/2014/03/studying-us-families -men-are-where-women-were-30-years-ago/284515/.

"marriage is hard work": In her book *It's Not You: 27 (Wrong) Reasons You're Single* (New York: Perigee, 2007), Sara Eckel writes, "Married people like to say marriage is 'work,' often with a smug, Protestant pride—as if they were plowing fields all day while their single friends sipped appletinis" (page 64).

"In film and television": A. O. Scott, "The Hard Work in 'Before Midnight,'"

'Amour' and Other Films and Shows," *New York Times*, June 19, 2013, https://www.nytimes.com/2013/06/23/movies/the-hard-work-in-before -midnight-amour-and-other-films-and-shows.html?pagewanted=1&ref =weddings&_r=0.

damaging the average marriage: Eli J. Finkel, "The All-or-Nothing Marriage," *New York Times*, February 14, 2014, https://www.nytimes.com/2014/02/15 /opinion/sunday/the-all-or-nothing-marriage.html.

aren't measuring up: Eli J. Finkel, *The All-or-Nothing Marriage: How the Best Marriages Work* (New York: Dutton, 2017), 22.

Fewer Americans report: Tom W. Smith, Jaesok Son, and Benjamin Schapiro, *General Social Survey: Trends in Psychological Well-Being 1972–2014*, NORC, 2015, 5, https://www.norc.org/PDFs/GSS%20Reports/GSS_PsyWellBeing15 _final_formatted.pdf.

"means turning inward": Naomi Gerstel and Natalia Sarkisian, "Marriage: The Good, the Bad, and the Greedy," *Contexts* 5, no. 4 (2006): 16–21.

married Americans were less likely: Naomi Gerstel and Natalia Sarkisian, "Marriage Reduces Social Ties," Council on Contemporary Families, https:// sites.utexas.edu/contemporaryfamilies/2007/01/01/marriage-reduces-social -ties/.

often strains community ties: Gerstel and Sarkisian, "Greedy," 16.

less likely to spend time volunteering: Young-Il Kim and Jeffrey Dew, "Marital Investments and Community Involvement: A Test of Coser's Greedy Marriage Thesis," *Perspectives* 59, no. 4 (2016): 743–59, https://doi .org/10.1177/0731121415601270.

"greedy institution": Lewis Coser, *Greedy Institutions: Patterns of Undivided Commitment* (New York: Free Press, 1974).

people who disperse their emotional needs: Elaine Cheung et al., "Emotionships: Examining People's Emotion-Regulation Relationships and Their Consequences for Well-Being," *Social Psychological and Personality Science* 6, no. 4 (2015): 407–14, https://doi.org/10.1177/1948550614564223.

less physiological stress: Elizabeth Keneski, Lisa A. Neff, and Timothy L. Loving, "The Importance of a Few Good Friends: Perceived Network Support Moderates the Association Between Daily Marital Conflict and Diurnal Cortisol," *Social Psychological and Personality Science* 9, no. 8 (2018), https://doi .org/10.1177/1948550617731499.

on the path to Sodom: Anonymous, *Satan's Harvest Home: Or the Present State of Whorecraft, Adultery, Fornication, Procuring, Pimping, Sodomy, and the Game of Flatts* (London: Sold at the Change, St. Paul's, Fleet Street, 1749), 51–52.

authorities rounded up accused sodomites: Alan Bray, *The Friend* (Chicago: University of Chicago Press, 2006), 271.

kissing had been replaced: This comes from an account by a Prussian historian: Johann Wilhelm von Archenholz, *A Picture of England: Containing a Description of the Laws, Customs, and Manners of England. Interspersed with Curious and Interesting Anecdotes* (Dublin: P. Byrne, 1791), 198.

Men's power relative to women: John Ibson, *Picturing Men: A Century of Male Relationships in Everyday American Photography* (Chicago: University of Chicago Press, 2002), 55. As Ibson explains, this new masculinity was quite literally muscular. During this time, the "middle-class culture's ideal male body went from 'lean and wiry' to one of 'physical bulk and well defined muscles.'"

category of homosexuality: Richard Godbeer, *The Overflowing of Friendship: Love Between Men and the Creation of the American Republic* (Baltimore: Johns Hopkins University Press, 2009), 197.

hadn't been hidden: George Chauncey, *Gay New York: Gender, Urban Culture, and the Making of the Gay Male World, 1890–1940* (New York: Basic Books, 2008). The story is similar in England. The historian Deborah Cohen writes about how, in working-class areas of Britain, what marked a man as queer wasn't the type of sex he had but how he dressed and acted. See Deborah Cohen, *Family Secrets: The Things We Tried to Hide* (New York: Penguin Books, 2014), 145.

new label of "homosexual": Chauncey, *Gay New York*, 22.

a euphemism for homosexuality: Martha Vicinus, *Intimate Friends: Women Who Loved Women, 1778–1928* (Chicago: University of Chicago Press, 2004), xxii.

not as widely criminalized: In England: Cohen, *Family Secrets*, 144; in the United States: Margot Canaday, *The Straight State: Sexuality and Citizenship in Twentieth-Century America* (Princeton, NJ: Princeton University Press, 2009), 11–12.

chaste love for her friends: Here are more details of what she wrote: "The very nature of my affections for my friends precludes the possibility of any element entering into it which is not absolutely sacred."

"feelings like mine were 'unnatural'": Lillian Faderman, *Surpassing the Love of Men: Romantic Friendship and Love Between Women, from the Renaissance to the Present* (New York: HarperCollins, 1998), 244.

Freud, whose influence: Cohen, *Family Secrets*, 154; for a summary of Freud's complex and sometimes contradictory ideas about homosexuality, see Sara Flanders et al., "On the Subject of Homosexuality: What Freud Said," *International Journal of Psychoanalysis* 97, no. 3 (2016): 933–50, https://www .freud-zentrum.ch/wp-content/uploads/2017/10/Flanders_et_al-2016-Freud -and-Homosexuality_IJP.pdf.

***The Lancet* found the novel troubling:** Vicinus, *Intimate Friends*, 220.

love is infinite but time is not: Samantha Cooney, "What Monogamous Couples Can Learn from Polyamorous Relationships, According to Experts," *Time*, August 27, 2018, https://time.com/5330833/polyamory-monogamous -relationships/.

CHAPTER 3: WHAT'S SEX GOT TO DO WITH IT?

"Sometimes it seems": From "Dearest Friend," chapter 6 of *Ruins*, an unpublished epistolary novel by Andrea Dworkin, excerpted by permission of the Estate of Andrea Dworkin.

"Our relationship was so intense": Lisa M. Diamond, "Passionate Friendships Among Adolescent Sexual-Minority Women," *Journal of Research on Adolescence* 10, no. 2 (2000): 194, https://doi.org/10.1207/SJRA1002_4.

emotionally intense as a romantic relationship: Diamond, 197.

far more likely than conventional friendships: Diamond, 201.

quotes on the walls: Kiran Misra and Robin Ye, "The Satellite Dorms: Culture, Traditions, and the Making of Home," *Chicago Maroon*, May 14, 2015, https:// www.chicagomaroon.com/article/2015/5/14/satellite-dorms-culture-traditions -making-home/.

lust and love are associated: Lisa M. Diamond and Janna A. Dickenson, "The Neuroimaging of Love and Desire: Review and Future Directions," *Clinical Neuropsychiatry: Journal of Treatment Evaluation* 9, no. 1 (2012): 39; Lisa Diamond, *Sexual Fluidity: Understanding Women's Love and Desire* (Cambridge, MA: Harvard University Press, 2008), 218.

androgens and estrogens: Diamond, 219.

serve different evolutionary functions: Christopher Munsey, "Love's Not Sex," *Monitor on Psychology* 38, no. 2 (February 2007): 42, https://www.apa.org /monitor/feb07/lovesnot.

an "attachment" relationship: Beyond Lisa Diamond, psychologists Cindy Hazan and Phillip Shaver have made this argument. See Cindy Hazan and Phillip Shaver, "Romantic Love Conceptualized as an Attachment Process," *Journal of Personality and Social Psychology* 52, no. 3 (1987): 511–24.

motivate a pair of adults: Diamond, *Sexual Fluidity*, 225.

attachment as the second stage: Cindy Hazan makes this argument, as does the philosopher Robert Nozick, in his book *The Examined Life* (New York: Simon & Schuster, 1990): "Perhaps here lies one function of infatuation, to pave and smooth the way to uniting in a *we*; it provides enthusiasm to take one over the hurdles of concern for one's own autonomy, and it provides an initiation into we-thinking too, by constantly occupying the mind with thoughts of the other and of the two of you together" (page 78).

sexual orientation only orients sexual attraction: Lisa Diamond, "What Does Sexual Orientation Orient? A Biobehavioral Model Distinguishing Romantic Love and Sexual Desire," *Psychological Review* 110, no. 1 (2003), doi:10.1037/0033-295x.110.1.173.

61 percent of women: Dorothy Tennov, *Love and Limerence: The Experience of Being in Love* (New York: Scarborough House, 1979), 244.

a survey agreed with: G. Oscar Anderson, "Love, Actually: A National Survey of Adults 18+ on Love, Relationships, and Romance," AARP Research, November 2009, 3, https://assets.aarp.org/rgcenter/il/love_09.pdf.

"I am always thinking": Elaine Hatfield et al., "Passionate Love: How Early Does It Begin?," *Journal of Psychology and Human Sexuality* 1, no. 1 (1988): 35–51.

"made in the shape of a human": Angela Chen, *Ace: What Asexuality Reveals About Desire, Society, and the Meaning of Sex* (Boston: Beacon Press, 2020), 37.

asexual respondents felt more stigma: Esther D. Rothblum et al., "Asexual and Non-Asexual Respondents from a U.S. Population-Based Study of Sexual Minorities," *Archives of Sexual Behavior* 49, no. 2 (2020): 757–67, https://doi.org/10.1007/s10508-019-01485-0.

shape their identity: Gary Gutting and Johanna Oksala, "Michel Foucault," *Stanford Encyclopedia of Philosophy*, Fall 2022, ed. Edward N. Zalta and Uri Nodelman, https://plato.stanford.edu/archives/fall2022/entries/foucault/.

more about producing pleasure: For instance, psychotherapist Matt Lundquist writes, "The insistence by society that sex must always exist within the context of intimacy is oppressive and negates the fact that all sorts of healthy people throughout the world and history find great pleasure and meaning in sex that isn't intimate." This quote appears in his post "Intimacy and Sex Aren't the Same Thing," Tribeca Therapy, June 15, 2017, https://tribecatherapy.com/4780/sex-intimacy-couples-therapy/.

Frequently Asked Questions: "Relationship FAQ," Asexual Visibility and Education Network, http://www.asexuality.org/?q=relationship.html#gq1.

CHAPTER 4: BE YOUR OWN MAN

"Lord, to whom shall we go": John 6:68 (New International Version)

men like Nick constrain their behavior: Mark McCormack and Eric Anderson, "The Influence of Declining Homophobia on Men's Gender in the United States: An Argument for the Study of Homohysteria," *Sex Roles* 71, nos. 3–4 (2014): 109–120.

10 percent of the population: McCormack and Anderson, 13.

homophobia has waned: Tina Fetner, "U.S. Attitudes Toward Lesbian and Gay

People Are Better Than Ever," *Contexts* 15, no. 2 (2016): 20–27, https://doi.org /10.1177/1536504216648147; McCormack and Anderson, "The Influence of Declining Homophobia," 6.

By adolescence: Niobe Way, *Deep Secrets: Boys' Friendships and the Crisis of Connection* (Cambridge, MA: Harvard University Press, 2011).

trained to act competitively: In the book *The Psychology of Friendship*, David R. Hibbard and Gail E. Walton explain that research shows "boys are 'trained' from an early age to be competitive" and that "norms for male-male friendships seem to discourage communal expression or sentimentality at all cost while encouraging direct competition and 'one-upmanship'" (page 222)." Way's work in *Deep Secrets* also traces how boys stamp out emotional intimacy.

bond over activities: Geoffrey Greif, *Buddy System: Understanding Male Friendships* (New York: Oxford University Press, 2008). Greif distinguishes between "shoulder-to-shoulder" friendships, which he says are typical for men, and "face-to-face" friendships for women.

"skinship": Jaeyeon Yoo, "Korean American Stories About Kinship and Intimacy," *Electric Literature*, August 18, 2021, https://electricliterature.com/yoon-choi -stories-skinship-korean-american/.

in India: Rekha Basu, "U.S. Men Must Embrace Their Friends, Literally," *Des Moines Register*, December 10, 2013, https://www.desmoinesregister.com/story /opinion/columnists/rekha-basu/2013/12/11/basu-us-men-must-embrace-their -friends-literally/3980935/.

an aberration: For instance, in 2007, Iran's then-president Mahmoud Ahmadinejad said homosexuality is less common in Iran than in the U.S. "President Misquoted over Gays in Iran: Aide," Reuters, October 10, 2007, https://www.reuters.com/article/us-iran-gays/president-misquoted-over-gays-in -iran-aide-idUSBLA05294620071010. Robert Mugabe, the former president of Zimbabwe, called homosexuality "un-African" and a "white disease." Bernardine Evaristo, "The Idea That African Homosexuality Was a Colonial Import Is a Myth," *Guardian*, March 8, 2014, https://www.theguardian.com/commentisfree /2014/mar/08/african-homosexuality-colonial-import-myth.

incursion of Western values: For example, see Leah Buckle, "African Sexuality and the Legacy of Imported Homophobia," Stonewall, October 1, 2020, https:// www.stonewall.org.uk/about-us/news/african-sexuality-and-legacy-imported -homophobia.

openly engaged in physical intimacy: Ibson, *Picturing Men*, 30. He explains that until the 1930s, it was a common ritual for men to be photographed together in a studio (page 47).

normative male alexithymia: Ronald F. Levant and Mike C. Parent, "The

Development and Evaluation of a Brief Form of the Normative Male
Alexithymia Scale (NMAS-BF)," *Journal of Counseling Psychology* 66, no.
2 (2019), doi:10.1037/cou0000312; Emily N. Karakis and Ronald F.
Levant, "Is Normative Male Alexithymia Associated with Relationship
Satisfaction, Fear of Intimacy and Communication Quality Among Men in
Relationships?," *Journal of Men's Studies* 20, no. 3 (2012), https://doi.org/10
.3149/jms.2003.179.

socialized to be tough and stoic: *APA Guidelines for Psychological Practice with
Boys and Men* (Washington, DC: American Psychological Association, 2018),
http://www.apa.org/about/policy/psychological-practice-boys-men-guidelines
.pdf.

women felt more emotional intimacy: Anna Machin, *Why We Love: The New
Science Behind Our Closest Relationships* (New York: Pegasus Books, 2022).

survey from 2021: Cox, "The State of American Friendship."

told a friend they loved them: Cox.

didn't want to "burden" others: Reiner, "Budding Social Safety Nets."

"emotional gold digging": "Men Have No Friends and Women Bear the Burden,"
Harper's Bazaar, May 2, 2019, https://www.harpersbazaar.com/culture/features
/a27259689/toxic-masculinity-male-friendships-emotional-labor-men-rely-on
-women/.

"Essentially, Art and Nick": Ray Fava, "Revoice Conference Exposed:
Perverting Friendship, Marriage, and Promoting Queer Theory," Evangelical
Dark Web, April 8, 2021, https://evangelicaldarkweb.org/2021/04/08/revoice
-conference-exposed-perverting-friendship-marriage-and-promoting-queer
-theory/.

John lying on Jesus's bosom: John 13:23.

advice in a recent book on friendship: This is an argument in the "Pursuing
Authenticity" chapter of Marisa Franco's book *Platonic: How the Science of
Attachment Can Help You Make—and Keep—Friends* (New York: G. P. Putnam's
Sons, 2022).

John Mulaney joked: "John Mulaney Monologue—SNL," YouTube video, 8:21,
posted by *Saturday Night Live*, March 1, 2020, https://www.youtube.com/watch
?v=jRLH8E_CpP0.

fewer close friends is associated: For example, from Cox's 2021 survey: "For
Americans with three or fewer close friends . . . more than half say they have
felt [lonely] at least once in the past seven days. In contrast, only one in three
Americans with ten or more close friends report feeling lonely in the past seven
days."

negative health outcomes: Julianne Holt-Lunstad et al., "Social Relationships
and Mortality Risk: A Meta-Analytic Review," *PLOS Medicine* 7, no. 7 (2010),

https://doi.org/10.1371/journal.pmed.1000316; "Social Isolation, Loneliness in Older People Pose Health Risks," National Institute on Aging, April 23, 2019, https://www.nia.nih.gov/news/social-isolation-loneliness-older-people-pose -health-risks.

more diverse systems of social support: Jialu L. Streeter, "Gender Differences in Widowhood in the Short-Run and Long-Run: Financial, Emotional, and Mental Wellbeing," *Journal of the Economics of Ageing* 17, suppl. 1 (2020), https://doi.org/10.1016/j.jeoa.2020.100258; Janice Kiecolt-Glaser and Tamara L. Newton, "Marriage and Health: His and Hers," *Psychological Bulletin* 127, no. 4 (2001): 472–503, https://doi.org/10.1037/0033-2909 .127.4.472.

women supposedly lacked the character: Women are absent from Cicero's discussion of *amicitia*. Aristotle says that friends reproduce each other's virtuous characteristics, and he defines virtue as public and political, spheres from which women were excluded.

"a rash and wavering fire": Michel de Montaigne, "On Friendship," in *Shakespeare's Montaigne: The Florio Translation of the Essays, a Selection*, ed. Stephen Greenblatt and Peter Platt (New York: New York Review Books, 2014), 43.

aspired to live up to: Donald Yacovone, "Surpassing the Love of Women," in *A Shared Experience: Men, Women, and the History of Gender*, ed. Laura McCall and Donald Yacovone (New York: New York University Press, 1998), 196.

letter-writing manuals advised men: Richard Godbeer, *The Overflowing of Friendship: Love Between Men and the Creation of the American Republic* (Baltimore: Johns Hopkins University Press, 2009), 10.

British college students who had "bromances": Stefan Robinson, Adam White, and Eric Anderson, "Privileging the Bromance: A Critical Appraisal of Romantic and Bromantic Relationships," *Men and Masculinities* 22, no. 5 (2017): 850–71.

more shades of acceptable masculinity: Eric Anderson and Mark McCormack, "Inclusive Masculinity Theory: Overview, Reflection and Refinement," *Journal of Gender Studies* 27, no. 5 (2018): 547–61; Wendy Luttrell, "Making Boys' Care Worlds Visible," *Boyhood Studies* 6, no. 2 (2012): 186–202, https://doi.org /10.3149/thy.0601.186.

friendship behaviors that are stereotyped: In *Buddy System*, Greif's study of hundreds of men's and women's friendships, he found that women's friendships tend to be built around intimacy and men's around activities.

CHAPTER 5: FUNCTIONAL FAMILIES

two rounds of anonymous donor sperm: "Co-Parenting Elaan," YouTube video, 4:21, posted by *National Post*, March 24, 2018, https://www.youtube.com /watch?v=apJ_7ow1ifU.

close to 20 percent of children: "Portrait of Children's Family Life in Canada in 2016," Statistics Canada, August 2, 2017, https://www12.statcan.gc.ca/census -recensement/2016/as-sa/98-200-x/2016006/98-200-x2016006-eng.cfm.

proportion of children living with two parents: Paul Hemez and Chanell Washington, "Percentage and Number of Children Living with Two Parents Has Dropped Since 1968," U.S. Census Bureau, April 12, 2021, https://www .census.gov/library/stories/2021/04/number-of-children-living-only-with-their -mothers-has-doubled-in-past-50-years.html.

no longer one "typical" family form: "Parenting in America: Outlook, Worries, Aspirations Are Strongly Linked to Financial Situation," Pew Research Center, December 17, 2015, https://www.pewresearch.org/social-trends/2015/12/17/1 -the-american-family-today.

"We must make it possible": Marco Rubio, "Protecting Family as the Center of Culture," Edify, November 15, 2022, https://edify.us/video/protecting-family-as -the-center-of-culture/.

"Too many fathers are MIA": Julie Bosman, "Obama Sharply Assails Absent Black Fathers," *New York Times*, June 16, 2008, https://www.nytimes.com/2008 /06/16/us/politics/15cnd-obama.html.

the first person to hold him: Julie Ireton, "Raising Elaan: Profoundly Disabled Boy's 'Co-Mommas' Make Legal History," CBC, February 21, 2017, https:// www.cbc.ca/news/canada/ottawa/multimedia/raising-elaan-profoundly-disabled -boy-s-co-mommas-make-legal-history-1.3988464.

common experience in immigrant communities: Helen Rose Ebaugh and Mary Curry, "Fictive Kin as Social Capital in New Immigrant Communities," *Sociological Perspectives* 43, no. 2 (2000), https://doi.org/10.2307/1389793.

nearly any anthropologist would claim: For example, see Marshall Sahlins, *What Kinship Is—and Is Not* (Chicago: University of Chicago Press, 2013).

legal strangers to their biological mother: Joanna L. Grossman, "We Are Family: Connecticut Passes New Parentage Law to Embrace Modern Families," Verdict, June 23, 2021, https://verdict.justia.com/2021/06/23/we-are-family -connecticut-passes-new-parentage-law-to-embrace-modern-families.

weren't entitled to inheritance rights: "Illegitimacy," Law Library, https://law .jrank.org/pages/7473/Illegitimacy-Modern-Law.html; for financial support, see "Inheritance Rights for Legitimate and Illegitimate Children," HG.org, https:// www.hg.org/legal-articles/inheritance-rights-for-legitimate-and-illegitimate -children-47186; Stephanie Coontz, "Illegitimate Complaints," *New York Times*,

February 18, 2007, https://www.nytimes.com/2007/02/18/opinion/18coontz
.html.

The court reasoned: These cases, *Levy v. Louisiana* and *Glona v. American
Guarantee & Liability Insurance Co.*, are summarized in Doug NeJaime,
"The Constitution of Parenthood," *Stanford Law Review* 72, no. 2 (2020):
261–379.

"familial bonds": Doug NeJaime, "Marriage Equality and the New Parenthood,"
Harvard Law Review 129, no. 5 (2016): 1194.

number of single people: "Parenting in America," Pew Research Center.

easier for stepparents to adopt: Stepparent or second-parent adoption is a more
streamlined process than ordinary adoption.

A man's ex-wife revealed: Susan H. v. Jack S., 30 Cal. App. 4th 1435 (Cal. Ct.
App. 1994).

"This social relationship": Susan H. v. Jack S., quoting Estate of Cornelious, 35 Cal.
3d 461 (Cal. 1984).

"lesbian baby boom": Charlotte J. Patterson, "Families of the Lesbian Baby
Boom: Parents' Division of Labor and Children's Adjustment," *Developmental
Psychology* 31, no. 1 (1995): 115, http://citeseerx.ist.psu.edu/viewdoc/download
?doi=10.1.1.454.9133&rep=rep1&type=pdf.

1989 survey: Stephanie Coontz, *The Way We Never Were: American Families and the
Nostalgia Trap* (New York: Basic Books, 2001), 19.

"Yes, my world feels better": Ashley Csanady, "Meet the Co-Mammas: Women
Who Are Partners in Raising a Son, but Not Romantic Partners," *National Post*,
April 4, 2017, https://nationalpost.com/news/canada/meet-the-co-mommas
-women-who-are-partners-in-raising-a-son-but-not-romantic-partners.

likely related to the knot: "*The Current* Transcript for July 7, 2017," CBC, July
7, 2017, https://www.cbc.ca/radio/thecurrent/the-current-for-july-7-2017–1
.4193157/july-7–2017-full-episode-transcript-1.4195184.

"He's going to have a wonderful life": Ireton, "Raising Elaan."

Lynda was asked at Elaan's appointments: "Co-Parenting Elaan."

Lynda turned forty: Radhika Sanghani, "Platonic Parenting—Is This the
Way of the Future?," *West Australian*, April 13, 2017, https://thewest.com
.au/lifestyle/parenting/platonic-parenting-is-this-the-way-of-the-future-ng
-b88446248z.

Wow, I have a family: Sanghani.

eager to support people: Ireton, "Raising Elaan."

assumed the women were a couple: "*The Current* Transcript," CBC.

Natasha had to forfeit: Natasha Bakht and Lynda Collins, "Are You My Mother?
Parentage in a Nonconjugal Family," *Canadian Journal of Family Law* 31, no. 1
(2018): 105–150.

one-third of US states: See Table 2 in Susan Hazeldean, "Illegitimate Parents," *UC Davis Law Review* 55, no 3 (2022): 1583–1715.

"How could we have": "Co-Mammas Fight Rights," *New Family*, http://thenewfamily.com/2017/04/podcast-episode-131-co-mammas-fight-rights/.

Richard V. Reeves: Reeves classifies marriages similarly to Wilcox and is also skeptical of marriages chiefly rooted in romance. He doesn't argue for returning to what he calls "traditional marriage," with its retro gender roles, but instead that the future of American marriages is "High-Investment Parenting" marriages—where the glue isn't sex or tradition but a shared commitment to raising kids. Richard V. Reeves, "How to Save Marriage in America," *The Atlantic*, February 13, 2014, https://www.theatlantic.com/business/archive/2014/02/how-to-save-marriage-in-america/283732.

"family-first" model: W. Bradford Wilcox and Alysse ElHage, "COVID-19 Is Killing the Soulmate Model of Marriage. Good," *Christianity Today*, June 22, 2020, https://www.christianitytoday.com/ct/2020/july-august/coronavirus-covid-19-killing-soulmate-model-marriage-good.html.

societal and legal recognition: Bakht and Collins, "Are You My Mother?," 11.

"Is There Sex After Kids?": Brandie Weikle, "Is There Sex After Kids?," *New Family*, http://thenewfamily.com/2016/02/podcast-episode-44-is-there-sex-after-kids/.

misplaced emphasis on sexual love: Sacha M. Coupet, "Beyond Eros: Relative Caregiving, Agape Parentage, and the Best Interests of Children," *Journal of Gender, Social Policy & the Law* 20, no. 3 (2012): 611–21.

"the New Illegitimacy": Nancy Polikoff, "The New Illegitimacy: Winning Backwards in the Protection of the Children of Lesbian Couples," *Journal of Gender, Social Policy & the Law* 20, no. 3 (2012): 721–40.

Dobson shared his disapproval: James C. Dobson, "Two Mommies Is One Too Many," *Time,* December 12, 2006, https://content.time.com/time/subscriber/article/0,33009,1568485,00.html.

gained prominence centuries, not millennia, ago: Researchers have debated how much industrialization is tied to the nuclear family. Some scholars date the nuclear family to the Industrial Revolution, others a few centuries prior. Either way, it's not nearly as old as Dobson suggests. See Paul Puschmann and Arne Solli, "Household and Family During Urbanization and Industrialization: Efforts to Shed New Light on an Old Debate," *History of the Family* 19, no. 1 (February 2014): 3–5, https://doi.org/10.1080/1081602x.2013.871570.

cooperative child-rearing: Sarah Blaffer Hrdy, "How Humans Became Such Other-Regarding Apes," National Humanities Center, https://

nationalhumanitiescenter.org/on-the-human/2009/08/how-humans-became
-such-other-regarding-apes/.

"Without alloparents": Sarah Blaffer Hrdy, *Mothers and Others: The Evolutionary Origins of Mutual Understanding* (Cambridge, MA: Harvard University Press, 2011), 109.

"The legendary white middle-class family": Elaine Tyler May, *Homeward Bound: American Families in the Cold War Era* (New York: Basic Books, 2008), 13–14.

constantly threatened: Philip Cohen, *The Family: Diversity, Inequality, and Social Change* (New York: W. W. Norton, 2020), 44.

"networks of mutual obligation": Herbert G. Gutman, *The Black Family in Slavery and Freedom* (New York: Vintage, 1977), 222.

fictive kin: "Kinship and Family" in *African American Psychology: From Africa to America*, ed. Faye Z. Belgrave and Kevin W. Allison (Los Angeles: SAGE, 2009), 125.

they remain a vital feature: Robert Joseph Taylor et al., "Older African American, Black Caribbean, and Non-Latino White Fictive Kin Relationships," *Annual Review of Gerontology & Geriatrics* 41, no. 1 (2021), https://www.ncbi.nlm.nih .gov/pmc/articles/PMC9005029/.

Split-household families: Cohen, *Family*, 54–55.

white American men and Japanese women: Rose Cuison Villazor, "The Other Loving: Uncovering the Federal Government's Racial Regulation of Marriage," *New York University Law Review* 86, no. 5 (2011).

Anti-immigrant sentiment: Coontz, *The Way We Never Were*, 8.

labored outside the home: Coontz, 5.

forge "chosen families": Kath Weston, *Families We Choose: Lesbians, Gays, Kinship* (New York: Columbia University Press, 1992), 109. Chosen families were a major part of the Black and Latinx ballroom scene. For instance, see Marlon M. Bailey, *Butch Queens Up in Pumps: Gender, Performance, and Ballroom Culture* (Ann Arbor: University of Michigan Press, 2013).

single mothers by choice: Susan Golombok et al., "Single Mothers by Choice: Mother-Child Relationships and Children's Psychological Adjustment," *Journal of Family Psychology* 30, no. 4 (2016): 409–18, doi:10.1037 /fam0000188.

as critics claimed: Golombok also points out that any family that deviates from the "traditional family" is lumped together under the category "non-traditional families," regardless of the cause—whether they came about from divorce, or a single parent with an unplanned pregnancy, or families made possible by technological developments and changes in social attitudes.

kids fare well: Susan Imrie and Susan Golombok, "Long-Term Outcomes of Children Conceived Through Egg Donation and Their Parents: A Review of the Literature," *Fertility and Sterility* 110, no. 7 (2018): 1187–93, https://doi.org /10.1016/j.fertnstert.2018.08.040; Susan Golombok, "Love and Truth: What Really Matters for Children Born Through Third-Party Assisted Reproduction," *Child Development Perspectives* 15, no. 2 (June 2021): 103–9, https://doi.org/10 .1111/cdep.12406.

"those who have children": Susan Golombok, *We Are Family: The Modern Transformation of Parents and Children* (New York: PublicAffairs, 2020), 27.

"Children are most likely to flourish": Golombok, 270.

called themselves "vertical neighbors": Ireton, "Raising Elaan."

At 7:00 a.m. every day: "February 21, 2017, Full Episode Transcript," CBC, February 21, 2017, https://www.cbc.ca/radio/thecurrent/the-current-for -february-21–2017–1.3991287/february-21–2017-full-episode-transcript-1 .3993019#segment2.

people are happier: Elaine Cheung et al.,"Emotionships: Examining People's Emotion-Regulation Relationships and Their Consequences for Well-Being," *Social Psychological and Personality Science* 6, no. 4 (2015): 407–14, https:// doi.org/10.1177/1948550614564223.

"Having two adults who co-operate": Branwen Jeffreys, "Do Children in Two-Parent Families Do Better?," BBC News, February 5, 2019, https://www.bbc .com/news/education-47057787.

"Oh that all of the children": This quote is from a case in which multiple adults sought custody of a child after the biological mother's death. *In re* Clifford K, 217 W. Va. 625 (W. Va. 2005).

need to make a formal agreement: Csanady, "Meet the Co-Mammas."

applied for parental rights: Bakht and Collins, "Are You My Mother?," 134.

multiple US states allow a child: Doug NeJaime explained in an email to the author that, as of March 2023, the jurisdictions that allow a child to have more than two legal parents are California, Connecticut, Washington, D.C., Delaware, Maine, Nevada, Vermont, and Washington.

single mothers have created "Mommunes": Debra Kamin, "'Mommunes': Mothers Are Living Single Together," *New York Times*, May 12, 2023, https:// www.nytimes.com/2023/05/12/realestate/single-mother-households-co-living .html.

Tens of thousands of people: "Platonic Co-Parenting Goes Mainstream," Trends, June 22, 2021, https://link.trends.co/view/5f32c6fd3891211a672a9555ef5sc .2y7/13598f6e.

"the tidiest person she's ever met": Sanghani, "Platonic Parenting."

2017 survey of hundreds of women: "Key Findings: Survey on Today's Women,"

Lake Research Partners, July 2017, https://familystoryproject.org/wp-content /uploads/2018/10/LRP-Memo_Key-Findings_2017.07.25.pdf.

Natasha's father often says: Baidar Bakh, Affidavit, February 2, 2016, 2.

CHAPTER 6: THE LONG HAUL

Above age sixty-five: "2021 Profile of Older Americans," Administration for Community Living, November 2022, https://acl.gov/sites /default/files/Profile%20of%20OA/2021%20Profile%20of%20OA /2021ProfileOlderAmericans_508.pdf.

three times the number of widows: "2021 Profile of Older Americans," 6.

median income for older women: Bureau of Labor Statistics, "Median Weekly Earnings $971 for Women, $1,164 for Men, in Third Quarter 2022," *Economics Daily*, November 2, 2022, https://www.bls.gov/opub/ted/2022 /median-weekly-earnings-971-for-women-1164-for-men-in-third-quarter -2022.htm. For the poverty rates for older women and men, see United States Census Bureau, *Income and Poverty in the United States: 2020*, Report Number P60-273 (Washington, DC: U.S. Government Printing Office, 2021), 16, https://www.census.gov/content/dam/Census/library/publications/2021/demo /p60-273.pdf.

poverty rates for older Black women: Zhe Li and Joseph Dalaker, "Poverty Rates Among the Population Aged 65 and Older," Congressional Research Service, December 6, 2022, 14, https://sgp.fas.org/crs/misc/R45791.pdf.

by 2060, life expectancy will increase: Lauren Medina, Shannon Sabo, and Jonathan Vespa, *Living Longer: Historical and Projected Life Expectancy in the United States*, Report Number P25-1145 (Washington, DC: U.S. Government Printing Office, 2020), 1, https://www.census.gov/content/dam/Census/library /publications/2020/demo/p25-1145.pdf.

cancer and dementia cases will increase: The CDC predicts that the total number of cancer cases will increase by almost 50 percent because of the growth and aging of the US population—an extension of an existing trend. Hannah K. Weir et al., "Cancer Incidence Projections in the United States Between 2015 and 2050," *Preventing Chronic Disease* 18, no. 59 (June 2021): 1–8, https:// www.cdc.gov/pcd/issues/2021/pdf/21_0006.pdf. For dementia cases, see "Dementia Incidence Declined Every Decade for Past Thirty Years," August 14, 2020, Harvard T. H. Chan School of Public Health, https://www.hsph .harvard.edu/news/press-releases/dementia-incidence-declined-every-decade-for -past-thirty-years/; "Minorities and Women Are at Greater Risk for Alzheimer's Disease," Centers for Disease Control and Prevention, August 20, 2019, https:// www.cdc.gov/aging/publications/features/Alz-Greater-Risk.html.

about 6 percent of Americans sixty-five: Andrew W. Roberts et al., "The Population 65 and Older in the United States: 2016," U.S. Census Bureau, October 2018, https://www.census.gov/content/dam/Census/library/publications/2018/acs/ACS-38.pdf.

growing in younger cohorts: Wendy Wang and Kim Parker, "Record Share of Americans Have Never Married," Pew Research Center, September 24, 2014, https://www.pewresearch.org/social-trends/2014/09/24/record-share-of-americans-have-never-married/.

quarter of adults sixty-five and older: Wendy Wang, "The State of Our Unions: Marriage Up Among Older Americans, Down Among the Younger," Institute for Family Studies, February 12, 2018, https://ifstudies.org/blog/the-state-of-our-unions-marriage-up-among-older-americans-down-among-the-younger.

divorce rate for this group: Renee Stepler, "Led by Baby Boomers, Divorce Rates Climb for America's 50+ Population," Pew Research Center, March 9, 2017, https://www.pewresearch.org/fact-tank/2017/03/09/led-by-baby-boomers-divorce-rates-climb-for-americas-50-population/.

seventy-five-year-olds without a living spouse: Paola Scommegna, "Family Caregiving for Older People," Population Reference Bureau, February 24, 2016, https://www.prb.org/resources/family-caregiving-for-older-people/.

sociologists call "elder orphans": For a reference to "elder orphans," see Deborah Carr and Rebecca L. Utz, "Families in Later Life: A Decade in Review," *Journal of Marriage and Family* 82, no. 1 (February 2020): 346–63. For an example of "kinless," see Rachel Margolis and Ashton M. Verdery, "Older Adults Without Close Kin in the United States," *Journals of Gerontology: Series B, Psychological Sciences and Social Sciences* 72, no. 4 (2017): 688–93, doi:10.1093/geronb/gbx068.

likely to grow in coming years: Carr and Utz, "Families in Later Life," 357.

daughters spend far more time: "Daughters Provide as Much Elderly Parent Care as They Can, Sons Do as Little as Possible," ScienceDaily, August 14, 2014, https://www.sciencedaily.com/releases/2014/08/140819082912.htm.

children with aging parents: Paola Scommegna, "Family Caregiving."

older Americans want to stay: Joanne Binette, *2021 Home and Community Preferences Survey: A National Survey of Adults Age 18+ Chartbook*, AARP Research, 2022, 9, https://www.aarp.org/content/dam/aarp/research/surveys_statistics/liv-com/2021/2021-home-community-preferences-chartbook.doi.10.26419-2Fres.00479.001.pdf.

especially those who live alone: *2021 Profile of Older Americans*, The Administration for Community Living, 2022, 3, https://acl.gov/sites/default/files/Profile%20of%20OA/2021%20Profile%20of%20OA/2021ProfileOlderAmericans_508.pdf.

grew from 2 percent: Joanne Binette and Kerri Vasold, *2018 Home and Community Preferences: A National Survey of Adults Age 18-Plus*, AARP Research, August 2018, 18, https://doi.org/10.26419/res.00231.001.

Silvernest: Kaya Laterman, "Getting a Roommate in Your Golden Years," *New York Times*, January 12, 2018, https://www.nytimes.com/2018/01/12/realestate/getting-a-roommate-in-your-golden-years.html.

"Many baby boomers want to stay": Valerie Finholm, "More Renters over Age 50 Turning to 'Golden Girls' Trend," *USA Today*, August 19, 2018, https://www.usatoday.com/story/news/nation/2018/08/19/golden-girls-home-sharing/1019790002/.

financial concerns have motivated: Laterman, "Getting a Roommate."

"It's companionship": Alexa Liacko, "Home Sharing Is Helping Seniors Afford Housing," Denver 7 Colorado News, March 17, 2022, https://www.thedenverchannel.com/news/national-politics/the-race/home-sharing-is-helping-seniors-afford-housing.

Nesterly: "Intergenerational Homeshare," City of Boston, September 19, 2017, https://www.boston.gov/departments/new-urban-mechanics/housing-innovation-lab/intergenerational-homeshare-pilot.

expanded to several other regions: Their website (https://www.nesterly.com) has listings in central Ohio, coastal Massachusetts, Louisville, and Boston.

In 2011, a group of eight friends: Jeff Foss, "The True Story of the Llano Tiny Home Exit Strategy," *Outside*, February 10, 2016, https://www.outsideonline.com/outdoor-gear/gear-news/true-story-llano-tiny-home-exit-strategy/.

press dubbed it "Bestie Row": Alex Heigl, "'Tiny House Compound' in Texas Goes Viral as 'Bestie Row,'" *People*, May 13, 2015, https://people.com/celebrity/bestie-row-texans-tiny-house-compound-goes-viral/.

more than five hundred calls and emails: Foss, "The True Story."

a group of Chinese friends: "7個廣州閨蜜合力造民宿 7 Girlfriends in Guangzhou Build a House to Live Together," YouTube video, 3:56, posted by "一条Yit," June 28, 2019, https://www.youtube.com/watch?v=Rqt2rZ99X4U&feature=youtu.be.

three Australian couples: Eve Grzybowski, "Share-Housing in Your 60s: 'Six of Us Wanted to Do Retirement in an Extraordinary Way,'" *Guardian*, June 17, 2021, https://www.theguardian.com/lifeandstyle/2021/jun/13/share-housing-in-your-60s-six-of-us-wanted-to-do-retirement-in-an-extraordinary-way.

gather most evenings: Heather Bolstler, "The Power of Ritual," *Shedders* (blog), May 13, 2017, https://shedders.wordpress.com/2017/05/23/the-power-of-ritual/.

persistent paid-caregiver shortage: Phil Galewitz, "With Workers in Short Supply, Seniors Often Wait Months for Home Health Care," NPR, June 30,

2021, https://www.npr.org/sections/health-shots/2021/06/30/1010328071
/with-workers-in-short-supply-seniors-often-wait-months-for-home-health-care.

Low pay and difficult working conditions: Galewitz.

stereotyped as asexual: Ateret Gewirtz-Meydan et al., "Ageism and Sexuality" in
Contemporary Perspectives on Aging, ed. Liat Ayalon and Clemens Tesch-Römer
(New York: Springer, 2018), 151.

A study from 1987 found: Teresa E. Seeman et al., "Social Network Ties and
Mortality Among the Elderly in the Alameda County Study," *American Journal
of Epidemiology* 126, no. 4 (1987): 714–23.

friendships become more predictive of mortality: William J. Chopik,
"Associations Among Relational Values, Support, Health, and Well-Being Across
the Adult Lifespan," *Personal Relationships* 24, no. 2 (2017): 408–22, https://doi
.org/10.1111/pere.12187.

2020 AARP survey found: *Caregiving in the U.S. 2020*, AARP Family Caregiving,
2020, E-2, https://www.caregiving.org/wp-content/uploads/2020/06
/AARP1316_ExecSum_CaregivingintheUS_WEB.pdf.

LGBT baby boomers: *Still Out, Still Aging: The MetLife Study of Lesbian, Gay,
Bisexual, and Transgender Baby Boomers*, MetLife Mature Market Institute &
American Society on Aging, 2010, 3, https://www.asaging.org/sites/default/files
/files/mmi-still-out-still-aging.pdf/.

caregiving among queer friends: Anna Muraco and Karen Fredriksen-
Goldsen, "'That's What Friends Do': Informal Caregiving for Chronically Ill
Midlife and Older Lesbian, Gay, and Bisexual Adults," *Journal of Social and
Personal Relationships* 28, no. 8 (2011): 1073–92, https://doi.org/10.1177
/0265407511402419.

often viewed providing care: Muraco and Fredriksen-Goldsen, "'That's What
Friends Do,'" 10.

rejected by their families of origin: Shari Brotman et al., "Coming Out to Care:
Caregivers of Gay and Lesbian Seniors in Canada," *Gerontologist* 47, no. 4
(2007): 490–503, https://doi.org/10.1093/geront/47.4.490.

less likely to have kids: Victoria Sackett, "LGBT Adults Fear Discrimination in
Long-Term Care," AARP, March 27, 2018, https://www.aarp.org/home-family
/friends-family/info-2018/lgbt-long-term-care-fd.html.

Many worry they'll be refused care: From Sackett, "More than 60 percent
surveyed said they think they might be refused or receive limited care [in a long-
term care setting], and they also fear they would be in danger of neglect, abuse,
or verbal or physical harassment. Most are uneasy about acceptance and think
that entering long-term care might force them to hide or deny their LGBT
identity."

one-third of chronically ill: Andrew Nocon and Maggie Pearson, "The Roles of Friends and Neighbours in Providing Support for Older People," *Ageing & Society* 20, no. 3 (2000): 341–67, doi:10.1017/S0144686X99007771.

older adults surveyed felt more isolated: University of Michigan National Poll on Healthy Aging, "Loneliness Among Older Adults and During the COVID-19 Pandemic," December 2020, https://www.healthyagingpoll.org/reports-more /report/loneliness-among-older-adults-and-during-covid-19-pandemic.

CHAPTER 7: GIVE THEM GRIEF

"But it has been much harder": Ann Friedman and Aminatou Sow, *Big Friendship: How We Keep Each Other Close* (New York: Simon & Schuster, 2020), 19.

Without a well-defined conclusion: Pauline Boss et al., *Family Stress Management: A Contextual Approach*, 3rd ed. (Thousand Oaks, CA: SAGE Publications, 2017), 74–75.

"frozen grief": Meg Bernhard, "What If There's No Such Thing as Closure?," *New York Times*, December 19, 2021, https://www.nytimes.com/2021/12/15 /magazine/grieving-loss-closure.html.

romantic relationship takes up "two rations": Sheon Han, "You Can Only Maintain So Many Close Friendships," *The Atlantic*, May 20, 2021, https:// www.theatlantic.com/family/archive/2021/05/robin-dunbar-explains-circles -friendship-dunbars-number/618931/. Glynnis MacNicol writes poignantly about the experience of losing friendships to marriage in her memoir *No One Tells You This* (New York: Simon & Schuster, 2018), 65.

Traister writes about how: Rebecca Traister, *All the Single Ladies: Unmarried Women and the Rise of an Independent Nation* (New York: Simon & Schuster, 2016), 102.

"Well, it's like in life": Sheila Heti, *How Should a Person Be?* (New York: Henry Holt, 2012), 265–6.

Miller describes friend breakups: Patti Miller, "A Friendship Breakup Is a Radical Loss. Why Don't We Talk About It More?," *Guardian*, April 12, 2022, https:// www.theguardian.com/books/2022/apr/13/a-friendship-breakup-is-a-radical -loss-why-dont-we-talk-about-it-more.

diagnosed with stage 3c ovarian cancer: Hannah Friedrich, "Initial Diagnosis," CaringBridge, May 16, 2011, https://www.caringbridge.org/visit /hannahfriedrich/journal; Friedrich, "Cycle 3 day 8," CaringBridge, July 13, 2011, https://www.caringbridge.org/visit/hannahfriedrich/journal.

"I am literally defenseless": Friedrich, "IV Port," CaringBridge, May 16, 2011, https://www.caringbridge.org/visit/hannahfriedrich/journal.

"A suffocating blanket of fear": Friedrich, "Happy Fall!," CaringBridge, September 23, 2011, https://www.caringbridge.org/visit/hannahfriedrich/journal.

"I love you mom": Hannah Friedrich, "Change in Plans," CaringBridge, February 17, 2013, https://www.caringbridge.org/visit/hannahfriedrich/journal.

disenfranchised grief: Kenneth J. Doka, *Disenfranchised Grief: Recognizing Hidden Sorrow* (Lexington, MA: Lexington Books, 1989).

cause of disenfranchised grief: Pauline Boss and Janet R. Yeats, "Ambiguous Loss: A Complicated Type of Grief When Loved Ones Disappear," *Bereavement Care* 33, no. 2 (2014): 63–69.

"Try calling your boss": Friedman and Sow, *Big Friendship*, 176.

complicated grief: "Complicated Grief," Mayo Clinic, December 13, 2022, https://www.mayoclinic.org/diseases-conditions/complicated-grief/symptoms-causes/syc-20360374.

grief strikes in oscillations: George A. Bonanno, *The Other Side of Sadness: What the New Science of Bereavement Tells Us About Life After Loss* (New York: Basic Books, 2019), 21–22.

Terms like *closure* and *over it*: Pauline Boss, *The Myth of Closure: Ambiguous Loss in a Time of Pandemic and Change* (New York: W. W. Norton, 2019).

misguided use of the Protestant work ethic: Judith Butler, "Violence, Mourning, Policing," *Center for LGBTQ Studies News* 12, no. 1 (2002): 3–6, https://academicworks.cuny.edu/clags_pubs/54/.

the rite of shraddha: "Shraddha," *Encyclopedia Britannica Online*, October 9, 2015, https://www.britannica.com/topic/shraddha.

If we stop expecting relationships: Meg-John Barker, *Rewriting the Rules: An Anti Self-Help Guide to Love, Sex, and Relationships* (New York: Routledge, 2018), 143.

"as the people we've reached": Barker, 262.

"grieving what could have been": J.S. Park, "Intrapsychic Grief," Facebook, August 11, 2021, https://www.facebook.com/jsparkblog/posts/intrapsychic-grief-grieving-what-could-have-been-and-will-never-bethe-pain-of-lo/368905264828536/.

a fundamental feeling: For example, see Lalin Anik and Ryan Hauser, "One of a Kind: The Strong and Complex Preference for Unique Treatment from Romantic Partners," *Journal of Experimental Social Psychology* 86 (2020), https://doi.org/10.1016/j.jesp.2019.103899.

CHAPTER 8: FRIENDS, WITH BENEFITS

few enough gay and lesbian: Nancy Polikoff, "Equality and Justice for Lesbian and Gay Families and Relationships," *Rutgers Law Review* 61, no. 3 (2009): 529–65, http://rutgerslawreview.com/wp-content/uploads/2011/08/Equality-and-Justice-for-Lesbian-and-Gay-Families-and-Relationships.pdf.

Kowalski case as evidence: Nancy Polikoff, *Beyond (Straight and Gay) Marriage: Valuing All Families Under the Law* (New York: Beacon Press, 2009), 57–58.

an efficient way to gain rights: Thomas Stoddard, "Why Gay People Should Seek the Right to Marry," *OUT/LOOK*, Fall 1989, 9.

fell along gender lines: Nancy Polikoff, interview by the author, March 23, 2022.

"marital supremacy": Serena Mayeri, "Marital Supremacy and the Constitution of the Nonmarital Family," *California Law Review* 103, no. 5 (2015): 1277–1352.

Ettelbrick endorsed a different approach: Paula Ettelbrick, "Since When Is Marriage a Path to Liberation?," *OUT/LOOK*, Fall 1989, 14.

"the groundwork for revolutionizing": Ettelbrick, 17.

Massachusetts became the first US state: "Factbox: List of States That Legalized Gay Marriage," Reuters, June 26, 2013, https://www.reuters.com/article/us-usa-court-gaymarriage-states/factbox-list-of-states-that-legalized-gay-marriage-idUSBRE95P07A20130626.

political conversation happening in Maryland: The ACLU filed a lawsuit in 2004 for same-sex marriage rights in Maryland. "ACLU Files Lawsuit Seeking Marriage for Same-Sex Couples in Maryland," ACLU, July 7, 2004, https://www.aclu.org/press-releases/aclu-files-lawsuit-seeking-marriage-same-sex-couples-maryland.

learned important lessons: "Joan E. Biren and Amelie Zurn-Galinsky" in *Collective Wisdom: Lessons, Inspiration, and Advice from Women over 50*, ed. Grace Bonney (New York: Artisan, 2021).

separation is only valid: "Divorce," Maryland Courts, https://www.mdcourts.gov/sites/default/files/import/family/pdfs/familylawinformation-divorcelegaldigest.pdf. One Maryland law office's website states, "The most important part of remaining in a bona fide state of separation is that you cannot have sexual relations with your spouse. If you do so, you risk a Judge throwing out your divorce case." See "Sexual Relations with Spouse During Pending Divorce Action," Meriwether & Tharp, https://mtlawoffice.com/news/sexual-relations-with-spouse-during-pending-divorce-action.

"I was beside myself with joy": Joan E. Biren, interview by Kelly Anderson, transcript of video recording, February 27, 2004, Voices of Feminism Oral History Project, Sophia Smith Collection, 26, https://compass.fivecolleges.edu/object/smith:1342624.

sneak around in the bushes: Biren, 23.

met in student government: Biren, 25.

pornographic images and photos: Gem Fletcher, "The Camera as a 'Revolutionary Tool': Joan. E. Biren on Unifying Lesbians in Their Struggle for Freedom," It's Nice That, March 15, 2021, https://www.itsnicethat.com/features

/joan-e-biren-eye-to-eye-portraits-of-lesbians-photography-150321. Fletcher
writes, "Any representations in the culture were fake and ridiculous—from
highly romanticised images of straight women made for the male gaze shot by
David Hamilton to pornographic man-eating monsters in horror films."

a selfie before the term existed: Paul Moakley, "How a Groundbreaking Book
Helped a Generation of Lesbians See Themselves in the 1970s," *Time*, February
13, 2021, https://time.com/5938729/eye-to-eye-portraits-of-lesbians-jeb/.

rendered in black-and-white film: Carrie Maxwell, "Joan E. Biren aka JEB Talks
Portraits of Lesbians Book Journey and Re-issue," *Windy City Times*, April
21, 2021, https://www.windycitytimes.com/lgbt/Joan-E-Biren-aka-JEB-talks
-Portraits-of-Lesbians-book-journey-and-re-issue/70325.html.

"images I had never seen before": Sophie Hackett, "Queer Looking," *Aperture*,
2015, https://issues.aperture.org/article/2015/1/1/queer-looking.

a knockoff of marriage: NYU law professor Melissa Murray traces this history of
domestic partnerships in "Paradigms Lost: How Domestic Partnerships Went
from Innovation to Injury," *New York Review of Law and Social Change* 37, no.
291 (2013): 291–305, https://socialchangenyu.com/wp-content/uploads/2017
/12/Melissa-Murray_RLSC_37.1.pdf.

governor was skittish about the optics: Scott L. Cummings and Doug NeJaime,
"Lawyering for Marriage Equality," *UCLA Law Review* 57, no. 1235 (2010):
1235–1331.

"We are excited to see": Perry v. Brown, 671 F.3d 1052 (9th Cir. 2012), https://
casetext.com/case/perry-v-brown-3.

many states eliminated domestic partnership: John Culhane, *More Than
Marriage: Forming Families After Marriage Equality* (Oakland: University of
California Press, 2023), 26–27.

couples might not want to be married: Private employers made the same
assumption even earlier. In 1993, Oracle opened domestic partnership benefits
to same-sex couples. It required the couple to sign an affidavit that read, "We
would legally marry each other if we could, and we intend to do so if marriage
becomes available to us in our state of residence." See Polikoff's *Beyond (Straight
and Gay) Marriage*, 60–61.

"No union is more profound": Obergefell v. Hodges, 576 U.S. 644 (2015).

"The designation of 'marriage'": Perry v. Brown, 52 Cal. 4th 1116 (Cal. 2011).

presented platonic marriage: Jay Guercio spoke on TikTok and to different media
outlets about her platonic marriage. She and her friend have since broken off
their relationship. See "Viral Best Friends in Platonic Marriage Have a Shocking
Update," YouTube video, 5:54, posted by the *Tamron Hall Show*, February 6,
2023, https://www.youtube.com/watch?v=kmZzs5vh9Hk.

devoted older male friends: Ed O'Loughlin, "In Ireland, a Same-Sex Marriage

with a Tax Benefit," *New York Times*, December 24, 2017, https://www.nytimes
.com/2017/12/24/world/europe/ireland-gay-marriage-inheritance-tax.html.

never a private contract: Michael Warner, *The Trouble with Normal: Sex, Politics,
and the Ethics of Queer Life* (Cambridge, MA: Harvard University Press, 2000),
117.

a status and a contract: Kerry Abrams, "Marriage Fraud," *California Law Review*
100, no. 1 (2012): 1–67, 10.

often true for older Americans: Naomi Cahn et al., "Family Law for the One-
Hundred-Year Life," *Yale Law Journal* 132, no. 6 (2023): 1691–1768.

British sisters in their eighties: Hilary Osborne, "Sisters Lose Fight for Tax Rights
of Wedded Couples," *The Guardian*, April 29, 2008, https://www.theguardian
.com/money/2008/apr/29/inheritancetax.humanrights.

sole acceptable venue: Abrams, "Marriage Fraud," 56; see pages 39–40 for details
on fornication and adultery.

marital status determined eligibility: Abrams, 42.

less advantaged socioeconomic classes: Kim Parker and Renee Stepler, "As
Marriage Rate Hovers at 50%, Education Gap in Marital Status Widens," Pew
Research Center, September 14, 2017, https://www.pewresearch.org/short-reads
/2017/09/14/as-u-s-marriage-rate-hovers-at-50-education-gap-in-marital-status
-widens/.

"The stakes of marital supremacy": Mayeri, "Marital Supremacy," 1279.

"end the dependence of needy parents": "Personal Responsibility and Work
Opportunity Reconciliation Act of 1996," Public Law 104-193, U.S. Statutes at
Large 110 (1996): 2105–2355.

fewer people on government rolls: The feminist writer Lyz Lenz spells out a
critical take on this reasoning. She writes in her newsletter, "In sum, we need
women to buy into romantic partnerships so that they will become the social
safety net that our leaders and politicians refuse to create." Lyz Lenz, "Finding
New Narratives in Sex and the City," Men Yell at Me, January 12, 2022, https://
lyz.substack.com/p/finding-new-narratives-in-sex-and.

if only these women married: Angela Onwuachi-Willig, "The Return of the
Ring: Welfare Reform's Marriage Cure as the Revival of Post-Bellum Control,"
California Law Review 93, no. 6 (2005): 1647–96, http://www.jstor.org/stable
/30038499; Ife Floyd et al., "TANF Policies Reflect Racist Legacy of Cash
Assistance," Center on Budget and Policy Priorities, August 4, 2021, https://
www.cbpp.org/research/family-income-support/tanf-policies-reflect-racist-legacy
-of-cash-assistance. There's irony to the focus on marrying off Black mothers:
the American government historically prevented Black Americans from
marrying, as I discussed in chapter 5.

best environment in which to raise children: On the panel, AEI senior fellow Ian

V. Rowe talked about the "success sequence"—the idea that people who follow a series of steps, including marriage before having kids, are almost guaranteed not to end up in poverty. See Isabel Sawhill, "Modeling Opportunity in America: The Success Sequence and Social Genome Model," Institute for Family Studies, December 5, 2018, https://ifstudies.org/blog/modeling-opportunity -in-america-the-success-sequence-and-social-genome-model; also see the work of the sociologist Sara McLanahan, summarized here: Marcia J. Carlson, "Sara McLanahan: Pioneering Scholar Focused on Families and the Wellbeing of Children," *PNAS* 119, no. 16 (2022), https://www.pnas.org/doi/10.1073/pnas .2204143119.

a fierce debate: See this rundown of key sociological studies on the topic of family structure, stability, and children's well-being: "Family Stability," Urban Institute, May 18, 2022, https://upward-mobility.urban.org/family-stability.

little discernible effect on marriage rates: Emily Alpert Reyes, "Federal Funds to Foster Healthy Marriage Have Little Effect, Study Finds," *Los Angeles Times*, February 9, 2014, https://www.latimes.com/local/la-me-healthy-marriage -20140210-story.html; Philip N. Cohen, "More Marriage Promotion Failure Evidence," *Family Equality* (blog), June 1, 2018, https://familyinequality .wordpress.com/2018/06/01/more-marriage-promotion-failure-evidence/.

40 percent of children: "Unmarried Childbearing," Centers for Disease Control and Prevention, https://www.cdc.gov/nchs/fastats/unmarried-childbearing.htm.

built around the interests: Cahn, "Family Law," 1691.

two core functions: Vivian Hamilton, "Mistaking Marriage for Social Policy," *Virginia Journal of Social Policy & the Law* 11, no. 3 (2004): 307–72. The philosopher Elizabeth Brake makes this argument, too, in her book *Minimizing Marriage*.

"We didn't want": Culhane, *More Than Marriage*, 61.

covering many of the core rights: Michele Zavos, in an email to the author, listed which rights from Colorado's DBA would be covered in a boilerplate estate-planning process.

legislators knew many people don't: Culhane, *More Than Marriage*, 67–68.

city-level domestic partnership: For example, Cambridge, Massachusetts, and Somerville, Massachusetts. See the Polyamory Legal Advocacy Coalition, https:// polyamorylegal.org/.

domestic partnerships spiked: Emily Zentner, "I Do: California Domestic Partnerships Surge After More Opposite-Sex Couples Allowed to File," Capitol Public Radio, September 22, 2020, https://www.capradio.org/articles/2020/09 /22/i-do-california-domestic-partnerships-surge-after-more-opposite-sex-couples -allowed-to-file/.

roles they'd slipped into: Zentner.

PACS, is nearly as popular: "Is the Number of PACS Civil Unions in France the Same as the Number of Marriages?," Institut National d'Etudes Démographiques, June 2022, https://www.ined.fr/en/everything_about _population/demographic-facts-sheets/faq/is-the-number-of-pacs-civil-unions -in-france-the-same-as-the-number-of-marriages/.

Justice Kennedy links marriage to autonomy: He writes in *Obergefell*, "A first premise of the Court's relevant precedents is that the right to personal choice regarding marriage is inherent in the concept of individual autonomy. This abiding connection between marriage and liberty is why *Loving* invalidated interracial marriage bans under the Due Process Clause."

nearly 40 percent of Americans: Richard Fry and Kim Parker, "Rising Share of U.S. Adults Are Living Without a Spouse or Partner," Pew Research Center, October 5, 2021, https://www.pewresearch.org/social-trends/2021/10/05/rising -share-of-u-s-adults-are-living-without-a-spouse-or-partner/.

EPILOGUE

console himself with songs: Terry Gross, "'New Yorker' Culture Critic Says Music and Mixtapes Helped Make Sense of Himself," *Fresh Air*, October 18, 2022, https://www.npr.org/2022/10/18/1129644971/new-yorker-culture-critic-says -music-and-mixtapes-helped-make-sense-of-himself.

zoning laws that create obstacles: Kate Redburn, "Zoned Out: How Zoning Law Undermines Family Law's Functional Turn," *Yale Law Journal* 128, no. 8 (2019), https://www.yalelawjournal.org/note/zoned-out.

live in danger: "Somerville Passes Historic Non-Discrimination Ordinance Protecting Polyamorous Families and Other Diverse Relationships," Chosen Family Law Center, March 24, 2023.

expand eligibility: The Healthy Families Act, which has been introduced in Congress every year since 2004 to establish a federal sick leave policy, defines eligibility broadly: "a child, a parent, a spouse, a domestic partner, or any other individual related by blood or affinity whose close association with the employee is the equivalent of a family relationship."

alternatives to marriage are scattered: There are state-level legal structures, such as civil unions in Illinois and domestic partnerships in Washington, D.C. Municipal domestic partnerships in Cambridge, MA, and Somerville, MA, don't have a romantic connotation to them. See the Polyamory Legal Advocacy Coalition, https://polyamorylegal.org.

courts have recognized multiparent households: Courtney G. Joslin and Douglas NeJaime, "Multi-Parent Families, Real and Imagined," *Fordham Law Review* 90 no. 6 (2022): 2561–89. In this paper, Joslin and NeJaime analyze forty years of case law in West Virginia and find that multiparent households were recognized by the courts. These cases generally involved children conceived by different-sex couples in which a third adult became part of the parenting picture.

first nondiscrimination ordinance: "Somerville Passes Historic Non-Discrimination Ordinance."

Sweden's Supreme Court ruled: "Sex Is Not a Condition for Cohabitation," LexPress, July 8, 2022, https://www.lexpress.se/doc/482020.

rights that are similar to marriage: "Adult Interdependent Relationships," Canadian Legal FAQs, https://www.law-faqs.org/alberta-faqs/family-law/adult -interdependent-relationships/.

Germany's Federal Ministry of Justice: "Germany Considers Granting Friends Similar Legal Rights to Married Couples," YouTube video, 3:42, posted by DW News, February 28, 2023, https://www.youtube.com/watch?v=VTkU9SFPPuI.

INDEX